At the Crossroads

At the Crossroads

Old Saint Patrick's and the Chicago Irish

Ellen Skerrett, Editor

Foreword by Richard M. Daley

Wild Onion Books

an imprint of Loyola Press
Chicago

Wild Onion Books
an imprint of Loyola Press
3441 North Ashland Avenue
Chicago, Illinois 60657

Copublished with Old Saint Patrick's Church
700 West Adams Street
Chicago, Illinois 60661

Wild Onion Books publishes provocative titles on Chicago themes that offer diverse perspectives on the city and surrounding area, its history, its culture, and its religions. Wild onion is a common nickname for Chicago.

Wild Onion Books staff:
Imprint editors: June Sawyers, Jeremy Langford
Production coordination: Jill Mark Salyards

Cover design and interior design: Juanita Dix

Cover illustration: Postcard, Saint Patrick's Church, c. 1916. Printed in Germany and published by the Rembrandt Art Company, Chicago. (Courtesy, Len Hilts)

Library of Congress Cataloging-in-Publication Data

At the crossroads : Old Saint Patrick's and the Chicago Irish / Ellen Skerrett, editor.
    p. cm.
  Includes bibliographical references (p.) and index.
  ISBN 0-8294-0935-1
  1. Saint Patrick's Church (Chicago, Ill.) 2. Irish Americans—Illinois–Chicago–History.
3. Chicago (Ill.)–Church history. I. Skerrett, Ellen.
BX4603.C5S253 1997
977.3'11049162–dc21
                                                               96-45450
                                                               CIP

97 98 99 00 01 / 10 9 8 7 6 5 4 3 2 1

Contents

Illustrations

Foreword

Chicago has always been a city of strong and diverse ethnic communities. If you traced the history of these communities, you would usually find an institution like Old Saint Patrick's Church at its core, at its very foundation—a place that is the heart and soul of its community.

People throughout Chicago recognize Old Saint Pat's as the historical center of the Irish community, but its story is not simply the story of one church in one community serving one ethnic group in Chicago. It is the story of communities throughout our city.

When immigrants came to Chicago to establish new lives for their families, they looked to religion for guidance and sustenance. As these settlements grew, parishioners demanded more and more from their religious institutions as well as from individual members of the clergy. The churches of the archdiocese of Chicago answered the call and, in the process, became the centers of education, social activity, and political activism in the city.

These churches not only gave people a sense of belonging to their community but also a sense of belonging to Chicago as a whole. They taught people to work together for the future welfare of their families, their neighborhoods, and their city. When people did move away, they carried those important values with them.

Churches still play a vital role in the development of Chicago. Old Saint Pat's is but one shining example. Over the years, Saint Pat's has evolved with the times—from a place that helped assimilate Irish immigrants in the nineteenth century to a church that reaches out to young people and, indeed, Chicagoans from many backgrounds.

I am proud to be a part of Old Saint Pat's, and I am confident that Father Jack Wall will continue the fine tradition that began 150 years ago into the next century.

Richard M. Daley
Mayor of Chicago

Acknowledgments

It has been a distinct pleasure collaborating with leading scholars of the American Irish experience on a book that examines the Chicago Irish and their 150-year-old mother parish, Old Saint Patrick's. With keen appreciation for the history of the Irish in this city, Reverend John J. Wall endorsed my proposal for a book of essays and generously contributed his own insights about the rebirth of Saint Patrick's. From our very first meeting, Sue A. Lupori, director of Saint Patrick's Sesquicentennial, has offered crucial support and commitment to the project. Special thanks are also due Roger Hughes, Old Saint Patrick's executive director; Elizabeth Keating, director of communications; Jackie Van Oost, executive assistant; and Jeremy Langford, acquisitions editor at Loyola Press. It has been a delight to work with June Sawyers, Wild Onion imprint editor, and Jill Salyards, trade production coordinator for the Press, and I thank them for their enthusiasm and diligence.

In editing *At the Crossroads: Old Saint Patrick's and the Chicago Irish,* I have been doubly blessed by the scholarship and friendship of Lawrence McCaffrey, Charles Fanning, Suellen Hoy, Janet Nolan, Eileen Durkin, and Timothy Barton. Not only were these contributors willing to draw on their own expertise in writing their essays, they also shared insights and important documentary evidence. Suellen Hoy epitomizes the genius behind this approach. It was Suellen's provocative question, "What do we know about Finley Peter Dunne's schoolteacher-sister?" that prompted a collective search for Amelia. It is a journey that led to the recovery of one of Chicago's most important

public school teachers and principals at the turn of the century: Amelia Dunne Hookway.

Illustrating *At the Crossroads* has also been an adventure. Thanks to the generosity of Len and Kay Hilts, precious Dunne family photos are published here for the first time, providing us with renewed appreciation for the differences families make in the life of a parish, a city, and a nation. I extend special thanks to Paul Lane of Photo Source in Evanston for his patience and skill in restoring and enhancing fragile portraits and documents. I am also grateful to Jim Pollick, Patrick Kavanaugh, and Erin Jaeb for their contemporary photos of parish life.

Few places in Chicago have been as blessed as Saint Patrick's. Immortalized in literature by Finley Peter Dunne, the church today is the best known example of Celtic Revival art in America, thanks to the genius of Thomas A. O'Shaughnessy. All Chicago owes a special debt to this visionary artist, who breathed new life into the city's oldest church. I am particularly grateful to Joseph J. O'Shaughnessy. He generously shared personal stories about his father with Timothy Barton and me and enriched the book with rare photographs and documents.

In preparing these essays for publication, I have benefited from the expertise of many archivists, including Nancy Sandleback and Julie Satzik, archdiocese of Chicago; Brother Michael Grace, S.J., Loyola University; Sister Patricia Illing, R.S.M., Mercy Archives; Sister Alice Whitehead, I.B.V.M., Loretto Archives (Wheaton, Illinois); Lois Martin, Daughters of Charity Archives (Evansville, Indiana); and Sister Virginia Gaume, B.V.M. Archives, Clarke

College. I owe a long-standing debt of gratitude to John J. (Jac) Treanor, assistant chancellor and archivist for the archdiocese of Chicago. Thanks to his vision, the archdiocesan archives is beginning a new chapter in its history at 711 West Monroe Street, just around the corner from Old Saint Patrick's Church. As they have so often in the past, Mary Claire Gart, Dolores Madlener, and Heidi Schlumpf of the New World Publishing Company welcomed my requests for information and photographs. John E. Corrigan, a long-time scholar of Chicago Irish history, provided each of the authors with important references from his voluminous research. I admire Dominic A. Pacyga's scholarship and love of Chicago, especially his loyalty to De La Salle Institute. And I am grateful for the assistance of Steve Rosswurm, who proofread the entire manuscript.

I would also like to acknowledge the legendary staff of the Chicago Historical Society, especially Archie Motley, Linda Evans, Janice McNeill, Eileen Flanagan, Linda Ziemer, Cynthia Mathews, and Sharon Lancaster as well as Daniel Meyer and the librarians in Special Collections at the University of Chicago Library. But above all, I owe a debt of gratitude to the energetic staffs in the microfilm room and the Special Collections and Preservation Division of the Chicago Public Library: John P. Chalmers, curator; Beverly Cook, assistant curator; Andrea Mark Telli, senior archival specialist; Constance J. Gordon, librarian II; and Turina T. Harris and Wallace Wilson, library pages, give new meaning to the term public service.

Among the many individuals who contributed to *At the Crossroads* are Carole Cahill; Megan Healy; Meggan Youpel; Julie and James Patrick Dunne; Peter Finley Dunne; Brother Konrad Diebold, F.S.C., president and Donald Palermini, director of public relations, Saint Patrick High School; Michael F. Funchion; Thomas M. Keefe; Brenda J. Bailey, Mark Twain Project, The Bancroft Library; Peter Blekys, Calvary Cemetery; Eileen Burke; John D. Burke; Paul C. Gearen; Reverend James Burke, O.P.; Karen Crotty, Irish-American Teachers Association, Chicago; James B. Sloan, Irish Music Foundation; Joan Radtke; Jerry O'Sullivan; William F. Jones; Anna Dlugopolski; Dan McFalls; Sister Hortense Marie Ponthieux, D.C.; Sister Bernadita Finnegan, B.V.M.; Ellen Wadey; and Catherine Wall.

In this project, as in all my past scholarly work, I am indebted to John C. O'Malley. Little did I know when we walked down the aisle at Old Saint Patrick's Church on October 6, 1979 and out the door that our future would include Mary, Ellen, and Maisie O'Malley. I thank them all.

Introduction

This book of essays explores the complex history of the Chicago Irish through the prism of a particular place, Old Saint Patrick's. Founded at the time of the Great Famine in Ireland, the parish has been a microcosm of the American Catholic and urban experience for 150 years. Against the background of this special place, individuals and their accomplishments come into clear relief: Sister Mary Agatha O'Brien and Reverend Denis Dunne, pioneer builders of urban Catholicism; Civil War hero Colonel James A. Mulligan; Finley Peter Dunne, journalist and custodian of Irish-American cultural memory; Amelia Dunne Hookway, innovative educator and dramatist; and visionary artist Thomas A. O'Shaughnessy.[1]

In a city shaped by sacred space, Saint Patrick's is unique. Its yellow brick church at the corner of Adams and Desplaines Streets is Chicago's oldest public building, a landmark for generations of city dwellers. Moreover, thanks to the genius of Thomas O'Shaughnessy, Saint Patrick's constitutes the best known example of Celtic Revival art in America.

At the Crossroads: Old Saint Patrick's and the Chicago Irish emphasizes the role religion has played in creating community and identity in an urban neighborhood from the 1840s to the present day. Not only did Saint Patrick's contribute to Chicago's expansion, it also responded to the needs of the larger city. Despite dramatic economic, social, and demographic changes in its surrounding neighborhood, this mother parish of the Chicago Irish endured, providing stability and continuity for diverse groups of immigrants and their American-born children.

One of the paradoxes of the urban Catholic experience is that the churches and schools that anchored Chicago neighborhoods and shaped communal life also contributed to Irish mobility. Yet, as Eileen Durkin demonstrates, Old Saint Patrick's retained its central place in the lives of the Chicago Irish and played a crucial role in sustaining group identity through ritual celebrations every March 17. No other parish in Chicago has observed Saint Patrick's Day for a longer period of time or done more to infuse the day with meaning than Old Saint Patrick's. And no one is better suited to tell this story than Durkin. For the past ten years, she has been the creative genius behind the church's unique Saint Patrick's Day liturgies. In her lively essay, Durkin reconstructs the fascinating history of Saint Patrick's Day in Chicago and sheds new light on the way in which the celebration has mirrored changing conceptions of Irish-American identity.

A key theme that emerges in this volume is the primacy of place. Since its dedication in 1856, Saint Patrick's Church has been a sacred site embodying the dreams and aspirations of hundreds of thousands of Chicagoans. In few neighborhoods have the bricks and mortar mattered so much. By building Saint Patrick's Church and establishing schools and charities, I argue that Irish Catholics claimed a distinct place for themselves in Chicago and left their imprint on the urban landscape. Maintaining parochial institutions in the fastest growing city in America was no easy task. Indeed, Mark Twain could have been describing Saint Patrick's neighborhood when he declared in 1883 that, "It is hopeless for the occasional visitor to try to keep up with Chicago . . . for she is never the Chicago you saw when you passed through the last time."[2]

Beautiful houses of worship such as Saint Patrick's didn't just happen nor was their success guaranteed. The same held true for parochial schools and charitable organizations. As Suellen Hoy documents, Chicago's "walking nuns" set the pace for social reform in 1846, establishing elementary schools and convent academies, nursing the sick in cholera epidemics, organizing Mercy Hospital, orphanages, and Sunday schools. Drawing on her own extensive research on public works, Hoy makes a convincing case that the Mercys created institutions that contributed to the well-being of Chicago and, at the same time, materially improved urban neighborhoods. Indeed, long before the founders of Hull-House were born, the Irish Sisters of Mercy had compiled a record of service unequaled by any other group of women. In her provocative essay, Hoy questions why nuns such as the Sisters of Mercy were "known by contemporaries, but lost to history."

Recovering the past of an immigrant group is difficult under ordinary circumstances. But, as Lawrence J. McCaffrey, one of the founders of Irish studies in America has shown, it is not an impossible task. Using extensive newspaper articles from the 1860s, McCaffrey has painted vivid portraits of Colonel James A. Mulligan and Reverend Denis Dunne. No other individuals did as much to revise negative stereotypes about the Chicago Irish during the Civil War than Mulligan and Dunne. The regiments they raised gave new meaning to the term *fighting Irish* and helped to improve the public image of Irish Catholics. It was not coincidental that Chicagoans of all classes mourned the deaths of Mulligan and Dunne with elaborate funerals fit for Irish chieftains.

Like many immigrant institutions, Saint Patrick's never enjoyed the luxury of document-

ing its past, but thanks to Finley Peter Dunne, the parish lives on in literature. When Chicago's brightest young journalist created the popular "Mr. Dooley" newspaper columns in the 1890s, he drew upon his family's stories and his own childhood memories of Old Saint Patrick's. Charles Fanning, the internationally known authority on Irish-American writers, asserts that the Chicago Dooley pieces "constitute the most solidly realized ethnic neighborhood in nineteenth-century American literature." In this book Fanning takes a new look at Dunne's pioneering accomplishments and discovers why his voice "still rings true across the hundred years since it first appeared."

At the time these essays were being written, Old Saint Patrick's Church embarked on a major restoration campaign aimed at completing the artistic vision of Thomas A. O'Shaughnessy. Timothy Barton, research director for the Chicago Landmarks Commission, recounts O'Shaughnessy's remarkable career as an artist and civic promoter. Barton draws on a wide range of sources to explore O'Shaughnessy's genius and his unique vision that transformed Chicago's oldest church into a masterpiece of Irish ecclesiastical art between 1912 and 1922. In his essay, Barton demonstrates that in addition to reconnecting the Chicago Irish with their Celtic past, O'Shaughnessy's luminescent stained glass windows and stencils also challenged contemporary notions of sacred art and transcended cultural boundaries.

At the Crossroads: Old Saint Patrick's and the Chicago Irish is a model for the multidisciplinary approach to urban, ethnic, and religious studies in America. While historians have acknowledged the important role Catholic churches and schools played in the formation of immigrant communities, they have not explored the influence these institutions exerted in the larger city. Janet Nolan, who has done pioneering work on the history of Irish and Irish-American women, redresses this imbalance. By focusing on Amelia Dunne Hookway, who grew up in Old Saint Patrick's parish and graduated from Saint Patrick's High School, Nolan documents the way in which Irish Catholic women shaped the city's public school system at the turn of the century. Trained by nuns, Catholic girls such as Amelia, Kate, and Mary Dunne used their education to better the lives of their own families as well as the city of Chicago. Indeed, the Dunne family's upward mobility was directly linked with their daughters' occupations as teachers in the city's public schools. While much research remains to be done on the connections between parochial and public institutions, *At the Crossroads* breaks new ground in discussing the public presence of Chicago Catholicism.

Now restored to its former beauty, Old Saint Patrick's Church has also reclaimed its central place in the life of Chicago. In the concluding essay in this volume, Reverend John J. Wall recounts the rebirth of Chicago's oldest church. It is a dramatic story, an eyewitness account of the challenges involved in creating a metropolitan church. Known throughout the city and nation as a place of initiative and imagination, Old Saint Patrick's has charted a bold course, blending the innovative with the traditional. In opening the Frances Xavier Warde School, for example, Old Saint Patrick's reclaimed the legacy begun by earlier generations of Catholics in this enchanted, holy place. Once again a thriving parish at the crossroads of urban life, Old Saint Patrick's is a powerful reminder that sacred space continues to make a difference in the lives of people and their city, generation after generation.

At the Crossroads: Old Saint Patrick's and the Chicago Irish enlarges our understanding of the way in which Irish immigrants used their churches and schools to create identity, community, and a place for themselves in Chicago. In addition, this book documents the equally daunting challenges facing succeeding generations who have attempted to "hold fast to the spot made precious by labors so evidently blessed."[3] Published in conjunction with the 150th anniversary of Saint Patrick's parish, these essays provide compelling evidence to support the creed of Irish poet Patrick Kavanaugh: "Parochialism is universal; it deals with the fundamentals."[4]

Saint Patrick's Day at Saint Patrick's Church

Eileen Durkin

Fifteen thousand Irishmen tramped through muddy streets last Tuesday to honor St. Patrick and Ireland. . . . Women with swarms of children were happy to take their stand in the muddy thoroughfare . . . alternately holding aloft babies and skirts if only they might see the clans go by and hear again the music of dear old Ireland. At St. Patrick's old church another multitude had blocked even the approaches in Adams street for half a block on both sides of Desplaines street. . . . [S]everal thousands who liked to mix pleasure with sentiment crowded about the old church to watch the honors done for their patron saint.

The Chicago Citizen, *March 21, 1896*[1]

On March 17, 1896, the start of Chicago's Saint Patrick's Day parade was delayed for an hour by a one-hundred-year-old Irishman dancing a jig at the crossroads of Adams and Desplaines. A crowd blocked the line of march as Jimmy Lane celebrated in the shadow of an "old" Saint Patrick's Church just half his age.

Jimmy told the *Times-Herald* reporter that he had left Ireland more than sixty years earlier "for being too active at the drilling by the rising of the moon." As Chicago's earliest meat packer, turned grocer, alderman, boarding-house proprietor, and real-estate investor, Jimmy was "intimately associated" with the spectacular growth of the metropolis. In 1837

he distributed Chicago's first municipal charter to its citizens. A member of the prestigious Old Settlers' Club with its many descendants of Yankee stock, the proud recipient of the German society's "Oldest Settler" award, and a familiar sight to "every Irishman of any account in Chicago," Jimmy enjoyed a wide audience for stories. His memory as sharp as his blue eyes, he regaled listeners with tales of how the frontier settlement had erupted into a speculative boom town, a national crossroads where America shopped. Jimmy never missed a Saint Patrick's Day parade, an election, or "all the dances that were going."

In 1896 he stood in a carriage in Haymarket Square at Randolph and Desplaines (the site of the original, wooden Saint Patrick's Church) at the head of a platoon of police and marchers in top hats and green sashes. At the scheduled starting time of the parade, he excused himself to Grand Marshal Martin Mulcahy and drove off down Desplaines Street.

Earlier, he had heard a German band playing "The Wind That Shakes the Barley" at the crossroads of Saint Patrick's Church. The tune and its setting made Jimmy think of the Sunday dances at the crossroads back in Ireland. "There was the music . . . the 'four roads' crossing each other . . . colleens and bouchals [lads] galore all around." Memory and mischief combined in the old man as he descended to the street and shouted, "Bring the back of a door!"

Dennis Wade, pipe sergeant (left) and Peter Conroy, pipe major (right), members of the Shannon Rovers Irish Pipe Band, founded in 1926, play a spirited, traditional march at the conclusion of a Saint Patrick's Day liturgy. (Photo by Jim Pollick)

He battered the floor—in this case the door—with a lively dance. The band knew only one Irish tune but kept playing when Jimmy saluted Patsy Brannigan, the champion dancer of the Irish Village at the 1893 World's Columbian Exposition. Patsy and two other lads did a three-handed reel in the brisk March air.

Back at the Haymarket, Grand Marshal Mulcahy of the Ancient Order of Hibernians was beside himself with the unknown delay. His aide, Frank Morgan, rode south to disperse the crowd. Though tempted to join the dance, Morgan "kept his saddle and cleared the way" as an angry Mulcahy finally caught up with Jimmy. They reconciled at the crossroads of Saint Patrick's, then turned east on Jackson toward Michigan Avenue and the reviewing stand at the Auditorium.[2]

One hundred years later, Jimmy Lane's great-nephew, Reverend John Lane, S.J., led the offertory procession up the aisle of Old Saint Patrick's Church during the 1996 liturgy honoring Saint Patrick and the 150th anniversary of the founding of his church in Chicago. Following the scripture readings, Jimmy's dance at the crossroads was reenacted by the pastor, Reverend John J. Wall, sporting a cap and blackthorn stick. Irish-American dancers, players, and musicians joined him for a tragic and comic retelling of the history of the church and its people in Chicago. At the conclusion of the Mass, the Shannon Rovers Pipe Band led the congregation out into the streets and down into the church hall for a lively brunch. Those assembled then moved on to Dearborn and Wacker to kick off the official Saint Patrick's Day Parade.

A Moveable Feast, A Memorable Date

For 150 years, Saint Patrick's Day at Saint Patrick's Church has captured the spirit and soul of the Irish in Chicago. If the publishers of the popular *Day in a Life* books ever chose to feature Chicago's Irish, they would dispatch their photographers on March 17 and direct them to Old Saint Patrick's Church. No place in the city has celebrated over a longer period of time or done more to sustain the rituals of the day and infuse them with meaning. As the neighborhood around Saint Patrick's and the ethnic makeup of parishioners changed, church leaders adapted not only their pastoral ministries but also their celebration of Saint Patrick's Day. At the same time, they preserved the day's spiritual and cultural value for the Irish throughout Chicago and maintained the church building as a sacred space at the crossroads.[3]

Mel Loftus, the 1996 parade coordinator, describes the activities of Saint Patrick's Day in Chicago as corresponding to the leaves of a shamrock: the Mass at Old Saint Patrick's, the downtown parade, the Irish Fellowship Club dinner. This trinity of events takes place at different places for different people, yet the celebration in Chicago has always been a moveable feast. From the beginning, crowds have processed from religious services to parades or other gatherings and then on to banquets, balls, or entertainments. While known primarily for "The Mass," Saint Patrick's has hosted festivities both sacred and secular where "almost imperceptibly the religious ceremony ends and the community celebration takes over."[4]

Bishop William J. Quarter dedicated the first Saint Patrick's Church on Easter, April 12, 1846, but the current congregation was historically accurate in launching their sesquicentennial celebration on the feast of their patron saint. March 17 has always been the most important public date on the church's calendar. With an ancient Irish belief in the turning points of the seasons and a Celtic Christian affection for saints, the people of Old Saint

Patrick's knew that on this day, things could happen at the crossroads—and things could be made to happen.

On March 17, 1853, Bishop James O. Van de Velde celebrated a Pontifical High Mass in the frame church at Randolph and Desplaines. He used the occasion to exhort the overflow crowd to build a larger structure down the street. During his sermon on the saint the year before, the Belgian-born bishop had asked the Irish to contribute generously to this "pious and as regards yourselves, truly national purpose." (In the next breath, he told them not to drink so much!)[5]

For poverty-stricken Irish immigrants, building a brick church in the 1850s was an heroic undertaking. Keeping that building open through the years has been equally daunting. As early as the turn of the century, the "mother parish" of Chicago's Irish stood isolated in the midst of a commercial district. In 1911, determined to restore Saint Patrick's to its role as "the central Catholic parish in the city,"[6] Reverend William J. McNamee commissioned Thomas A. O'Shaughnessy to redecorate its interior. The following Saint Patrick's Day, McNamee held special religious services to introduce the artist's ongoing work to the city and her Irish citizens. Over the next ten years, O'Shaughnessy transformed the old church into a masterpiece of Celtic Revival art. By 1922 Saint Patrick's Day mass-goers were marveling at his luminous stained glass windows and resplendent, interlacing stencils covering the ceiling and walls.

To this day, the histories of Saint Patrick's Church and Saint Patrick's Day are interlaced as tightly as O'Shaughnessy's designs in paint and glass. These ongoing histories are, in turn, intimately associated with the broader history of the Irish in Chicago. The Illinois and Michigan Canal, the Great Hunger in Ireland, prejudice against immigrants, the rapid growth of the Catholic Church, the "fighting Irish" in American wars, the bizarre complexities of Irish nationalist organizations—all contributed to the evolving celebration of Saint Patrick's Day. So, too, did the political aspirations of aldermen, the power of the press, labor struggles, cultural lobbying by the Gaelic League, and changing immigration patterns. Mass-goers and marchers were buffeted by natural disasters and economic depressions on both sides of the Atlantic.

Journalists covering Saint Patrick's Day in Chicago often reported on pontifical masses, parades, trans-Atlantic politics, and the prominent men behind these activities. Reading between the lines of 150 years of newspaper accounts, however, I began to imagine the individual histories of the men and women who lined the parade route or waited on the steps of the church. What had been the impact of this annual feast, I wondered, on them and their children and grandchildren? What were the dreams of the hotel maid who leaned out the balcony in 1862 to wave at Irish Civil War veterans carrying the "torn and tattered flag" from Lexington? What became of the shivering cadet from Saint Patrick's Total Abstinence, Temperance, and Benevolent Society who tramped through "mud thick upon the streets" in the 1870s? One March 17 in the early 1920s, a choirboy wept beside the communion railing in Saint Patrick's Church. No photographs exist of him or the visiting priest who towered over him describing—in detail—the gruesome executions during the Irish war for independence. Frank Brown, the choirboy, confessed recently that he still associates March 17 with sorrow.[7]

At the crossroads of Saint Patrick's Church, the religious, political, and cultural dramas of Saint Patrick's Day have been played out by individual characters, such as Brown, McNamee, O'Shaughnessy, and the irrepressible Jimmy Lane. In 1987 Father Wall invited me to narrate the saga of Chicago's Irish, to interview individuals and families and creatively weave together their stories for the Saint Patrick's Day liturgy. Every March 17 since that time, a chorus of dramatic voices has evoked the best and worst of Chicago's Irish—their experiences of family, neighborhood, faith, work, immigration, and becoming American. With resounding music, hushed invocations—and a strong dash of humor—we have reconstructed a community's memory and reclaimed the spirituality and symbols of the feast. In the sanctuary of the church, we have given voice to Irish women as well as men.

If, as Irish president Mary Robinson says, "Understanding comes with remembering," then in Chicago each March 17, the day, the place, and the people must be remembered together to be understood by Chicago's Irish and the multiethnic congregation of Old Saint Patrick's Church. Saint Patrick's Day is part of the phenomenal story of how one nation's holy day became an American national holiday, how "Kiss Me, I'm Irish" buttons and green beer came to coexist alongside traditional step dancers and fiddlers. In Chicago, as elsewhere, valentines are taken down and shamrocks put up without much thought as to that remarkable journey.[8]

From Holy Day to Holiday

The journey began, of course, in the early fifth century when Patrick was abducted and enslaved by an Irish chieftain. The youth underwent a profound religious conversion before escaping home to Britain. Against great odds, he became a priest, then bishop, and returned to bring Christianity to the Irish, who adopted him as their patron saint. During the centuries when the Irish were themselves oppressed, this ex-slave became a source of hope and the wandering saints and scholars he

inspired a source of pride to generations denied religious freedom and education.

Reporters often contrast the quiet, reverent commemorations of Saint Patrick's Day in Ireland with the boisterous celebrations in the United States. The Irish who fled the Great Famine of the 1840s and settled in parishes such as Saint Patrick's had had few opportunities for feasting. Later arrivals had grown up during Ireland's "devotional revolution" when feasting and dancing were discouraged.[9] The Irish had older traditions, however, of breaking the Lenten fast by "drowning the shamrock" in deference to the good saint. When not forbidden by law, their pilgrimages combined private commemorations of saints with public celebrations of life.

When the gregarious Irish came to America, they took advantage of their new freedoms to develop Saint Patrick's Day traditions in the New World: religious services, processions of military companies and charitable societies, banquets with guests from "sister societies" of other nations, gatherings in taverns for those not attending banquets, appeals for Irish liberty, and staunch proclamations of allegiance to the United States.[10] Annual sermons reminded Irish immigrants that their patron saint had himself been a stranger in a new land.

Jimmy Lane and Irish canal workers carried these holiday traditions with them when they came to Chicago in the 1830s via the East Coast. By 1843 they accounted for only 773 of Chicago's 7,580 residents, yet their first public celebration of Saint Patrick's Day captured the attention of a city with, even then, "a disposition to festivals." On March 17 the Montgomery Guards, an all-Irish militia that included Jimmy, marched with the newly formed Catholic Temperance Society from the public hall to Saint Mary's Cathedral at Madison and Wabash. After Mass—celebrated by a French priest—the crowd marched back to the hall for a lecture by the well-known Dr. William Bradshaw Egan. Less than six months earlier, Dr. Egan had formed "an association for the repeal of the Union between England and Ireland," the first of many local organizations of Protestants and Catholics dedicated to Irish freedom.[11]

At the crossroads of the continent, the Irish ritual of springtime also encountered the tenacity of Chicago's winters, introducing the most enduring character of all our Saint Patrick's Day celebrations: the weather. From 1843 until 1901, when the original parade was disbanded, blowing dust from unpaved streets coated magnificent banners and muddy snow dampened boots, if not spirits. Journalists marvelled at the perplexing optimism of the Irish, who insisted that the day brought "color to sunless streets" and that "breezes made the flags wave better."

Irish-born Bishop Quarter held great hopes for Chicago's Irish immigrants and began his first Holy Week in the new diocese with a special Mass on Saint Patrick's Day, 1845. The following August, however, blight destroyed the potato crop in Ireland, as it would five times over the next seven years. Ireland had alternative sources of food, yet agricultural and social conditions, market ideology, government mismanagement in Britain, and prejudice against the Irish character led to a devastating famine. During the decade surrounding this tragedy, Ireland lost one quarter of her population, approximately one million to starvation and disease and one and a half million to emigration. Weeks before the first Saint Patrick's Day at Saint Patrick's Church, the city's Irish took up a subscription for relatives back home suffering from "Black '47." So great was the "influx of immigrants" in 1848, that Quarter and others founded the Hibernian Benevolent Emigrant Society to raise funds for the poor in both Ireland and Chicago. They sponsored an impressive series of lectures and hosted a banquet on March 17. Saint Patrick's young pastor, Reverend Patrick McLaughlin, attended on behalf of those crowding the pews of his wooden church.[12]

Biographies of Chicagoans involved in Saint Patrick's Day celebrations in the nineteenth century reveal the direct influence of the Famine on them and their families. In 1849 Jimmy Lane sent money for his brother's entire family to journey to Chicago. Only an orphaned niece and nephew disembarked at the Dearborn Street Bridge. William J. Onahan was a businessman and philanthropist whose involvement in Irish organizations over the years reads like a "Who's Who" of where the prosperous Irish were dining on Saint Patrick's Day. He lost his mother to cholera in Liverpool in 1849, when that city was a crowded way station for Irish fleeing to Canada and the United States. An early member and life-long friend of Saint Patrick's parish, Onahan helped organize the Irish Catholic Colonization Association, coordinating its national convention in Chicago on March 17, 1879. Archbishop James E. Quigley's parents survived a treacherous crossing from Liverpool to Quebec in 1850. Fifty-three years later, their son arrived in Chicago from Buffalo, New York, and one of his first public appearances was on Saint Patrick's Day at Saint Patrick's Church.

Speeches and sermons during early Saint Patrick's days in Chicago clearly alluded to the Famine's aftermath, linking "the ruin by which Ireland is at present surrounded" to her people's lack of nationhood and history of suffering for Patrick's faith. While tears for Erin flowed freely and often, they never erased smiles on Saint Patrick's Day since enthusiasm for the festival united the diverse Irish community. On March 17, 1852, for example, Englishmen, Scotchmen, Irishmen, and "Americans" gathered at the annual banquet of the Hibernian Benevolent Emigrant Society. When the chairman proposed the opening toast, Jimmy Lane surely raised his glass and, in accordance with custom, echoed back loudly, "The Day We Celebrate!" After the chairman's lengthy oration on the meaning of "The Day," the band struck up "Saint Patrick's Day in the Morning," followed by toasts to the president, the Constitution, and "The Memory of Washington."[13] In 1864 toasting at one banquet continued until three in the morning. Only then could the dancing begin!

After the Famine, almost one in five Chicagoans were Irish-born. Religious and political leaders could not ignore the number of Irish faces lining an expanding parade route. The resulting anti-immigrant backlash of the 1850s caused "Irish" to become equated only with "Catholic" and Chicago's Saint Patrick's Day celebrations to lose their ecumenical quality.[14] Among Irish Catholics, however, both the prosperous and the laboring took advantage of the annual, public opportunity to confront stereotypes. Appearance was everything, and

from the beginning that appearance was green . . . and red, white, and blue.

According to a correspondent for the *Western Tablet,* Chicago's first Catholic newspaper, "the solemn proceedings" at Saint Patrick's Church in 1853 "were well calculated to excite the deepest respect and veneration." Bishop Van de Velde "was seated under a handsome canopy erected for the occasion. . . . The altar was tastefully decorated and had a beautiful green drapery neatly festooned and prettily adorned with emblems truly befitting the day." The "choir in attendance was excellent and the various pieces of music selected, were executed with admirable taste and precision."[15]

The "ladies who took part in the celebration" at Saint Mary's the following year "imparted to the church a most brilliant

News reports of the Great Famine in Ireland described Irish peasants as "crawling skeletons," practically naked, with "little protection against inclement weather." Survivors who settled in Chicago in the late 1840s and 1850s found refuge at Saint Patrick's Church. (Illustrated London News)

appearance." Over at Saint Patrick's, Father McLaughlin celebrated Mass in an imposing ceremony assisted by a French priest and a German priest. Evening banqueters feasted on sumptuous dinners surrounded by ornate round towers, harps, and shamrocks.[16] By the 1890s, American-born Irish poked fun at "paraders and diners" dressed up in green neckties, stovepipe hats, and regalia with "gaudy sashes." Yet for those who had fled Ireland hungry and demoralized, what a luxury to attend a banquet where "abundant attention" was given to both food and conversation. For those who had arrived in rags, clothing—even costumes—conveyed dignity and the color green, distinctiveness.

American patriotism became an increasingly important theme of Saint Patrick's Day as battles raged in the editorial pages over whether Irish Catholics could be loyal to both the pope and the president. Chicago's Irish regiments and their bands were stationed in front of the altar each March 17 at Saint Patrick's Church. Irish Americans born after the election of John F. Kennedy may be unaware of the depth of anti-Catholic and anti-Irish prejudice experienced by their ancestors. And yet, in 1856, Saint Patrick was hung in effigy in New York days before the feast. No wonder Chicago's Irish draped countless star-spangled banners throughout the city on his feast day.

Although crowd violence was not a feature of Saint Patrick's Day in Chicago, the organizers of the day's events worried about public drunkenness, greatly increased by the Famine immigration. Both clergy and laity encouraged parade-goers to emulate the virtues of Saint Patrick and avoid "sinful excesses." At times, their efforts prevailed. Before the 1865 parade, "Catholic ladies of Chicago" presented American and Irish flags to the Roman Catholic Temperance Society while Miss Mary White addressed a crowd at Bishop James Duggan's

residence. In 1878 a *Chicago Tribune* reporter was forced to concede that he saw "not one intoxicated person . . . upon the line of march."[17]

In spite of scarce resources, Chicago's Irish regularly practiced the virtue of charity, especially on the emotional feast of their patron. The local Society of Saint Vincent de Paul, founded in the basement of Saint Patrick's in 1857, took up collections for the poor at the church door each March 17. In 1879 the Daughters of Charity from the school began their own campaign, standing in a carriage in the middle of Desplaines Street and soliciting contributions to Saint Joseph's Orphan Asylum from those streaming out of Mass. By the 1890s Chicago's pastors had long recognized the fundraising potential of the day. They vied with each other to deliver lectures or stage entertainments that drew large crowds and raised money for new churches and schools.[18]

Following the Civil War, organizations promoting Irish freedom began competing with the Catholic Church for these significant charitable dollars. For many immigrants and their children, bitterness over the Famine transformed the day into an occasion to rally around the cause of Irish nationalism. Bishop Duggan condemned the new Fenian brotherhood as a secret society dedicated to the violent overthrow of the British government in Ireland, and he chastised those who would remember the patriot on March 17 but forget the saint.[19] Until the end of the century, conflict between organizers of religious and civic celebrations became a recurring feature of Saint Patrick's Day in Chicago, first between Fenians and the Catholic Church and later between proliferating nationalist organizations.

On March 17, 1866, the parade and Mass were deliberately scheduled for the same time. Grand Marshal David Walsh stepped out with Fenian volunteers from the corner of Orleans and Lake Streets while Bishop Duggan was

SEVENTH ANNUAL BANQUET

OF THE

IRISH LITERARY ASSOCIATION

AT THE

SHERMAN HOUSE,

CHICAGO,

MARCH 17th, 1876.

MENU.

OYSTER SOUP.

Raw Oysters.   Fried Oysters.   Scolloped Oysters.   Spiced Oysters.

Broiled Whitefish, Steward Sauce.   Boiled Fresh Codfish, Oyster Sauce.
Baked Bluefish, Wine Sauce.

Boiled Turkey, Oyster Sauce.   Boiled Leg of South Down Mutton, Caper Sauce.
Boiled Ham.   Boiled Jole and Cabbage.

Roast Beef.   Roast Turkey, Cranberry Sauce.   Roast Chicken, Giblet Sauce.
Roast Saddle of Mutton, Jelly Sauce.

Boned Turkey with Jelly.   Cold Roast Turkey.   Cold Roast Chicken.
Cold Boiled Tongue.   Oyster Salad.   Lobster Salad.   Sardines.
Salmon Trout a la Myonaise.

ENTREES.

Fillet of Beef with Croquets Potatoes.   Mutton Cutlets en Carbonade a la Financere.
Macaroni en Timbole a la Parisann.   Rock Bass a la Turban.
Fulton Market Scallops fried in Crumbs with Anchovy Essence.

RELISHES.

Lettuce.   Pickles.   Chow Chow.   Horseradish.   Worcestershire Sauce.
Nabob Sauce.   Tomato Catsup.

VEGETABLES.

Mashed Potatoes.   Lima Beans.   Stewed Tomatoes.   Sweet Corn.
Boiled Potatoes.   Green Peas.   Boiled Turnips.   Boiled Cabbage.

GAME.

Roast Mallard Ducks with Grape Jelly.   Roast Bluewing Ducks, Game Sauce.
Roast Saddle of Antelope with Currant Jelly.

PYRAMIDS.

Pound Cake.   Lady Cake.   Fruit Cake.   Orange Cake.

DESSERT.

Oranges.   Apples.   Raisins.   Walnuts.   Almonds.
Filberts.   Pecan Nuts.   Figs.
Vanilla Ice Cream.   Roman Punch.
Tea and Coffee.

Menu from the Irish Literary Association's 1876 dinner, one of several patriotic banquets and balls held in Chicago to commemorate the Saint Patrick's Day Centennial celebration in America. (Courtesy, Special Collections and Preservation Division, the Chicago Public Library) celebrating Mass "with full choir and orchestra" over at Adams and Desplaines. Irish citizens were forced to choose between demonstrations of nationalist power or religious respectability. Those at mass meetings raised funds for a Fenian "invasion" of Canada, while those at Mass offered alms for the poor. The following year, the Knights of Saint Patrick broke away from the Saint Patrick's Society "over the question of whether to toast the hierarchy." They staged an alternate banquet, although Reverend John McMullen, D.D., a leading clergyman, discounted the rift. He claimed, "When Irishmen do differ, they make a great deal of noise about it."[20]

Less than ten years later, laity and clergy, the parade and the Mass linked up again, and Saint Patrick's Church stood at the crossroads of the city's grand celebrations. The "point of rendezvous" for the parade was moved in front of the church, which had survived the Great Chicago Fire of 1871 and boasted a new gallery to accommodate mass-goers. Although newspapers devoted almost all their attention to the afternoon and evening festivities, anecdotal evidence reveals that the Irish community depended on morning Mass to keep the saint in Saint Patrick's Day.

In 1875 Grand Marshal John F. Finerty, a prominent Irish nationalist and newspaper editor, attended religious services in his own parish but was forced to delay the parade because many key participants were still inside Saint Patrick's Church. As "the day was particularly cold and blustery, and the Mass was unusually long," Finerty dispatched an aide to see what was happening. The aide returned with assurances that Mass was almost over, but Finerty, "chilled to the marrow," cried, "O, botheration to the Mass." The following November, he ran for clerk of the superior court, and the alleged remark was "brought up against him." As John Kelley remembered, "It was told with

variations and resulted in his defeat." John J. Healy, who was Jimmy Lane's son-in-law, won the election.[21]

In 1876, immediately after Mass at Saint Patrick's Church, Bishop Thomas Foley and Mayor Harvey D. Colvin reviewed the parade from the rectory balcony. No doubt they admired Reverend Patrick Conway's new brick school buildings and marvelled at the growing influence of the Irish—and their churches—throughout the city. The parade that passed below them united nationalist groups and parish-based societies into a four-hour procession that ventured all the way north to the cathedral of Holy Name, south to Saint John's, and west to Holy Family.

During this time, the nationalist cause increasingly occupied the attention of the city's Irish—and sympathetic clergy as well. The Clan-na-Gael Guards and Ancient Order of Hibernians (AOH) replaced the Fenians, lobbying vigorously for tenants' rights in Ireland and Charles Stewart Parnell's "Home Rule" bill. Beginning on the eve of Saint Patrick's Day, 1883, however, and for several years thereafter, the Chicago clan masterminded a dynamite campaign in England. So enthusiastically did John Finerty support the bombings at Whitehall, Victoria Station, and the Tower of London that the British press labeled him "Finerty the Dynamitard."[22] The bombings and subsequent scandals involving Irish politicians and organizations at home and abroad alienated a new generation of Irish Americans.

As Charles Fanning has demonstrated, newspaper editor Finley Peter Dunne was among those who sought to distance themselves from the bombastic rhetoric and nationalist displays of Saint Patrick's Day. Dunne had grown up across the street from Saint Patrick's Church during the years following the Great Fire when, each March 17, crowds "surged around the church and the priests' house, the central points of interest." He abhorred the transformation of Saint Patrick's Day from a religious and cultural event into a political one. In editorials in the *Chicago Evening Post* in the 1890s, Dunne lambasted the endless political maneuvering around the parade as "an insult to religion and a disgrace to the much abused Irish cause." He applauded those who found "more appropriate, more intelligent and practical ways" to celebrate the day than traipsing over cobblestones.[23]

Dunne was not alone in his criticism. The Irish-American Council that met each February to plan the parade canceled the procession several times in the 1880s and 1890s to avoid scandal or to divert money to relief work in Ireland and Chicago. Bewildered immigrant parents and priests complained, "Irish boys and girls do not take part in our parades—they mutter and refuse."[24] The pro-parade contingent pressed on, however, emboldened by the support of several hundred thousand spectators and the "stout lads" of the Gaelic Athletic Association. They moved the starting point of the parade to Haymarket Square at Randolph and Desplaines (where Irish policemen had died during the riot of 1886) and shifted the reviewing stand to different neighborhoods. By 1896, when Jimmy Lane danced at the crossroads, Saint Patrick's had aged along with the Famine immigrants and was only a sentimental stop on the parade route.

Although Dunne campaigned seriously against the parade, it provided rich—often humorous—material for his columns featuring the saloonkeeper-philosopher, "Mr. Dooley." Noting that the 1896 parade had turned east from Saint Patrick's toward the lakefront instead of west towards Holy Family, Mr. Dooley observed: "What business have we in Mitchigan Avenoo? There ain't a vote or a subscriber to th' Citizen there an' they'se twinty-sivin blocks iv unfrindly houses without enough dhrink to

start a fight on. Sure we'd a-done betther if we'd stuck where we belonged. Displaines street . . . south to Harr'son, wist to Bloo I'l'and avnoo, south-wist to Twilfth, where th' procission'll counthermarch befure th' Jesuit Church an' be reviewed be his grace th' archbishop, be th' clargy an' th' mayor an' th' board iv aldhermin . . . . 'Twas Pathrick's day thin."[25]

Dunne's facts were a bit off—Jimmy had marched many times down Michigan Avenue—but his satire provides us with an invaluable glimpse into the complex social history of the parade. In one column Mr. Dooley ridicules the bravado of parade organizers yet admits that come Saint Patrick's Day, even he feels "like goin' up on th' roof an' singin' O'Donnell Aboo so all may hear." Addressing the parade's reputation for starting late, Mr. Dooley explains, "It's a long wait, but nobody minds. It's nachral. It takes time f'r to start a Pathrick's day parade, because ivrybody looks as though they ought to be out in front."[26]

After 1901 Chicago's weather quieted the noisy parade debate. Veteran newspaper reporter John Kelley explained that the parade organizers could no longer depend upon the "'old timer' from the Emerald Isle who would rather march than eat." So many aged marchers had died of pneumonia following parades in the 1890s that the Roman Catholic clergy "discouraged the annual turnout." They blamed the deaths on the Celts' "love of marching" and appealed to the Irish-American Council to abandon the procession in 1902.

Post-Parade Festivities

With the parade "leaf" of the shamrock gone, no single activity united the Irish community on Saint Patrick's Day. The number of religious and civic events multiplied, however. On the morning of March 17, 1902, for example, Chicago's Irish attended Masses at churches

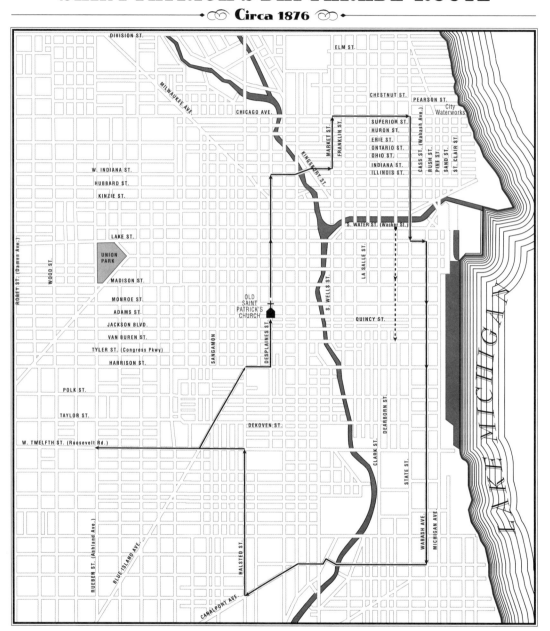

SAINT PATRICK'S DAY PARADE ROUTE
⟨⟨ Circa 1876 ⟩⟩

Saint Patrick's Day Parade Route, circa 1876
The 1876 parade route (solid line) started on Desplaines to Indiana (Grand Avenue), continued east to Market (Orleans), north to Chicago Avenue, east to State Street, south to Lake Street, east to Wabash Avenue, south to Eighteenth Street, west to the intersection of Canal and Canalport, southwest to Halsted Street, north to Twelfth Street (Roosevelt Road), and west to Reuben (Ashland Avenue). A countermarch (also solid line) then began on the north side of Twelfth Street to Blue Island Avenue, northeast to Harrison Street, east to Desplaines Street, and north to the final destination of Old Saint Patrick's Church. The modern parade route (dashed line) is considerably shorter, beginning at Dearborn and Wacker, traveling south down Dearborn, and terminating at Dearborn and Van Buren.

Saint Patrick's Day parade route, 1876. Anyone who has ever complained about the cold march down State Street or Dearborn Street need only imagine the stamina required to follow Grand Marshal Hugh J. Maguire through the streets of Chicago 120 years ago. (Map by Robert Voigts) throughout the city. At Saint Thomas the Apostle in Hyde Park, many heard the acclaimed Reverend J. J. Carroll preach his annual sermon in Gaelic. That evening, the Gaelic League and other Irish organizations held a mass political and cultural meeting. Presiding was Reverend A. J. Burns of Saint Patrick's Church, "one of the most widely known advocates of the revival of the Irish spirit in the Irish people." Other activities included a benefit ball supporting the Irish-American Boer Ambulance Association and a joint Irish-Polish celebration where "pictures of Robert Emmet and Thaddeus Kosciusko were draped with the flags of both countries."[27]

That same year Judge Edward F. Dunne joined other distinguished citizens in forming the Irish Fellowship Club "for the purpose of promoting friendship and good fellowship among Americans of Irish birth and descent; to give recognition to and keep alive Irish cultural traditions; and to fittingly celebrate Saint Patrick's Day." Archbishop Quigley spoke at their first banquet, and the *Chicago Tribune* noted that the "toasts, while keeping Ireland's patron as the central theme, were not of race, politics, or religion, but of America and Americanism."[28] In 1910 President William Howard Taft agreed to be the featured speaker at the annual Saint Patrick's Day banquet, the first of several heads of state to appear before the club. As a token of their appreciation and in keeping with their aim to promote Irish culture, the club commissioned Thomas O'Shaughnessy to design an ornamental tribute to the president.

During the nineteenth century, official Saint Patrick's Day events had been primarily male affairs. Newspapers praised the elaborate banners carried by marchers but rarely commented on the women who created them. Patricia Kelleher has argued that Irish women may have found greater opportunities in parish-

based and charitable work than in the broad movement of Irish nationalism.[29] By the turn of the century, however, women were orchestrating annual dramatic and musical productions that benefitted parishes, schools, and charities. The Knights of Columbus and Catholic women's groups soon drew the children of the AOH and its Ladies Auxiliary to their more modern St. Patrick's Day gatherings. As the Irish met success and suburbia, interest in the Gaelic revival waned. Instead their children attended such Americanized activities as Saint Patrick's Day card parties, dances, and fashion shows sponsored by sodalities and Holy Name societies.

The yearly celebration at Saint Patrick's Church continued to evolve throughout the twentieth century. From 1911 until his retirement in 1933, Father McNamee relied on special programming to attract Chicago's Irish back to the aging neighborhood. He transformed the high feast into a series of events that showcased O'Shaughnessy's art and provided funds for parish and school operations. To promote Irish culture and spirituality, he invited Irish organizations to concerts, lectures, groundbreaking ceremonies, and "impressive religious services" to which "hundreds sought in vain for admittance."

"Father Mac" certainly made the unexpected happen on Saint Patrick's Day. He invited a woman, Agnes L. Byrne, to unveil a large Celtic cross at Adams and Desplaines, the Chicago Symphony to accompany Dr. J. Lewis Browne's 150-voice choir, and a professor to raise funds for a chair in Irish history at the University of Chicago. For the blessing in 1915 of O'Shaughnessy's mosaic shrine to Saint Patrick, McNamee appropriated all the popular symbols of the day: the organist played "River Shannon" and "Saint Patrick's Day in the Morning" while the Ladies Auxiliary of the AOH placed "a mass of shamrocks" at the foot of the statue. With all this activity, *The New*

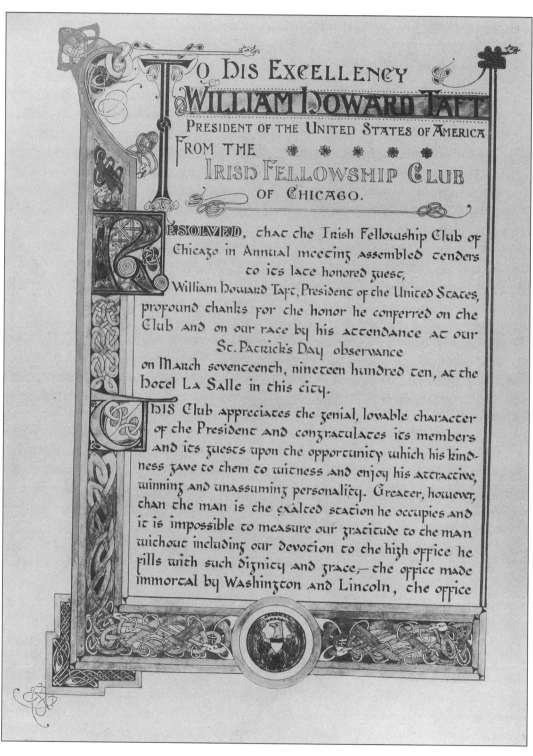

To His Excellency
WILLIAM HOWARD TAFT
PRESIDENT OF THE UNITED STATES OF AMERICA
FROM THE ✱ ✱ ✱ ✱ ✱
IRISH FELLOWSHIP CLUB
OF CHICAGO.

RESOLVED, that the Irish Fellowship Club of Chicago in Annual meeting assembled tenders to its late honored guest,

William Howard Taft, President of the United States, profound thanks for the honor he conferred on the Club and on our race by his attendance at our St. Patrick's Day observance on March seventeenth, nineteen hundred ten, at the Hotel La Salle in this city.

THIS Club appreciates the genial, lovable character of the President and congratulates its members and its guests upon the opportunity which his kindness gave to them to witness and enjoy his attractive, winning and unassuming personality. Greater, however, than the man is the exalted station he occupies and it is impossible to measure our gratitude to the man without including our devotion to the high office he fills with such dignity and grace,— the office made immortal by Washington and Lincoln, the office

In 1910 Thomas A. O'Shaughnessy designed the Irish Fellowship Club's tribute to President Taft with his signature Celtic designs. Between 1912 and 1922 O'Shaughnessy transformed Saint Patrick's Church into the best known example of Celtic Revival art in America. (Courtesy, Chicago Historical Society)

World hailed the renaissance of Saint Patrick's, once again "the heart of the city's life."

McNamee was pastor during a period of intense Irish nationalism coinciding with World War I and the Irish war for independence. The dreams of generations of Irish began to be realized in 1921 when Ireland and Great Britain signed a treaty granting dominion status to twenty-six counties, known as the Irish Free State. On Saint Patrick's Day, 1922, Bishop Edward F. Hoban and 100 priests cabled greetings from Saint Patrick's Church to Arthur Griffith, president of Dáil Eireann (the Irish Parliament), and Michael Collins, chairman of the provisional government. Jubilation turned to sorrow, however, when civil war engulfed Ireland. Finally, in 1926, peace came to their ancestral home, and the Irish in Chicago united on Saint Patrick's Day at Saint Patrick's Church to rejoice and give thanks. A local radio station agreed to broadcast the Mass, with preaching by Irish scholar Reverend Hugh P. Smyth and commentary by Father McNamee. An overflow crowd poured into the rectory and listened to McNamee's radio "as devoutly as though they were in church." When the Mass ended, the community moved into the new gymnasium to continue the celebration.[30]

The Great Depression and a growing "Skid Row" district put a halt to McNamee's ambitious plans for Saint Patrick's Church. With few resident parishioners, Saint Patrick's struggled to maintain its parish plant, social services, and the three schools run by the Daughters of Charity and the Christian Brothers. Like his predecessor, Reverend Thomas J. Hayes hosted seasonal fund-raising events, such as "The Triumph of St. Patrick," a 1936 concert in Orchestra Hall. Sister Margaret Quinn, D.C., attended the grammar school during this time. She remembers March 17 as a colorful, exciting day that drew a choir of over 100 voices and a standing-room-only crowd of parishioners and Irish Americans who had journeyed back to their mother church.

Contributions from mass-goers each March 17 helped educate Sister Margaret and her hundreds of classmates. Their Irish, Italian, Mexican, and Puerto Rican names attest that Saint Patrick's was one of the most ethnically diverse parishes in the city. Many of these students sang in the choir on March 17, 1946, when Samuel Cardinal Stritch celebrated the one hundredth anniversary of the founding of the parish. In preparation for this centennial, Reverend Richard F. Wolfe invited Chicago's Irish to a traditional banquet at a downtown hotel. One hundred years after the Great Famine, they feasted in grand style—and helped reduce the parish's $100,000 debt.[31]

For schoolchildren like Margaret Quinn, "Saint Patrick's Day was always a big day at Saint Patrick's Church." Yet for most children with Irish names scattered throughout the city and suburbs, the feast meant only the day off school, eating candy in the middle of Lent, and a determined search for something green to wear. In the 1950s, however, South and West Side Irish Catholics decided to revive Saint Patrick's Day parades and Irish culture. Older people lining Western Avenue at the current South Side Irish Saint Patrick's Day Parade recall the big procession down Seventy-Ninth Street in the 1950s. Proceeds from the 1955 neighborhood parade along Madison Street near Laramie were sent back "home" to Saint Patrick's, the original West Side parish. An ad for the annual corned-beef-and-cabbage fund-raising dinner described new challenges facing the old church. For example, land clearance for the superhighway had reduced the number of neighborhood employees. Even more troubling, the new Saint Peter's Church was attracting Loop hotel workers and guests who formerly worshiped at Saint Patrick's![32]

Restarting the Parade

Irish immigrants present at the dedication of Saint Patrick's brick church on Christmas Day, 1856, could never have predicted that their "up and coming" neighborhood would attract so few residents fifty years later. In 1956 only a handful of visionaries held out hope that the Near West Side and Old Saint Patrick's could reinvent themselves yet again. Nevertheless, as Virginia LeFevour points out, Chicago had a new mayor—Richard J. Daley. "It would be hard," she wrote, "to separate the things he loved most: his family, his heritage, his religion, and his city. An idea was presented to him by the West Side Saint Patrick's Parade committee that would honor all four and involve Saint Patrick's." Reminiscing to reporter Steve Neal, parade stalwart Daniel P. Lydon insisted, "Old Saint Pat's Church is really the reason that the parade started." Apparently, Lydon and Reverend Thomas Byrne "went down to see Mayor Daley and got a permit to hold the first downtown parade."[33]

When the Chicago Journeymen Plumbers Union stepped forward as sponsor, Lydon and others united the South and West Side marchers into the first central-city parade in more than fifty years. Celebrating the "100th Anniversary of Old Saint Patrick's," Chicago's Irish marched

In 1956 Mayor Richard J. Daley and Admiral Daniel V. Gallery led the first Saint Patrick's Day parade downtown in over five decades. The celebration also marked the 100th anniversary of the building of Old Saint Patrick's Church. (Courtesy, Saint Patrick's Day Parade Committee)

from Wacker Drive down State Street to Adams and then over to Desplaines for a Mass celebrated by Cardinal Stritch. Joining Mayor Daley in the front line was the Grand Marshal, Admiral Daniel V. Gallery, who had grown up in Saint Patrick's parish next door to his famous grandfather, William J. Onahan. Gallery knew, firsthand, the important role Saint Patrick's had played in the history of Chicago. In addition, he embodied Irish-American patriotism: he had commanded the naval task force that captured the German U-505 submarine in World War II, and he had worked to bring it to Chicago's Museum of Science and Industry.

In the four decades of the modern parade, organizers have worked closely with Old Saint Patrick's Church to unite the religious and civic celebrations. The current program includes Mass at Old Saint Patrick's, brunch in the church hall, and the parade down Dearborn to Van Buren. The ritual begins before Mass with the parade queen, grand marshal, mayor, and representatives of the Irish government processing up the aisle of the church past politicians and grandmothers crowding the pews. As chaplain to the parade committee, the pastor of Old Saint Patrick's reciprocates by marching "out in front" each year.

As in the last century, dressing, dining, and decorating remain important on Saint Patrick's Day in Chicago. Stephen Bailey, long-time chairman of the downtown parade, proudly wore his green bow tie and derby weeks before the feast. The Irish Literary Society's elegant menu from 1876 boils down, at Old Saint Patrick's, to corned beef, eggs, and soda bread—but there had better be plenty of it. Symbolically, Chicago makes its biggest splash with green vegetable dye tossed into the river. In the 1980s painted shamrocks mysteriously appeared on the sidewalk in front of the church—to the delight of some and the consternation of others. (It was very durable paint.)

Yet how many church members knew that Queen Victoria had forbidden Irish troops to wear Saint Patrick's symbol of the trinity on his feast day? To early parishioners, shamrocks and "The Wearin' o' the Green" symbolized defiance against cultural and religious cleansing. In Ireland people still go "down the field" the morning of March 17 to gather a fresh sprig. Older immigrants who stepped over the green paint at Adams and Desplaines recall those fields and the Saint Patrick's Day letter from home containing wilted shamrocks and vivid memories. When those mass-goers opened the doors of Old Saint Patrick's, young ushers wearing green-tinged carnations welcomed them "home" again in spirit.

Following Father Byrne's example, succeeding pastors have relied on the parade committee and those attending the "parade" Mass to support the church beyond March 17. As a result of this partnership and in conjunction with Mayor Daley and the city council, Old Saint Patrick's gained landmark status in 1964, the first house of worship so designated in the city. After morning Mass and before the parade that year, Reverend Stephen J. O'Donnell invited archdiocesan and civic leaders to a commemorative ceremony at the crossroads. Through the years, committee members have also generously supported fund-raising efforts, including the "Renaissance Campaign" aimed at restoring O'Shaughnessy's artistic vision for Saint Patrick's Church. Their annual parade book educates mass-goers with articles on the Irish in Chicago and the church that first ministered to them. In 1996, on the occasion of Old Saint Patrick's sesquicentennial, the parade committee named Father Wall guest of honor for the day.

An Old Celebration, A New Millennium

After more than 150 years, Saint Patrick's Day in Chicago remains a moveable feast of symbol and spirit. As the twentieth century draws to a close, the parade route may be shorter, but the Mass is just as long, the church as crowded, the rain and snow just as inevitable. While speeches may end earlier in the evening, banqueting and fund-raising go on all month, and those organizing events continue to be vigilant against underage and public drinking. We observe less political activism on the feast but still plenty of politics—particularly during primary season when "ivrybody" hustles to be out in front. In addition there appears to be less need for the Irish to unite for power and more need for shared remembering. The tragic story of the Great Famine, for example, was lost to Chicago's Irish until it was revived in 1995 on Saint Patrick's Day at Saint Patrick's Church, along with a challenge to aid victims of hunger around the globe.

As yearly newspaper accounts attest, Chicago's Irish consistently have used this feast of their patron saint to remember who they are, where they have come from, and how they can make an impact on their city and world. The immigrants who built Saint Patrick's survived great hardships and seized unimaginable opportunities. Each March 17 their descendants honor them and give thanks to God with prayer that turns into a party. During Father Wall's tenure, church membership has grown dramatically to include city dwellers and suburbanites as well as descendants of immigrants from many nations. Today, the people of Old Saint Patrick's stand at a new crossroads as they determine how to celebrate for all this great Irish feast of belonging. The historical record suggests a tradition, worthy of revival, of reaching out on Saint Patrick's Day to other ethnic groups and religions, of assisting those in need even while investing in the sacred space at the crossroads.

Of March 17, Mr. Dooley said: "It's like a dhream. It don't last more thin a minyit, but a millyon things can happen in it." For 150 years, a million things have happened on this holy day at the crossroads. Jimmy Lane and the assorted individual characters who made things happen belong eternally to Saint Patrick's Day at Saint Patrick's Church. Surely they march beside us as we step off—with Mr. Dooley—into a new century of celebration: "Glory be, me saddle's slippin'. Ar-re ye ready? For-wa-ard, march!"[34]

Stepdancers from the Sheila Tully School of Irish Dance at Saint Patrick's Church, March 17, 1996 (from left to right) *Mary Ellen Sheil, Courtney Driscoll, Annie Sebastian, Nancy Ziemba, Cortney Donahugh, and Cheryl Ziemba. When the religious ceremony ends, the community celebration takes over.* (Photo by Jim Pollick)

Creating Sacred Space in an Early Chicago Neighborhood

Ellen Skerrett

Mr. Dooley "stood with his hat off while the first communicants passed . . . and he watched them till they turned the corner to illuminate another grimy street."

Finley Peter Dunne
The Ladies' Home Journal, *December 1899*

Since its dedication on Christmas Day 1856, Saint Patrick's has dominated the crossroads at Adams and Desplaines Streets. The "mother parish" of the Chicago Irish, it is the oldest public building in the city, a landmark in the fullest sense of the word. Few American cities have been as profoundly shaped by sacred space as Chicago. Yet at the time Saint Patrick's was constructed, conventional wisdom held that church-building was a luxury that poor Irish immigrants could ill afford. Instead of investing scarce resources on masonry churches, critics suggested that money would be better spent on reformatories, larger prisons, and orphanages. Did sacred space matter? As the history of Saint Patrick's illustrates, creating a beautiful house of worship in an urban neighborhood was a monumental undertaking, with no guarantee of success.[1]

Although historians of the American Irish have devoted much attention to politics and nationalism, they have given short shrift to parochialism. Despite the fact that the parish was far and away the most important institution in the lives of Irish immigrants and their children and grandchildren throughout the nineteenth century and well into the twentieth, we know only the barest outlines of this story. And we know virtually nothing about the role sacred space played in shaping identity and creating community in the urban neighborhood, which is a tragedy because since the earliest days of Chicago, church-building has been a defining element of the local Irish experience.

When I started researching Chicago Irish parishes and neighborhoods more than twenty years ago I was struck by the conspicuous absence of material on "brick and mortar" Catholicism.[2] Considering that you cannot travel very far in Chicago without encountering massive parish complexes I found this a curious omission, indeed. Official histories rarely discussed how or why parishes financed beautiful churches and schools, much less the influence these places exerted on their surrounding neighborhood. Although sources were fragmentary at best, little by little I began to realize that church-building was a complex process that profoundly affected individual congregations as well as the larger city. One day while reading microfilm at the Chicago Public Library, I happened to find a review of significant Chicago buildings. A single item under the heading "Desplaines Street" caught my eye. There, in the tiniest print imaginable, was specific

✝ ✝ ✝

information on the construction of Old Saint
Patrick's, crucial details that had been lost to
history. The news story in the January 8, 1857
issue of the *Chicago Weekly Times* took less than
a minute to read. After all, it was only 16 lines, a
total of 133 words. But as I subsequently
learned, every phrase packed a wallop. Here was
incontrovertible evidence that for the Chicago
Irish, creating sacred space was as much about
competition as it was about worship.

Nothing has pleased me more than finding
the names of the architects of Chicago's oldest
church. In the middle of the nineteenth century,
the firm of Carter and Bauer was one of the
city's most prestigious. Asher Carter had worked
with the famous architect James Renwick on the
original Smithsonian building in Washington,
D.C. His German-born partner, Augustus Bauer,
played a leading role in the design and construction of New York's Crystal Palace. Together they
designed a Romanesque church that put Saint
Patrick's parish on the map.

The decision to build a brick church spoke
volumes about the aspirations of Irish immigrants. In a city still largely composed of wood,
every new masonry structure became a powerful symbol of permanence, of commitment.
Saint Patrick's was the first Catholic church
constructed west of the Chicago River, and as
the *Times* account suggests, appearances did
indeed matter. Despite the existence of nearby
limestone quarries, Saint Patrick's was built "of
Milwaukee brick, of a much better quality and
prettier color than is usually seen here." The
choice of cream-colored brick from Wisconsin, a
material preferred by wealthy Americans
because of its resemblance to Italian marble,

indicated that this was no ordinary house of worship. Moreover, as the *Chicago Times* noted, Saint Patrick's "differs, in style of architecture, from all other churches in the city" and the newspaper predicted that it "will be by far the most imposing looking edifice in the West Division." Especially noteworthy was its "grand entrance" between two octagonal towers. The architectural review concluded with the news that the congregation intended to make the church interior "in all respects worthy of the beautiful exterior."[3]

Although more than half a century would pass before the prediction was fulfilled—thanks to the genius of Thomas A. O'Shaughnessy—in 1912 Saint Patrick's became the first church in the United States decorated "entirely in the ancient Catholic art of the Irish people."[4] Just as the creation of this edifice defied the conventional wisdom of its day in 1856, O'Shaughnessy's Celtic windows and stencils redefined contemporary notions of sacred art. In reconnecting the Chicago Irish with their Celtic past, O'Shaughnessy also reclaimed Saint Patrick's central place in the life of the city, no small feat considering the vast changes that had occurred in the neighborhood around Adams and Desplaines.

Hopes and Dreams, Bricks and Mortar

At the time Saint Patrick's was constructed in the 1850s, the Irish were the largest—and poorest—ethnic group in Chicago. Although they had grown up with the city, their numbers did not automatically confer power or respectability. When Chicago was incorporated in 1837 it was little more than a frontier town on the shores of Lake Michigan. But change came swiftly, thanks in part to Irish immigrant labor, first on the Illinois and Michigan Canal and later on the railroads and in the stockyards and

steel mills. While the Irish played an important role in building the city, their political contributions were less appreciated. In 1840 William B. Ogden, Chicago's first mayor, complained bitterly that "the Irish entirely control'd the [recent] election" and the *Chicago American* agreed, noting that "the foreign population in Cook and Will counties have asserted the right . . . to elect officers for the sole reason that they are Irishmen."[5]

If some Chicagoans thought their city was becoming too foreign, they had cause. In 1850 fully half of its thirty thousand residents were immigrants. The Irish accounted for 20 percent of the population with the Germans not far behind. Although most of the Irish spoke English, which made them in one sense the least foreign of ethnic groups, it did not compensate for their behavior. As the daily newspapers confirmed, the Irish were a formidable force in politics; they filled the criminal court docket and the Bridewell (the Irish nickname for the local jail); and they strained the charitable resources of the young city. Equally alarming to many was their close identification with Roman Catholicism, a religion popularly depicted as mysterious and alien to American democratic ideals. Although early Irish immigrants were not as devout in their practices as later arrivals, in the public mind Irish and Catholic were synonymous.[6]

To an extent that I don't think we fully appreciate, Irish Catholics in Chicago used the process of church-building to create a place for themselves—and leave their imprint on the landscape. No one was more conscious of the great symbolic value of "brick and mortar" Catholicism than William J. Quarter, Chicago's first bishop. A native of Kings County (Offaly), Ireland, Quarter emigrated to America at the age of sixteen and was ordained in New York in 1829. As a young parish priest he had witnessed the difficulties of immigrant life in the fastest growing city in the United States. But he also knew from experience that the Catholic Church was compatible with American society and that it could flourish in urban slums as well as in middle-class neighborhoods.

When he arrived in Chicago on May 5, 1844, Quarter found only a single parish in the city, Saint Mary's. Although the new cathedral at Madison and Wabash was a "respectable building," it was far from complete. In his episcopal journal, the bishop noted that the walls were unplastered, "the sanctuary was enclosed with rough boards. . . . There were neither columns, nor steps, nor doors . . . and worse than all, even that much of a church was burdened with about three thousand dollars of debt . . . bearing interest at from 10 to 12 percent." Despite the precarious finances of the new diocese, Quarter regarded the completion of Saint Mary's as a first but crucial step in putting the city's Catholics on equal footing with their Protestant neighbors. Not only did its neo-classical design compare favorably with nearby houses of worship but also, the bishop was proud to note, the cathedral steeple was "the first and only spire, as yet, in the city of Chicago." If there were any doubts about Quarter's belief in the absolute necessity of sacred space, they were dispelled on October 5, 1845. For his dedication sermon he invoked Isaiah, Chapter 25: "The wilderness and the solitary place shall be glad for them and the desert shall rejoice and blossom as the rose."[7]

As his journal and correspondence with other bishops confirms, Quarter viewed church-building as a pragmatic response to the problems of immigration. Far from being a luxury, the bishop believed that houses of worship—as well as schools and charitable institutions—were essential to the well-being of Chicago immigrants and their city. Indeed, less than six months after he dedicated Saint Mary's Cathedral, he created three new parishes: Saint

Patrick's for the Irish and Saint Joseph and Saint Peter for the Germans. While church-building remained an important activity for native-born Americans as well as immigrants of different ethnic backgrounds, it took on new layers of meaning for the Irish.

Church-Building: The Irish Experience

Although millions in Ireland remained Catholic in the face of British colonial rule, centuries of oppression had left their mark on the people and also on their landscape. Some of the country's oldest Catholic monasteries and churches were in ruins; others had been converted into Protestant houses of worship. One of the most positive developments to occur since Catholic Emancipation in the 1820s was an ecclesiastical building boom. While thousands of families still worshiped in "long, low thatched chapel[s] in a state of indifferent repair," new permanent church buildings began to appear throughout the Irish countryside.[8] In 1842, for example, Catholics donated more than twelve-thousand pounds for the construction of a new Gothic cathedral in Killarney designed by world-famous architect Augustus Welby Northmore Pugin. A powerful sign of increasing Irish Catholic prosperity and respectability, Saint Mary's Cathedral was considered by many to be the finest example of Gothic revival architecture. But then disaster struck. The potato blight of the mid-1840s killed at least one million Irish and forced the emigration of nearly 1.5 million more. The cathedral of Saint Mary's became a scar on the Irish landscape, a painful reminder of lost hopes and dreams.

When a reporter for the *Illustrated London News* visited the Lakes of Killarney to investigate the effects of the Great Famine, he discovered visible signs of decay. Irish peasants were living in mud cabins with festering dung heaps at the door and the town's streets "absolutely swarm[ed] with ragged and miserable-looking people." Two landmarks stood out: the poorhouse where thirteen hundred men, women, and children struggled for survival; and the unfinished cathedral, "a melancholy monument of pride and poverty." According to the English correspondent, "Its lofty walls are bare and blank; its oriel windows are blocked up with planks of wood; and a swamp, a foot deep in water, lies between it and the public road."[9]

Survivors of the Great Famine in Ireland knew how difficult it was to create and sustain sacred space. It was not a pious activity for the faint-hearted. It involved vision, cooperation, financial commitment, and healthy doses of competition. As the history of Saint Patrick's demonstrates, church-building represented a new beginning for the Chicago Irish, one full of potential. Whatever else the larger society might have thought or said about them, Irish Catholics considered the construction of churches to be an investment in their future. What is striking about Saint Patrick's is the speed with which the congregation established its first house of worship and the extent to which it was a family affair.

When Bishop Quarter established parishes for Irish and German Catholics in 1846 he sparked a competition that Saint Patrick's won, hands down. Although all three congregations hired A. D. Taylor to design frame structures, Saint Patrick's was the first dedicated on Easter Sunday, April 12, 1846. What made the difference? To begin with, the bishop's brother, Reverend Walter Quarter, took a personal interest in Saint Patrick's, helping to raise the $750 construction fee. And it certainly didn't hurt

that the Quarter brothers knew the contractor, William Dunne, from his work on Saint Mary's Cathedral at Madison and Wabash.[10]

The first member of the legendary Dunne family to settle in Chicago, William arrived in 1843 from New Brunswick, Canada, where his father, uncles, and brothers were well-known ship carpenters. In a classic case of chain migration, within five years, the entire Dunne family—and their Riordan in-laws—had followed William to Chicago.[11] While plenty of work existed for skilled carpenters in the city, there was another, equally compelling reason to put down roots. In 1848 Denis, the youngest Dunne brother, was ordained for the Chicago diocese and began his rapid rise through the ranks of the Catholic Church.

By all accounts, the church William Dunne and his Irish laborers built at the southwest corner of Randolph and Desplaines Streets was a modest affair. Unlike the city's wealthy Protestant churches that lined fashionable streets such as Wabash and Michigan, Saint Patrick's stood in the heart of a working-class district west of the river. Already by the mid-1840s, this part of Chicago included shipyards, sawmills, and boardinghouses where poor immigrants crowded together. Thanks in part to the flood-tide of refugees from the Great Famine, the parish population grew dramatically, and by 1848 it was necessary to double the size of the original church.

Although Saint Patrick's had become a familiar landmark on the West Side, its location was precarious. In fact, less than four years after its organization, the mother parish of the Chicago

✛ ✛ ✛

Chicago's Irish Catholics reinvested in their West Side neighborhood by completing Saint Patrick's in 1856 and converting their original church (at right) *into classrooms.* (Courtesy, Old Saint Patrick's Church)

Irish found itself in the midst of a classic confrontation between sacred and secular space. The surrounding neighborhood had become such an important commercial center by 1850 that the city decided to open its fourth municipal market—popularly known as "Haymarket"—on Randolph Street near Desplaines. If this parish were to survive, Reverend Patrick McLaughlin and his Irish congregation decided, a new location was needed. Creating sacred space in urban neighborhoods has always been difficult, but in the early 1850s it involved a giant leap of faith. As it turned out, the purchase of property at Adams and Desplaines was a blessing in disguise because it guaranteed that Saint Patrick's could build a permanent church and establish parochial schools.

Transforming Urban Space

In the middle of the nineteenth century, Chicago was the fastest growing city in the nation. Almost overnight, it seemed, miles of prairie were built up into broad avenues that stretched as far as the eye could see. Americans, especially Easterners, were enthralled by the magnitude of the "Garden City" and newspapers regularly speculated about Chicago's potential to become the center of commerce for the whole Northwest. In May 1853 the *Daily Chicago Journal* acknowledged that while Chicago's future was unlimited, immediate measures were necessary to insure the health and well-being of its citizens. Unless the city established a system of drainage, the newspaper warned, its alleys and streets would continue filling up with garbage and filth "to poison the air we breathe and scatter with a liberal hand, the fruitful seeds of disease." Moreover, the newspaper argued that no matter how bright the prospects for Chicago investments, the city must offer "some inducements as a place of residence." Transforming prairies into business districts and neighborhoods was a tremendous undertaking, but the *Journal* expressed confidence that Chicagoans were equal to the task. It encouraged them to plant shade trees on public grounds and around individual homes. Such an effort, claimed the *Journal*, "will go farther towards convincing a stranger of the morality, industry and thrift of a community than would forty churches."[12]

However, the history of Saint Patrick's suggests that the construction of houses of worship did have long-term positive consequences for the larger city. Although church-building originated as a religious activity and had a spiritual purpose, its influence extended far beyond a single congregation. Whether located in industrial slums or middle-class areas, churches and synagogues contributed to the growth and development of Chicago. Poor immigrants especially took pride in their ability to finance places of beauty in their own neighborhoods. But creating sacred space had another, deeper meaning for Chicago's Irish Catholics. Each new church symbolized in a very visible way that, against overwhelming odds, these newcomers had captured a part of the city for themselves.

In parishes throughout Chicago, cornerstone layings and dedications became public acts of faith that linked congregation, church, and neighborhood. James A. Mulligan, a prominent lawyer who later became Chicago's first Irish Catholic Civil War hero, has left us an enduring image of the cornerstone laying of Saint Patrick's Church on Trinity Sunday, May 22, 1853. Among others, "a great number of the Sunday School children," led by the Sisters of Mercy, marched in procession from the original frame building to the new parish property. Mulligan also described the painstaking preparations involved in this ritual event: "the foundation marked out, the stone prepared, and a tin box to contain . . . coins of the country, and some of the religious and political newspapers

of the day." Other symbolic items in the cornerstone included the names of the pope, the president of the United States, the governor of Illinois, leading office holders, the bishop, vicar-general, president of the University of Saint Mary of the Lake, and last but not least, Saint Patrick's pastor. Linked to Chicago as well as the larger world, the Irish crowd listened "with marked attention" to Reverend J. A. Kinsella's sermon, after which they contributed to a collection for the new church. In his episcopal journal, Bishop Van de Velde summed up the event in five words: "Weather rainy, still great crowd."[13]

No sooner had the walls of the new brick church begun to rise, however, than Saint Patrick's was dealt a near deathblow by the cholera epidemic of 1854. Father McLaughlin and scores of parishioners died along with Mother Agatha O'Brien and three other Sisters of Mercy who had nursed victims of the dread disease. Work on the church came to an abrupt halt as residents buried their dead. While Chicagoans of all classes and ethnic backgrounds were touched by cholera, among Irish families the epidemic evoked painful memories of Ireland's devastating Famine. As the daily newspapers were quick to point out, Chicago's unpaved dirty streets and alleys had aggravated the spread of cholera. "During some of the hottest days of the season," noted the *Weekly Chicago Democrat*, "we have seen through the crevices in the sidewalks water, foul and reeking with disease."[14] The Near West Side's low street grade and rotting plank sidewalks posed definite health risks, but few of its residents could afford to seek refuge in the country or at the city's edge. Yet, far from giving up turf, Irish Catholic families reinvested in their neighborhood by completing Saint Patrick's Church.

Saint Patrick's neighborhood included Chicago's bustling Haymarket at Randolph and Desplaines Streets. This intersection achieved international notoriety after a bomb exploded during a workers' rally on May 4, 1886, killing eight police officers and an equal number of civilians. The statue dedicated in 1889 by civic and business leaders was modeled after a Chicago Irish policeman, Thomas Birmingham. (Courtesy, Chicago Historical Society, ICHi–09281)

Parish and Neighborhood, Church and Turf

In a number of important ways, the appointment of thirty-year-old Denis Dunne as pastor in November 1854 represented new life for this mother parish of the Chicago Irish. Without his "influence and zeal," remarked a contemporary observer, Saint Patrick's Church would have remained "in embryo." While official parish histories do not shed light on Dunne's decision to begin construction anew, the *Chicago Times* later recalled that he altered the plan of the present church "upon a more extended scale, commensurate with his own idea of the future growth of Chicago."[15] Although it was not unusual for a priest to pledge personal funds for such a project, the depth of his commitment extended beyond the church to the neighborhood. So strongly did Dunne believe in the future of Saint Patrick's parish that he persuaded his uncle, four of his brothers, and his sister's family to purchase homes across the street from the unfinished church![16] Construction proceeded rapidly through the summer of 1856, and by Christmas, worshipers filled the Romanesque structure.

While the Chicago Irish left few written records that state unequivocally their attitudes toward church-building, the 1857 map produced

29

by J. T. Palmatary leaves no doubt that the process had dramatic consequences for the larger city. One of the first bird's-eye views of Chicago, this lithograph captured the fullness of the rapidly expanding city with its grid of streets at right angles. In addition to depicting such landmarks as the Illinois Central Railroad, grain elevators and shipyards, the courthouse, and the "Haymarket" on Randolph Street, the map offered visible proof that churches had become an important part of the fabric of urban life. Just four squares south of Haymarket, Saint Patrick's new brick church towered over the corner of Adams and Desplaines. Although some of Palmatary's etchings were fanciful (he added steeples to Saint Patrick's that didn't exist until 1885!), he faithfully portrayed the relationship between sacred and secular space in the city. At a glance, Chicagoans could see for themselves that houses of worship vied with the city's commercial buildings to dominate the landscape. But the competition didn't end there.

Located a few blocks from each other on the city's North Side, for example, were the Catholic cathedral of Holy Name and the Protestant Episcopal church of Saint James, both designed by the noted architect Edward Burling. Press accounts hailed the Episcopal church as "the most magnificent church edifice in Chicago," reflecting the good taste of its wealthy congregation. Especially impressive were its stained glass windows, designed by New York expert Robert Carse, which "surpass in richness and beauty of coloring anything of the kind in the West." Although newspapers rarely mentioned competition between Protestant and Catholic congregations, the Palmatary map made it clear that Holy Name overshadowed Saint James Episcopal. As one Chicagoan later recalled, the buttresses of the Gothic cathedral "were massive enough to have sustained an edifice the size of St. Peter's [in Rome] and millions of bricks were stowed away in the massive tower."[17]

While newspapers generally applauded the efforts of wealthy Protestant congregations to finance brick or stone churches, opinion was sharply divided when it came to Irish parishes such as Holy Name. The disparate treatment accorded Protestants and Catholics reflected an underlying critical debate: should poor immigrant congregations spend limited resources on constructing beautiful houses of worship? In a scathing editorial in 1857, the *Chicago Tribune* asserted that three-fourths of the city's hungry and nine-tenths of its beggars were Irish. Part of the reason for such widespread poverty, argued the newspaper, occurred because Irish "servant girls and laboring men" had contributed their wages to the Catholic Church. The *Tribune* suggested that Bishop Anthony O'Regan surrender his home "to the widows and orphans of his flock" and turn the unfinished cathedral of Holy Name "into a workshop for the unemployed" where the "hum of satisfied industry" would replace lavish religious ceremonies.[18]

What critics of "brick and mortar" Catholicism failed to understand or appreciate was the role sacred space played in the lives of ordinary people. For immigrants and their children, churches such as Saint Patrick's and Holy Name represented a crucial beginning in creating community, identity, and a sense of belonging in their new urban neighborhoods. Moreover, they helped to revise negative stereotypes about Irish Catholics. In 1857 an out-of-town correspondent for the *Chicago Daily Journal* expressed amazement at the immense crowd that gathered on Saint Patrick's Day for the "sublime and impressive" ceremonies, which included the singing of Mozart's Twelfth Mass. Besides listening to an eloquent tribute to Ireland's patron saint, the reporter found himself "very much captivated" by Father Riordan's remarks to the Irish congregation. Warning his immigrant countrymen against "too great warmth" that might lead to violence, the priest nevertheless praised their "faith and chastity as the bright jewels of their national character." The correspondent admitted, "I must acknowledge that the Irish Catholics in Chicago are not such as I have been accustomed to believe." Far from denouncing Saint Patrick's as a luxury the Irish could ill afford, the writer predicted that when finished, the church "will be an honor to the saint and reflect credit on themselves."[19]

Parochialism: The Legacy

Although it may have appeared that Chicago's Irish devoted all their resources to church-building, in fact the opposite occurred. Because of their commitment to parochial schools and work with the poor, it took years for them to complete their "mother" church. The oldest surviving photo of Saint Patrick's provides a rare glimpse of how an urban parish complex evolved over time. Anchoring the south end of Desplaines Street at Adams is the present church (without its distinctive steeples), and, at the north end, the original Saint Patrick's, transformed into a school. Standing on the wooden sidewalk with the Christian Brothers of De La Salle is a group of young students. Although their names are lost to history, their presence provides eloquent testimony that schools, like churches, represented investments in the future of the Irish as citizens and Catholics.

The history of Saint Patrick's illustrates clearly that creating sacred space was a difficult business because there were few guarantees of success. Competition was fierce, and more and more it came from Catholic quarters. Just months after the present Saint Patrick's was opened for services, the Jesuits established a new parish for Irish immigrants on the prairie around what is now Roosevelt Road and Blue Island Avenue. Although Holy Family quickly eclipsed Saint Patrick's in size and scale, Irish Catholics did not abandon their mother church. On the contrary, they redoubled efforts to complete Saint Patrick's. Despite a debt of $11,700, in June 1859 parishioners voted "to proceed at once with the carpenter-work and plastering of the church" and they elected a committee, including the pastor's brother, Peter Dunne, to collect funds.[20]

A popular method of fund-raising in Saint Patrick's involved dividing up the parish into districts, similar to the precincts of a city ward. Collectors went door-to-door in the neighborhood, while others used personal contacts to solicit contributions in offices, factories, saloons, and hotels. Although the voluntary aspect of such building campaigns was decidedly American, it also resonated deeply with the experience of Irish immigrants who had given to "penny-a-week" collections for new chapels in Ireland. Raising large amounts of money for a permanent church brought together diverse groups in a parish, and it also forced the wider city to take notice. In October 1859 Saint Patrick's sponsored a four-day fair and concert at Metropolitan Hall downtown as part of its campaign to complete the church. Publicity for the event made clear that this was no ordinary bazaar. In addition to "a splendid band" and a lavish musical entertainment by the popular Ghent sisters, the program included a grand drawing of a city lot, valued at $200, donated by John Davlin. Thus church-building not only enhanced the public image of Irish Catholics, it also afforded them a unique opportunity to shape and improve Chicago's physical landscape. Indeed, the *Chicago Daily Times* went so far as to argue that: "St. Patrick's Church should be assisted, for, when completed, it will be one of the ornaments of our city."[21]

Far from depleting scarce resources, as critics have charged, church-building may have made it easier for Catholics to meet other social needs. At the same time that parishioners worked to complete their church, for example, they contributed the lion's share of financial assistance to the poor. On New Year's Eve 1857 Saint Patrick's organized the first conference of the Society of Saint Vincent de Paul, a group well-known in Europe for its work with the sick and the poor. In a city that offered next-to-nothing in the way of charitable relief, local conferences of the Saint Vincent de Paul Society provided much-needed food, clothing, and fuel for impoverished Chicagoans. In Saint Patrick's parish alone, the group raised nearly $10,000 between 1859 and 1861 that was used to assist 6,499 persons.[22]

Stung by criticism that they were spending too much money on building churches, the Chicago Irish now found themselves lambasted for not contributing enough to charity. It was a charge hotly denied by Peter Dunne, secretary of the Saint Vincent de Paul Society and a generous contributor to Saint Patrick's parish. In 1867 Dunne took the director of the Young Men's Christian Association to task for suggesting that the city's Catholics "as a community, are a burden to their fellow-citizens." He noted that the Saint Vincent de Paul Society, unlike other sectarian groups, made no distinctions regarding the religious affiliation of poor families they assisted. Although Dunne willingly conceded that "the Catholics of Chicago are individually the poorest of all religionists found in this city," he reminded critics that Irish immigrants had suffered from "the wrongs and oppressions of a tyrannical government" that was largely Protestant. Yet the record was clear that the Irish, like their German Catholic neighbors in Chicago, established orphanages, hospitals, reform schools, and Magdalen asylums. Indeed, the greatest contribution of all, Dunne argued, was the city's Catholic schools

that saved the public treasury more than $82,000 a year.[23]

The increasing commitment of Irish Catholics to parochial schools was clearly reflected in Saint Patrick's parish. Since 1861 the Christian Brothers of De La Salle had operated an academy for boys; in September 1871 the Daughters of Charity assumed control of the girls' school. One month later the Great Chicago Fire destroyed more than three miles of the city, including its business district. Although the fire came within a few blocks of Saint Patrick's Church, the entire parish complex was saved. Chicago's well-known historian A. T. Andreas recalled that in October 1871 Saint Patrick's Church "was standing in the screws used to elevate it to the [street] grade," and he added that, "the improvement was completed as soon as practicable after the excitement occasioned by that great calamity had died away."[24]

Although many Protestant and Jewish congregations moved away from the center of the city after the fire, Catholics not only stayed put, they expanded their parish complexes.[25] The litany of improvements to Saint Patrick's Church was impressive, indeed: "a substantial and beautiful stone basement built at a cost of $20,000; the cold and cheerless interior of the church was enlivened by a new set of stations and frescoed in a beautiful manner, the sanctuaries were fitted up with elaborately carved altars, the pews upholstered, a gallery built both for the people and the choir, and the latter supplied with an organ of large dimensions and power . . . "[26] Not only did Irish Catholics reinvest in their mother church, they also financed two substantial brick schools, a strategy that had long-term, positive consequences for the parish, the neighborhood, and the city.

The new Saint Patrick's Academy on Desplaines Street was a showplace on the Near West Side. Four stories in height, its twelve rooms were furnished with "maple and walnut

On October 15, 1914, the old Beidler mansion on Jackson Boulevard took on new life and identity as a Catholic social settlement. In addition to operating a kindergarten and a day nursery for the children of working mothers, the Daughters of Charity sponsored noon-day lunches for workers in the nearby commercial district. (Courtesy, Daughters of Charity Archives, Mater Dei Provincialate, Evansville, Indiana)

floors, doors, and moldings, and supplied with water in every room." Of the seven hundred boys enrolled, those whose parents could afford it paid one dollar a month. According to a local newspaper, although the rest attended free of charge, they "are entitled to the same care and prosecute the same studies as do their more fortunate companions." Around the corner on Adams Street, nine Daughters of Charity instructed five hundred girls in their modern academy. Respected as skillful educators, the nuns also received praise because their "unostentatious lives" kept the operating costs of the school at a minimum.[27]

One of the continuing refrains echoed by civic leaders in the nineteenth century was the difficulty of keeping young boys in school. In 1881 the Christian Brothers pioneered a three-year commercial course that combined religious instruction with penmanship, bookkeeping, commercial law, and the composition of brief business letters "in correct English." Thanks to the use of "Remington machines in the classroom," students also achieved proficiency in the new skill of typewriting. Saint Patrick's Commercial Academy met with immediate success. In fact so great was the demand that within a few years the Christian Brothers opened De LaSalle Institute on the South Side. Chicago business leaders enthusiastically lent their support to both schools, contributing funds and hiring graduates. In addition to preparing young women for careers as teachers in Chicago's public schools, the Daughters of Charity also incorporated business courses into their curriculum. The end result was that long after Saint Patrick's lost its residential base, its schools continued to respond to the changing needs of the city.[28]

Despite criticism that Irish Catholics spent too much money on "brick and mortar" Catholicism, the experience of Saint Patrick's suggests that this investment yielded significant divi-

dends over time.[29] A powerful symbol of faith in the future of Irish Catholics—and Chicago—when it was constructed in 1856, Saint Patrick's dominated the neighborhood for decades to come. This was a minor miracle, considering the dramatic changes that had occurred in the surrounding area. Although the parish claimed a fairly extensive territory, roughly bounded by Kinzie Street on the north, Polk Street on the south, Loomis Street on the west, and the river on the east, more and more of its homes were being replaced by commercial buildings.

Redevelopment proved to be a mixed blessing: it insured a steady supply of jobs for young men and women from Saint Patrick's schools, but it hastened the departure of long-time supporters, among them the Dunne family. After living in the shadow of the brick church he helped to build thirty years earlier, Peter Dunne moved with his family to a more fashionable neighborhood on the West Side in the mid-1880s. Although the parish continued to lose population, there was no talk of giving up turf. In yet another grand gesture of commitment, the Irish of Saint Patrick's reinvested in their neighborhood by completing the church steeples in 1885.[30]

For thousands of immigrants, church-building represented a pragmatic—and inspired—response to the challenges of urban life. Establishing a permanent house of worship involved cooperation and financial commitment as well as competition (a fact rarely, if ever, mentioned in Chicago histories). These places of beauty didn't just happen, and their success wasn't guaranteed. Yet no similar endeavor, not politics or nationalism, did more for the future of the Chicago Irish. As the experience of Saint Patrick's demonstrates, creating sacred space in the city built community and laid the foundation for other important initiatives, especially parochial schools and social services.

By 1892 Saint Patrick's Commercial Academy had become well known throughout Chicago for its success in preparing "the boys of the masses for the battle of life, morally as well as educationally." (Courtesy, Brother Konrad Diebold, F.S.C., Saint Patrick High School)

*The Star and Garter Vaudeville program, August 28, 1918, reflects the ethnically diverse neighbor-
hood around Old Saint Patrick's Church.* (Courtesy, Department of Special Collections, University
of Chicago Library)

Although precious little documentation exists for Chicago's early Irish parishes, we know from Finley Peter Dunne's "Mr. Dooley" columns that sacred space made a difference in the lives of individual families and the larger city. Young "Pete" Dunne knew every nook and cranny of Chicago's oldest church. He was baptized in the sanctuary of Saint Patrick's in 1867 by his uncle, Denis Dunne, and he was six years old when the new carved altars and organ were installed. From his front stoop Finley Peter could watch the crowds pour into church every Sunday, and there is every reason to believe he attended the bazaars that helped to keep the parish solvent. Saint Patrick's fairs were legendary in the neighborhood, nine-day events featuring music, theatrical productions, and popular voting contests that pitted prominent Chicagoans against each other. Balloting was fast and furious, especially toward midnight, as friends purchased thousands of votes to ensure that their candidate won the gold-headed cane.[31] Drawing on his childhood memories of life in Saint Patrick's, Finley Peter Dunne, in 1894, painted this vivid picture of a Chicago Irish parish fair:

> They had Roddy's Hibernyun band playin' on th' cor-rner an' th' basemint iv th' church was packed. In th' ba-ack they had a shootin' gall'ry where ye got five shots f'r tin cints. . . . Th' booths was something iligant. Mrs. Dorsey had th' first wan where she sold mottoes an' babies' clothes. . . . Acrost th' hall was th' table f'r church articles, where ye cud get "Keys iv Hevin' an' St. Thomas a Kempises" an' ros'ries. It done a poor business, they tell me, an' Miss Dolan was that sore at th' eyesther shtew thrade done be Mrs. Cassidy next dure that she come near soakin' her with th' "Life iv St. Rose iv Lima."[32]

A New Vision for Chicago's Oldest Church

Creating Saint Patrick's Church in the 1850s had been a daunting task. But as the grandchildren of the Famine Irish discovered, so too was sustaining sacred space. The neighborhood immediately surrounding the parish complex had for many years been a mix of residential and commercial. On Monroe Street, right around the corner from the Christian Brothers Academy, was the Brinks Express Company and farther north on Desplaines Street were the Crane and Wolff manufacturing companies. Although John M. Smyth's furniture store remained a landmark on the West Side, the Schlesinger and Mayer department store moved from Madison and Desplaines Streets to State Street after it was absorbed by Carson Pirie Scott and Company. In a feature story about the changing West Side in 1910, the *Chicago Record-Herald* noted that the birthplace of Finley Peter Dunne had been razed "to make way for a modern factory structure to be used by an electric appliance company."[33]

Before long, Saint Patrick's was virtually surrounded by commercial buildings. Considering the vast network of English-speaking parishes that existed in the city at the time, it would have made rational sense to knock down the mother church of the Chicago Irish and sell its valuable land. But precisely the opposite occurred. In 1911 Irish-born Reverend William J. McNamee was appointed pastor, and he spent the rest of his life reclaiming Saint Patrick's central place in the life of Chicago. The effort began, simply enough, with a traditional parish bazaar that netted $8,000. After the $2,300 Christmas collection was counted, "all was spent in cleaning, decorating, and other necessary repairs of the church."[34]

As Timothy Barton demonstrates in this book, Thomas A. O'Shaughnessy's marvelous translucent windows and Celtic stencils did more than breathe new life into the city's oldest public building. They reconnected Irish Catholics with their Celtic past. In describing the transformation wrought in Old Saint Patrick's in 1912, Mary Onahan Gallery noted that O'Shaughnessy "has brought out the hidden treasures of the Book of Ardagh and the Book of Kells for us, the ordinary citizens of Chicago."[35]

Although some must have wondered about the wisdom of spending so much money on an aging downtown church, McNamee and O'Shaughnessy regarded the decoration of Saint Patrick's as reinvestment in the neighborhood and the city. Indeed, the pastor and artist sought out prominent Chicagoans who had ties to the parish and promised that "each can select his own special Irish saint." For brick manufacturer Alexander Burke, the choice was clear: Saint Finbar. Burke was born in Inchigeela, County Cork, on June 5, 1842 and baptized the same day in the tiny parish church of Saint Finbar. He dedicated the window in Saint Patrick's Church to the memory of his parents, Johanna Callaghan and Richard Burke.[36]

Others followed Burke's example. The Saint Colman window was a gift from the family of furniture magnate John M. Smyth, and the well-known banker A. J. Graham donated the Saint Brigid window in memory of his mother. Graham grew up just doors from Saint Patrick's Church. His father, John, operated one of the first Catholic bookstores in Chicago, and by the 1860s he had built up a thriving business as a steamship agent, arranging passages from Ireland for relatives of Saint Patrick's

parishioners. Donating stained glass windows is part of an ancient religious tradition. But it took on new layers of meaning in the mother parish of the Chicago Irish. Through their generosity, men and women were able to reclaim sacred space for new generations of worshipers and publicly acknowledge the crucial role Saint Patrick's had played in the life of their own families and the larger city.

Although it took years before O'Shaughnessy's artistic vision was completed, almost immediately the parish experienced a rebirth. Thanks in part to its central location on Chicago's major streetcar lines, Saint Patrick's drew a steady stream of worshipers from 1912 on. Increased revenues made it possible to upgrade the girls' high school—literally—in 1914, moving it farther east on Adams Street and placing it on a new foundation. Moreover, in the same year the Daughters of Charity expanded their mission by opening the Catholic Social Center in the old Beidler mansion at Jackson Boulevard and Sangamon Street.[37] Equally important for the future of the parish was the construction of a new brick building for Saint Patrick's Commercial Academy in 1917.

As the history of Saint Patrick's illustrates, creating and sustaining sacred space in an urban neighborhood has never been easy. Yet far from being a luxury that Irish immigrants could ill afford, churches such as Saint Patrick's were an absolute necessity. All Chicago would have been poorer if the yellow brick church at the corner of Adams and Desplaines had never been constructed in 1856. And Irish Catholics would have lost the most of all.

Walking Nuns
Chicago's Irish Sisters of Mercy

Suellen Hoy

*"The Sisters were everywhere, active and inde-
fatigable, visiting and ministering with tender
solicitude to the afflicted sufferers."*
　　　　　　　—William J. Onahan, 1908, on
　　　　　　　　　　Chicago's cholera epidemics[1]

Chicagoans, like Dubliners, called them "walking nuns," those first Sisters of Mercy who refused to remain behind convent walls. Upon arriving in Chicago in 1846, they took to heart the counsel of their Irish founder, Catherine McAuley, who encouraged them to remember the words of Saint Paul and "go into the middle of a perverse world." She told them not to dilly dally, nor to be afraid; for the poor, the illiterate, the sick all "need help today, not next week."[2] These instructions were unusual—revolutionary, in fact. Prior to the 1800s, nuns were seldom, if ever, seen in Ireland's streets or alleys. Yet several decades later, the Sisters of Mercy had high visibility in Irish towns and villages as well as in many English, Australian, and American cities.

Known by contemporaries, but lost to history—that, unfortunately, is the circumstance in which Catholic sisterhoods find themselves today. It's curious that such a competent and compassionate group of women have so small a place in the history of the Catholic Church, Chicago, and the United States, especially if we think how inclusive American history has

recently become. It has admitted minorities and women of nearly every stripe. But nuns, it seems, remain beyond the pale. Certainly, early on, they were ignored because they were women and also immigrants. But today American ethnic and women's history are rich and full fields. Have religious communities of women been overlooked or possibly dismissed because they are Catholic? It definitely appears so. Thus, as we celebrate the 150th anniversary of Chicago's Saint Patrick's parish and the Sisters of Mercy who first served there, let us place these Catholic women—who were once "everywhere"—and their public service on record. Let us also remember the Daughters of Charity of Saint Vincent de Paul who began their century of service to Old Saint Pat's in 1871.[3]

Not a Moment to Spare

On September 23, 1846, five Sisters of Mercy arrived in Chicago and established themselves as the first and, for the next ten years, the only community of nuns in the city. Mother Agatha (Margaret) O'Brien, born in County Carlow in 1822, was appointed superior. She and the other four traveled to Chicago in the company of Father Walter Quarter, brother of Bishop William Quarter who had invited them, and Mother Frances Warde, the American founder who had led the Mercys to Pittsburgh from Ireland in 1843. After a brief stay, Mother Frances

Mother Agatha O'Brien (1822–54), first superior of the Chicago Sisters of Mercy, died in the 1854 cholera epidemic and is buried in Calvary Cemetery, Evanston. (Courtesy, Sisters of Mercy Archives, Province Center, Chicago)

returned to Pittsburgh, leaving the future of this frontier foundation in the capable hands of Mother Agatha.[4]

Although she was only twenty-four years old when she came to Chicago, Mother Agatha was someone to be reckoned with. One of seventeen children, she had been educated by the Presentation nuns and entered the Sisters of Mercy in Carlow as a lay sister in 1843. It was common in Ireland at this time for working-class girls who could not provide a dowry and who were usually not well-educated to become lay rather than choir sisters. Lay sisters were responsible for "life-maintaining" tasks; they cooked, cleaned, and did whatever else needed to be done to keep a well-ordered home. But, although poor, Margaret O'Brien had abilities that distinguished her. Thus when she received the Mercy habit and her religious name in Pittsburgh in 1844, she did so as a choir nun. The Irish-born Bishop Michael O'Connor, who had invited the sisters to Pittsburgh, remembered her as a person "capable of ruling a

nation"; and he refused to be deprived of her services "because her father happened to be a poor man in Ireland."[5] However, Chicago rather than Pittsburgh would benefit from this astute and fortuitous assessment.

When the Sisters of Mercy arrived in Chicago, it was a rude western outpost of less than twenty thousand people. The sisters took up residence in what had been the bishop's house at Michigan and Madison. They remained at this location until November 1847, when they moved to a "commodious edifice" adjacent to the cathedral—of which Saint Xavier's Academy was a part—at 131 Wabash Avenue.[6] In this building, until fire destroyed it in 1871, the sisters would function as the church's shock troops (Chicago's Saint Vincent de Paul Society did not begin until 1857) and extend its public arm to a horde of desperate emigrants who escaped Ireland's Great Famine. Despised by Anglo-Protestants for their alien religion as well as their ignorance, filth, and strange ways, most of these uninvited newcomers secured public works jobs on railroads and canals. Living in makeshift, crowded shanties near their work, they were frequently sick and disorderly and thus regarded as health menaces.

Not surprisingly, when a cholera epidemic struck during the summer of 1849 and spread along the Illinois and Michigan Canal, a large number of Irish died. Although the Sisters of Mercy were already operating three schools, teaching Sunday School at Saint Patrick's, running an employment bureau for Irish working women, volunteering at a free dispensary opened by Rush Medical College, and holding night classes for illiterate adults, they began nursing cholera victims. It was a part of their tradition—Mother Catherine McAuley and her companions, along with the Irish Sisters of Charity, had enhanced their public image through the devoted care of strangers during Dublin's 1832 epidemic. When the Chicago outbreak subsided and the sisters' nursing assignments let up, they agreed to take charge of the city's first Catholic orphanage, "a haven for children who had lost their parents to the epidemic." Two years later, with an uneasy calm, Mother Agatha accepted control of what became Mercy Hospital.[7]

In Mother Agatha's letters of 1850–51, there is a continuing refrain. She wrote repeatedly that she had "not one moment to spare," that "time is real precious here," that "we are very busy," that "my hands are full."[8] Besides the sisters' heavy teaching obligations and their diverse program of social services, they had also opened a branch house in Galena in 1848, and Mother Agatha occasionally visited to advise and encourage her community and to prepare the young sisters for profession.

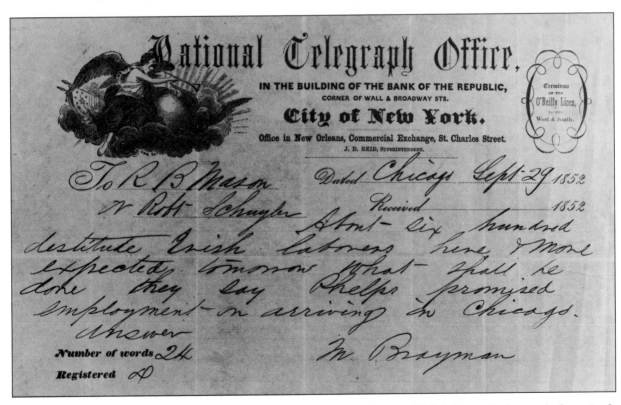

The Mercy Sisters had "not a moment to spare" because so many "destitute Irish laborers," who regularly arrived in Chicago during the 1850s, had such pressing needs. (Courtesy, Chicago Historical Society)

Although two nuns (both from the first band of five) died in Galena, this active community grew quickly. In 1851 Mother Agatha told her brother that there were forty-four Mercy sisters in the Chicago diocese: "Irish, American, German and French . . . a mixture of many nations, but all one with respect to religion." Yet, according to data from the federal census, a large majority were Irish.[9]

Because so many young women chose to enter religious life, Mother Agatha could begin new ministries. In late 1850 the Sisters of Mercy had begun nursing at the Illinois General Hospital of the Lake. Despite winter winds and clogged streets, they walked every day from their convent on Wabash to the hospital at Michigan and Rush. Because they were sometimes forced to wait "an hour at a time" to cross the Lake Street Bridge, which was "only a collection of planks chained together," they continually searched for better ways to reach their destination. When the Lake hospital was transferred to them in February 1851, Sister Vincent McGirr (whose brother, Dr. John McGirr, was a member of the hospital's staff) and three others moved there; the number of patients in their care averaged from sixteen to twenty. In June 1852 the Sisters of Mercy received a new charter in their name, creating an early version of today's landmark institution, Mercy Hospital.[10]

In 1852 Mother Agatha agreed to open another school. It was for the girls of Saint Patrick's parish and was located on Adams Street, near where the new church would stand (and still stands). Although it is not known exactly when the Mercy Sisters began teaching Sunday school in Father Patrick J. McLaughlin's old church at Randolph and Desplaines, they probably did so shortly after their arrival in 1846. Saint Patrick's was, after all, an 1846 offshoot of Saint Mary's, where the sisters lived. Therefore, when classes commenced on

Adams Street, these "walking nuns" trudged the distance from Madison and Wabash to Adams and Desplaines, crossing the troublesome Madison Street Bridge each day and in every kind of weather.[11] By the 1850s Chicago's Sisters of Mercy appear to have been "everywhere" and without a moment to call their own. Recognized on the street by Protestants and Catholics alike, they were certainly respected for their good intentions and quite possibly for their good works as well.

Without doubt, these pioneering sisters had Protestant students, friends, and supporters. Writing to a Mercy sister in Pittsburgh, Mother Agatha remarked that she had "so much to do with Protestants." She pointed out that "almost all the children in the select school [St. Xavier's Academy]" were Protestant, that Protestants visited them "constantly," and that they had "some very warm friends among them."[12] Thus, despite strong nativist sentiments regularly expressed in the press against Irish Catholics during the 1850s, no Chicago newspapers publicly criticized these Irish nuns. Perhaps by 1852 most Protestants realized the "vast and incalculable . . . good" that they had accomplished during their first six years.[13] In 1855 this goodwill was tested when an academy student, Mary Parker, who falsely claimed to have been held against her will, sued the sisters. The incident was reported only in the *Democratic Press,* and it supported the Mercys, correctly suggesting that the young woman, who had a lover, "fell into a very common error of thinking that her liberties were abridged." When given an opportunity to leave school, Mary Parker chose to stay and the case was dismissed.[14]

By comparison, the cholera epidemic of 1854 proved far more devastating. Still the only nuns in Chicago, the sisters were deeply involved during the early 1850s in plans to expand the Mercy network. Because Mother Agatha had quarreled with Bishop James Van de Velde over property rights (and won) in 1849, she was determined to avoid future disagreements over deeds. Thus, in 1852 and in 1853, she purchased two pieces of land: fifty acres in a suburb south of Chicago (Forty-Seventh and Cottage Grove) and a strip of prairie on the outskirts of Chicago (Twenty-Sixth and Calumet). On this slice of country property adjacent to the city, Mother Agatha intended to open a second academy and a resthouse for the community.[15]

Her plans were realized, but Mother Agatha lived only to see the beginnings of them. During the scorchingly hot summer of 1854, cholera returned to Chicago with terrific force. By the end of June more than two hundred people had died. Families who could afford to escape fled to Milwaukee, but even some of them did not get out in time. Cholera was a terrifying disease, largely because of the speed with which it killed—individuals who seemed healthy one day could be dead the next. Nevertheless, the indefatigable Sisters of Mercy went everywhere, walking to where they were needed and "ministering with tender solicitude." They set aside all their other duties to nurse the sick and dying. Overwhelmed by the crisis, they also organized bands of laywomen to assist them with their rounds of mercy.[16]

Following a full day of nursing on July 7, Mother Agatha became ill and died the next day. She was thirty-two years old. By July 11, three more nuns—all born in Ireland—had also become cholera victims. Later in the month, on July 31, Father McLaughlin, pastor of Saint Patrick's, died. He and the sisters were among the better known of the 1,424 people who succumbed that summer to a killer disease that was not very well understood. Shocked Chicagoans began to realize, however, that "cleanliness is conducive to health, and that filth is productive of disease." As a direct result of this tragedy and repeated appeals for preventive sanitary measures, the city council authorized construction of an underground sewer system and required homeowners to install drains.[17]

When the Sisters of Mercy opened their second Chicago academy in December 1854, it bore the name of Saint Agatha. In this way, they paid public tribute to their leading spirit, the young woman from County Carlow who had "succeeded by her zeal and wisdom" in laying a firm foundation for so many charitable and educational enterprises (both private and public) that would follow. By responding generously to the distressed and by trusting in Providence, she had unknowingly turned the convent on Wabash Avenue into something of a social settlement—the kind that so many of us have come to identify with Chicago in the late nineteenth century. Yet Mother Agatha O'Brien had completed her life's work before either Jane Addams and Ellen Gates Starr, the founders of Hull-House, were born.[18]

Setting the Pace

The McAuley-O'Brien legacy went a long way in directing the Irish women who led Chicago's Mercy Sisters during the late 1850s and Civil War years. The flexible, "can do" activism of Mothers Catherine McAuley and Agatha O'Brien worked well in a "can do" city bent on progress. Their energy and efforts to lift up their own contributed in no small way to the influence that Irish Catholics would have in Chicago—an influence that from the beginning was "all out of proportion to their numbers." Irish Catholics not only grew up with the city but their institutions became an essential part of its lifeblood.[19] In 1905 an observer of Chicago's cultural and social events commented that the Catholic Church was "unexcelled in charities."[20] No small part of this achievement can be attributed to women religious, particularly those pioneer Mercys who set the pace.

SAINT ANGELA'S
FEMALE ACADEMY,

CONDUCTED BY THE

SISTERS OF MERCY,

Corner of Desplaines & Adams Streets, West Chicago.

————◆•◆————

IN the various branches of a refined and solid education suitable to young Ladies ; in matters of propriety and elegance of deportment, the pupils of this Institution will receive the constant care and attention of the Sisters.

————◆————

THE branches taught are Orthography, Reading, Writing, Grammar, Arithmetic, Sacred and Profane History, Ancient and Modern Chronology, Mythology, Rhetoric and Poetry, Geography, Astronomy, and the use of the Globes, the elements of Natural Philosophy, Chemistry, Botany, and Mental Philosophy ; French and German Languages ; MUSIC—Piano, Guitar and Melodeon.

PAINTING—Poonah, Grecian, Antique, Oriental and Potichomanic. DRAWING—Pencil and Crayon. All kinds of Needle Work, Wax Flowers and Fruit.

FIRST TERM COMMENCES AUGUST 17, 1857,

And ends November 8th. Second Term commences November 9th, and ends January 30th, 1858. Third Term commences January 31st, and ends April 24th, 1858. Fourth Term commences April 25th, and ends July 17th, 1858.

TERMS, PAYABLE IN ADVANCE.

1st Class, for a term of twelve weeks,	- - - - - - -	$5 00
2d Class, do do	- - - - - -	4 60
3d Class, do do	- - - - - -	3 00

————o————

French, per quarter,	- - - - - - - -	$4 00
Piano, with use of Instrument,	- - - - - - -	9 00
Guitar, " " "	- - - - - - -	6 00
Melodeon, " " "	- - - - - - -	8 00
Painting,	- - - - - - -	5 00
Drawing,	- - - - - - -	5 00

Attendance from 9 1-2 A. M. until 12 1-2, and from 2 until 1-4 to 4 P. M.

....

Times Print, 43 La Salle Street.

The prospectus of Saint Angela's Female Academy, conducted by the Sisters of Mercy at the "Corner of Desplaines & Adams Streets, West Chicago," highlights the essentials of "a refined and solid education suitable to young Ladies" in 1857–58. (Courtesy, Sisters of Mercy Archives, Province Center, Chicago)

Mother Vincent McGirr, who came from Pittsburgh with Mother Agatha in 1846 and headed Mercy Hospital in 1851, opened Saint Angela's Academy on Desplaines Street, north of Saint Patrick's Church (facing east), in August 1857. Like the sisters' free school for girls, the academy was intended primarily for the young women of Saint Patrick's. Although no one knows why the school was named for Saint Angela Merici (founder of the Ursuline Sisters in sixteenth-century Italy), it is clear that Catherine McAuley was inspired by her nontraditional work among the poor, sick, and uneducated, particularly women and children.[21]

Saint Angela's Academy offered "a refined and solid education" as well as "the constant care and attention of the Sisters." Although religion and theology were not officially listed among the course offerings, they formed "the core of the curriculum." All students received instruction in the "Christian principles of solid virtue and strict morality" that was a part of a Mercy education.[22] Unlike Saint Francis Xavier and Saint Agatha academies, Saint Angela's was not a boarding school, but the tuition earned in these three institutions helped support the nuns' free schools and charities. Sister Angela Martin, the Canadian-born principal of Saint Angela's, and her teachers continued to live on Wabash Avenue and commuted across town on foot or by carriage until the Mercys left Saint Patrick's parish in 1863.[23]

For reasons that are not completely clear, Mother Francis Monholland (another Irish-born superior) refused Father Denis Dunne's request that the sisters who taught at Saint Patrick's reside there. It seems that she did not want "to place a branch so near the mother-house." Father Dunne's suggestion may also have come at a bad time. After opening Saint Angela's Academy in 1857, the Sisters of Mercy had again spread themselves dangerously thin in an attempt to serve a desperately poor immigrant population. In 1858, at the urging of

Sister Mary Angela (Louise) Martin, born in St. Leon, Canada, on April 12, 1833, was principal of Saint Angela's Female Academy in Saint Patrick's parish from 1857 to 1862. She had a long and full life as a Sister of Mercy; she died in Chicago on February 7, 1918. (Courtesy, Sisters of Mercy Archives, Province Center, Chicago)

✛ ✛ ✛

Father John McMullen, the nuns began the city's first Magdalen Asylum in a rented house not far from Saint Patrick's Church. They staffed the asylum until the following year, when four Irish Sisters of the Good Shepherd arrived from St. Louis and began their long history of service to Chicagoans. Relieved of this responsibility, Mother Francis then sent a group of five sisters to Ottawa, Illinois, to establish a foundation. Finally, and most importantly, in September 1861 she led her "soldiers of mercy" (all Irish) to nurse the sick and wounded in the Civil War. Colonel James A. Mulligan, leader of Chicago's Irish Brigade and a future war hero, secured the sister-nurses on behalf of his largely Catholic regiment.[24]

The Mercys were the first but not the only Chicago-based nuns to go to the front. The Daughters of Charity, who had begun teaching at Holy Name in September 1861 (and ten years later would transfer to Saint Patrick's), dramatically closed school early in June 1862 to answer "a call for more help for the sick." Sister Anne Regina Jordan, born in Donegal in 1821, then took Chicago's Daughters of Charity east, most likely to Satterlee Hospital in Philadelphia, where a large group of nuns from Emmitsburg, Maryland, began nursing in June 1862. The Sisters of Mercy, for their part, spent six months working in a field hospital in Jefferson City, Missouri, and then continued their labors on board the *Empress,* a hospital ship of the United States Sanitary Commission.[25]

The Mercys' wartime nursing did not end with their return to Chicago in May 1862. About two years later, they began visiting sick and wounded prisoners at Camp Douglas located on the city's South Side, within view from the roof of Saint Agatha's Academy. Built as a training center for Union recruits, it was converted into a prison camp for Confederate soldiers early in 1862. Colonel Benjamin Sweet, who became camp commander in May 1864, placed his daughter at Saint Xavier's Academy on Wabash. When he at first refused permission for the nuns to enter the camp, he was prevailed upon by Chicago's mayor—and perhaps by his bright, persistent daughter—to allow them to do so. Years later Ada C. Sweet recalled her own visits to Camp Douglas on weekends; the sisters, she said, often gave her "a great iced cake to carry to the Fifteenth Veteran Reserve Band." In return, on trips downtown, the band serenaded the nuns and their pupils.[26]

Long before the war's end, these "soldiers of mercy" had been transformed into "angels of mercy." Their "religious training and personal discipline, along with their practiced ability to treat soldiers with a compassion that remained devoid of sexual energy, won the respect of most people."[27] Thus, in April 1862, when Chicago's Protestant Female Nurse Association issued a call for nurses, it described the kind of women needed in familiar terms:

> They must be women of the most unimpeach-able integrity, religious in spirit, thoroughly kind and gentle-hearted, possessed of the rare gift of common sense, equal to the emergencies that constantly arise in the army hospitals . . . self-reliant, entirely subordinate and obedient to the surgeon. . . .They must be women of cheerful and active temperament, industrious and energetic — in short, model women.

Taking a cue from Superintendent of Nurses Dorothea Dix (whose anti-Catholic and anti-immigrant sentiments were well-known), the Chicago association also required that "every nurse shall be at least thirty years of age."[28] Many sister-nurses were younger.

At the war's end, the Sisters of Mercy had been in Chicago for nearly twenty years. Their nursing, teaching, and charitable activities had won for them an enviable place. There is little doubt that, as fearless and relentless caregivers on the fields of battle as well as on the streets of Chicago, they had won for Irish Catholics and their church an increased tolerance and a new

✢ ✢ ✢

This 1854 English caricature, drawn by T. H. McGuire (artist to the Queen), depicts an "Outward Bound" famine refugee at the quay in Dublin. He and many like him tested the mettle of Chicago's young and energetic Irish Sisters of Mercy. (Courtesy, Chicago Historical Society, ICHi–08506)

Chicago's "walking nuns" passed John R. Walsh's newsstand on Madison Street on their rounds of mercy. Although the newsstand did not survive the 1871 fire, Walsh did. He later became owner of the Chicago Herald and Evening Post. (Courtesy, Chicago Historical Society, ICHi–14245)

respectability. Moreover, they had caused earnest Protestant women to take serious notice. The remarkable Mary Livermore, who with Jane Hoge organized Chicago's highly successful Great Northwestern Sanitary Fair in 1863, became acquainted with the Mercys and other nursing nuns during the Civil War. Decades later, she still held them in high regard. In a series of lectures on *What Shall We Tell Our Daughters* (1883), she suggested that new communities of women "established on the basis of the Protestant religion . . . might be made very helpful to modern society." Livermore clearly recognized too how such organizations "would furnish occupation and give position to large numbers of unmarried women, whose hearts go out to the world in charitable intent."[29]

Daughters Called to Service

Mary Livermore was hardly the first, and certainly not the last, among prominent Protestant women to see Catholic sisterhoods as an effective and attractive force for good in American society. Earlier in the nineteenth century, Catharine Beecher had cast a jealous eye on the achievements of pioneer nuns on the western frontier. And at the century's end, Jane Addams and Ellen Gates Starr consciously or unconsciously chose a successful ecclesiastical form on which to model their social settlement. To live as neighbors among poor immigrants and work selflessly on their behalf would hardly have been considered new to Chicagoans who had witnessed or benefited from the labors of the Sisters of Mercy or other communities. By 1889, when Hull-House opened on Halsted Street, hundreds of Catholic women religious— the majority from Irish families—had already shown how single women could live useful and gutsy lives.[30]

Strange as it may seem today, religious life— especially in active communities, like the Sisters of Mercy—offered Catholic women an appealing alternative to the life choices available to most American women at that time: motherhood or spinsterhood. We should also remember that nineteenth-century society was far less secular than our own. Americans of every kind were generally churchgoers; both the schooled and unschooled found their faith, morality, and identity rooted in or shaped by religion. And for women, especially Catholic sisters and Protestant evangelicals, religion often stimulated "a life of Christian usefulness" that "replaced stylish idleness or aimless busywork with purposeful activities."[31]

The best hope for benevolent daughters of Protestants was to become the wives of ministers or missionaries. As such, they could lead "lives devoted to soul-winning" and assume "a public, assertive form of usefulness." In choosing husbands, therefore, these young women also selected careers or challenging ways to lead lives of service. Before the Civil War, Emily

Judson wrote to a friend about her decision to marry a missionary: "Did you ever feel as though all the things you were engaged in were so trivial, so aimless, that you fairly sickened of them, and longed to do something more worthy of your origin and destiny?" She wanted to spend her "short life in the way which would make [her] most happy—in doing real, permanent good." Despite these intentions, however, children and home duties made it difficult for women like Emily Judson "to function in the capacity of assistant missionary."[32]

Such was not case for the daughters of Catholics who became nuns. During the nineteenth century, when opportunities to save souls and do good were limitless, the restrictions on women religious were comparatively few. Until 1908 the Catholic Church officially recognized the United States as "mission territory," and the many Irish women who emigrated as nuns saw themselves as missionaries in their own right. Settling in faraway places, they remained flexible, responding as best they could to local needs and crises. The heavy influx of Famine refugees to American cities after 1847 forced the first wave of Irish sisters to emphasize the public dimension of their vows. Thus, it was only natural that the Mercy convent on Wabash Avenue became the center of so much social action.[33]

The hectic pace and the singular competence with which these determined nuns built respected urban institutions—ones largely free of male management—fueled the aspirations and idealism of young Chicago women who wanted to do something important in life. Most of them were the daughters of immigrants and working class. No doubt some saw religious life as an escape or possibly an adventure, but many entered convents because they "expanded the narrow range of what was possible for women who were coming of age" 150 years ago. By accepting a religious vocation, these first- and second-generation daughters of Erin were not only choosing what their families and friends considered "the better part" (rather than getting married or staying single) but also enlarging *their* sphere and infusing it with tough challenges.[34]

Living among and serving the poor, sick, and uneducated "demanded extraordinary stamina and dedication to the cause of religion." During the antebellum period, in particular, nuns lived and worked in convents and schools that were unattractive and often unhealthy. For Chicago's walking nuns, bitter cold or excessive heat heightened their discomfort and made their daily routine more difficult; bad weather also contributed to the terrible mortality among them. Large numbers of sisters died, as we have seen, during epidemics; but many more, especially among the Irish, were lost to tuberculosis, the result of poor living conditions and long hours of hard work. Sister Callista (Mary Ellen) Mangan, who was baptized in Old Saint Patrick's Church in November 1855 and subsequently became a Sister of Mercy, died of consumption twenty-eight years later. She was simply one of many.[35]

These hardships and early deaths did not lessen the attraction of the convent. Called to service by the growing number of Catholic poor and the threat of Protestant proselytism (especially among children), young women also saw that religious life offered them a way to do important work and be somebody. Nuns, who defined themselves in terms other than that of their husbands and children, most certainly challenged the "cult of true womanhood." As one historian has accurately observed: "their voluntary submergence of individual identity to a larger corporate identity within the convent gave them reason and opportunity to act in the world to a greater degree than was permitted to most women or was pursued by most men." The Sisters of Mercy were not only free to walk the streets of Chicago without male escorts,

they were also educated and self-supporting, held top administrative posts, and owned substantial amounts of property.[36]

Mother Agatha O'Brien, an Irish immigrant in her late twenties, must have offered a stunning example of how religious life could transform a bright, young woman into an able person of status and authority. In the 1849 property dispute with Chicago's Bishop Van de Velde, for example, the twenty-six-year-old Mother Agatha stood firm and refused to return a deed that she believed belonged to the sisters. Three years later, through the act that incorporated Mercy Hospital, she and the nuns elected to the board of trustees received sole corporate responsibility for the institution. Mother Agatha, who no longer needed the bishop's permission, could use the real estate as collateral to secure loans and mortgages to purchase more properties. Thus, she stands in stark contrast to Mary Livermore and Jane Hoge who realized after their successful sanitary fair that, although they had money in the bank, "our earnings were not ours, but belonged to our husbands."[37]

Unlike so many articulate Protestant women reformers who emerged in the post-Civil War years, however, the Sisters of Mercy and their successors claimed no public voice. They were, after all, products of their times *and* training — very much members of a patriarchal Irish church. Like other daughters of Erin, they "behaved aggressively and valued their economic prowess," but, despite "the web of support" they created for so many women of varied circumstances, they and their students generally "turned a cold shoulder to the organized women's rights movement." Its leaders were, of course, Protestant women of Anglo-Saxon stock whose religion permitted divorce and more sexual freedom than did the Catholic Church.[38]

Perhaps it is for this reason, most of all, that the Sisters of Mercy and other women religious, who provided the model and set the pace for social reform in the nineteenth century, remain absent from American history. It would be a mistake to dismiss them too readily, simply because they sought little public recognition and held a subservient place in the Catholic Church. Respect for and cooperation with bishops and priests did not always signify submission. As Mother Agatha O'Brien proved, sisters frequently resisted "patriarchy" with as much resolve as a suffragist or feminist. For those of us who value their indomitable spirit and know their rich legacy, we must insist that they not be ignored or forgotten.

Preserving the Union, Shaping a New Image
Chicago's Irish Catholics and the Civil War

Lawrence J. McCaffrey

No other individuals did more to change the public perception of the Chicago Irish during the Civil War than James A. Mulligan and Reverend Denis Dunne of Saint Patrick's. In organizing the Twenty-Third and Ninetieth Illinois Infantry regiments, Mulligan and Dunne delivered a stinging rebuke to critics who depicted the Irish as unwanted, ungrateful immigrants, reluctant to serve the country that had liberated them from poverty and oppression. While news reports for years had published Irish names in connection with crime stories and saloon brawls, now Chicagoans began to read about Irish bravery at Lexington, Vicksburg, and Missionary Ridge. It was a welcome change and long overdue.

Since the city's earliest days, Chicago's Anglo-Protestant nativists had heaped hatred and contempt on Irish Catholics, criticizing their lifestyle and conduct, their loyalty to the Democratic Party, but most of all their religious beliefs and practices. "Who does not know," thundered the *Chicago Tribune* in 1855, "that the most depraved, debased, worthless and irredeemable drunkards and sots which curse the community, are Irish Catholics? Who does not know that five-eighths of the cases brought up every day before the Mayor for drunkenness and consequent crime, are Irish Catholics?"[1]

When thirty-four-year old Colonel Mulligan died from battle wounds on July 26, 1864, the *Tribune* sounded a different note. It announced that "Another mighty one has fallen," in an obituary that continued for thirty-eight inches of column type. Not only did Chicago's leading newspaper brand Mulligan as a hero, but the entire city mourned the deceased colonel: "The flags on the Court House, Postoffice, and [fire] engine-houses were displayed at half mast, and at many of the principal business blocks the same sign of recognition was made." Before long, the nation would know of Mulligan's bravery during the Second Battle of Kernstown in the Shenandoah and his final command to his men who tried to rescue him as he lay wounded: "Lay me down and save the flag." During a short life, Mulligan had done much to inspire Chicago's Irish Catholics to gain acceptance as full-fledged Americans. Now in death his name became a household word throughout the Northwest, a blood-red symbol of American patriotism.[2]

Chicago's first Irish-Catholic, Civil War hero was born in Utica, New York in 1830. He moved with his widowed immigrant mother to Chicago six years later. When he arrived, the once small frontier town on the shores of Lake Michigan was on its way to becoming the fastest growing, most economically dynamic city in America. In the 1830s the Illinois and Michigan Canal linked it with commerce on the Mississippi, Missouri, and Ohio Rivers. Then in the 1850s, through the efforts of Chicago's own Senator Douglas, the Illinois Central Railroad connected the city with Mobile, Alabama, and other places in the South. By means of lake vessels, canal and river boats and railway cars, Chicago supplied much of the nation with grain, meat, and lumber. Its expanding economy stimulated a tremendous population growth. Between 1850 and 1860 the city's numbers increased from 29,963 to 109,260; many were either German or Irish. Although Irish Catholic immigrants found in Chicago a wide range of opportunities, from digging the Illinois and Michigan Canal to paving streets, laying railroad track, and working in packing houses, they also represented the city's first group social problem. Indeed, wretched Famine immigrants in the 1840s and 1850s had canceled out much of the progress earlier Irish settlers had made on the road to respectability and acceptability.[3]

James A. Mulligan literally grew up with Chicago and gained a reputation as an exceptionally articulate writer and speaker, a devout Catholic, an influential Douglas Democrat, and a committed Fenian. In 1850 he became the first graduate of the University of Saint Mary of the Lake. Founded by Bishop William Quarter, it was Chicago's first institution of higher learning, embodying the hopes and dreams of immigrant Catholics. Stricken with gold fever while reading law in the offices of Judge Isaac N. Arnold, Mulligan struck out for California. But he became ill in Panama where his funds ran out. After regaining his health, Mulligan assisted explorer John Lloyd Stephens map out a railroad route across the Isthmus. When Stephens died in 1852, Mulligan returned to Chicago, his legal studies, and the editor's chair at the *Western Tablet,* the city's first

Catholic newspaper. Against a rising tide of nativism that elected Know-Nothing Levi Boone, grand nephew of the famous Daniel, Chicago mayor in 1855, Mulligan championed Catholic civil rights. That same year he was admitted to the Illinois bar. In 1857 he served a brief stint as a clerk in the Department of the Interior's Bureau of Indian Affairs in Washington.[4]

A Call to Arms

Mulligan realized that the Civil War presented Irish Catholics, insecure about their place in America, with a great test and challenge. On April 15, 1861, the day after Fort Sumter in Charleston Harbor surrendered to Confederate forces, President Abraham Lincoln asked for volunteers to save the Union, an appeal he would make numerous times over the next four years. Irish Catholics had little reason to answer the president's call. During the 1850s they were the leading target for the anti-Catholic American (Know-Nothing) Party. As strong supporters of Senator Stephen A. Douglas of Illinois, they despised Lincoln's Republican Party that had absorbed the no-popery Know-Nothings and Whigs.[5]

Ending slavery was the great moral cause of the Civil War, but it did not appeal to the consciences or emotions of most Irish Catholics. Their racial prejudices reflected ignorance, fear of African-American competition in the unskilled labor market, anger that employers often employed blacks as strike-breaking scabs, and an inferiority complex that urged them to strike out against another hated minority group.[6] Irish Catholics considered Republican abolitionists who insisted on freeing plantation slaves in the rural South as their most implacable enemies in the industrial North. From the perspective of poorly paid Irish immigrant laborers, "The only difference between the negro slave of the South and the white wage slave of the North is that one has a master without asking for him, and the other has to beg for the privilege of becoming a slave. . . . The one is the slave of an individual; the other is the slave of an inexorable class."[7]

Many Irish immigrants had arrived technologically unskilled, often ignorant and illiterate. Agricultural laborers or small tenant farmers in Ireland, they had to make difficult social, economic, and psychological adjustments to urban, increasingly industrial America. Traumatized by a drastic environmental change and released from the restraining mores of a rural society, Irish immigrants frequently exhibited antisocial behavior involving drunkenness, disorderly conduct, petty crime, and family violence. Their conduct irritated the sensibilities of Anglo-American Protestants. Indeed, in some cities they were labeled "white niggers," socially inferior to free blacks. But American nativists found the Catholicism of the Irish even more obnoxious than their behavior. Rooted in British no-popery, American nativism considered Catholicism an alien creed, a nourisher of ignorance, superstition, and authoritarianism endangering American culture and institutions.[8]

Throughout the nineteenth century, American journalists, pamphleteers, and orators were so obsessed with Catholicism as a subversive force that they failed to appreciate its role in civilizing and polishing the Irish personality and adjusting it to the American situation. Devotional Catholicism was a spiritual and psychological comfort station, bridging Old and New Worlds, easing the transition between rural Ireland and modern America. Catholic moral teaching discouraged alcoholic excess and encouraged stable family life. Catholic nuns and brothers in parochial schools taught the faith, enforced discipline, and preached American patriotism, presenting poor and

Colonel James A. Mulligan (1830–64), Chicago's first Irish-Catholic Civil War hero. (Courtesy, Chicago Historical Society, ICHi–19964)

✛ ✛ ✛

working-class children with models of middle-class behavior. Parishes provided Irish Catholics with a social as well as a religious community that buffeted them against the harsh realities of a competitive, urban capitalism. Indeed, Irish Catholic affection and loyalty to their parishes were evident in the financial sacrifices they made to build and maintain magnificent churches such as Saint Patrick's.[9]

Despite their hostility to abolitionism and the Republican Party, a large number of Irish-American Catholics found motives to enlist in the crusade to preserve the Union. For some the decision was purely economic. Enlistment bounties or payments to substitute for Anglo-American Protestants attracted unskilled, often unemployed Irish Catholics. Military service also had an appeal for many jobless, recently arrived immigrants. In Ireland, young men, wanting to escape the boredom and destitution of rural life and searching for adventure, frequently joined the British army or navy; similar inducements also figured in Irish-American decisions to fight for the Union or Confederacy.

Mulligan's Irish Brigade

Approximately 150,000 Union soldiers were Irish born as were 40,000 who fought for the Confederacy.[10] It is reasonable to assume that the sons and grandsons of immigrants at least doubled the contribution to both sides. Altogether, the Union army contained about forty largely Irish regiments. New York's Irish Brigade, which included the "Fighting Sixty-Ninth," was the most famous, but Irish-American Catholics from other parts of the country made significant contributions to the eventual Union victory, including two from Chicago: the Irish Brigade (the Twenty-Third Illinois Infantry Regiment) and the Irish Legion (the Ninetieth Illinois Infantry Regiment).

Another compelling reason for enlistment was to gain military experience that might be used later to free the Irish from British rule. Most nationalists in Ireland sympathized with the desire of southern states to go their separate ways. However, leaders of the Fenian movement (the American wing of the Irish Republican Brotherhood) wanted a strong, united America as a potential ally in a future armed struggle with Britain to achieve a democratic Irish Republic. Although Chicago's County Kildare-born bishop, James Duggan, following the lead of the hierarchy in Ireland, condemned Fenianism, it was a strong force in the city's Irish community. In 1863 Chicago hosted the Fenian national convention, the next year their national fair. Fenian leaders encouraged enlistments in the Union army as a way of obtaining military experience for later use against the Sassenach enemy.[11]

But most Irish Catholics who risked lives for the stars and stripes or the stars and bars did so because they loved their country and appreciated the opportunities it either offered or promised. They were determined on proving to nativist foes that they were loyal, reliable citizens. When Senator Douglas reminded a Chicago audience in 1861 that now there were "only patriots—or traitors," his Irish Catholic admirers, who had voted for him in the 1860 presidential election, enthusiastically applauded his words.[12]

In April 1861 Chicago's Irish Catholics answered Lincoln's request for soldiers to defend the Union by organizing their own brigade dedicated to "the Honor of the Old Land . . . and the defense of the New."[13] Its core membership came from three Irish militia companies—the Montgomery Guards, the Fenian-supported Emmets, and the Shields' Guards. Brigade members elected Mulligan, captain of the Shields' Guards, their colonel. The Western Irish Brigade also included the Jackson Guards from Detroit, Michigan, and recruits from Earlsville, Morris, LaSalle County, and Ottawa, Illinois.

Support for the Brigade was immediate and enthusiastic. The city of Chicago presented Mulligan with a personal sword, and his wife, Marian Nugent Mulligan, took the lead in raising money for the Brigade's American flag. This highly symbolic act grabbed the attention of the *Chicago Tribune*. Calling on all Chicagoans to support "these warm-hearted patriotic ladies," it praised their efforts to "preserve the honor and integrity of the flag of our beloved country."[14]

Although more than one thousand men enlisted in the Irish Brigade, state officials rejected their services because Illinois had

MULLIGAN'S BRIGADE!

LAST CHANCE TO AVOID THE DRAFT!

$402 BOUNTY!

TO VETERANS!

$302 to all other VOLUNTEERS!

All Able-bodied Men, between the ages of 18 and 45 Years, who have heretofore served not less than nine months, who shall re-enlist for Regiments in the field, will be deemed Veterans, and will receive one month's pay in advance, and a bounty and premium of $402. To all other recruits, one month's pay in advance, and a bounty and premium of $302 will be paid.

All who wish to join Mulligan's Irish Brigade, now in the field, and to receive the munificent bounties offered by the Government, can have the opportunity by calling at the headquarters of

CAPT. J. J. FITZGERALD

Of the Irish Brigade, 23d Regiment Illinois Volunteers, Recruiting Officer, Chicago, Illinois.

Each Recruit, Veteran or otherwise, will receive

Seventy-five Dollars Before Leaving General Rendezvous,

and the remainder of the bounty in regular instalments till all is paid. The pay, bounty and premium for three years will average **$24** per month, for Veterans; and **$21.30** per month for all others.

If the Government shall not require these troops for the full period of Three Years, and they shall be mustered honor out of the service before the expiration of their term of enlistment, they shall receive, UPON BEING MUSTERED O the whole amount of BOUNTY remaining unpaid, the same as if the full term been served.

Chicago, December, 1863.

J. J. FITZGERALD.

Recruiting Officer, corner North Clark & Kenzie Stree

The Irish Brigade advertises for recruits. (Courtesy, Chicago Historical Society, ICHi–22049) already filled its army quota. Undeterred, Mulligan visited Senator Douglas as he lay dying at the Tremont House and secured a letter on behalf of the Brigade that he personally presented to President Lincoln. Douglas's plea, coupled with Mulligan's persistence, resulted in the War Department's acceptance on May 17, 1861, of the Brigade as the Twenty-Third Illinois Infantry, the state's first independent regiment.

Over nine hundred strong, the Irish Brigade left Chicago on July 14, 1861, for Quincy, Illinois, and then moved on to St. Louis. By the time it reached Jefferson City, Missouri, Mulligan's forces numbered 1,135 infantry soldiers, 133 cavalry, and 76 artillery. Less than three weeks later, the Brigade was dispatched to defend Lexington on the south branch of the Missouri, about forty miles from Kansas City. As senior officer, Mulligan also was in charge of the Thirteenth Missouri Infantry and the First Illinois Cavalry. Vastly outnumbered, inadequately equipped, and suffering food and water shortages, Mulligan's men bravely resisted General Sterling Price's Confederate troops for nine days, suffering the loss of twenty-four dead and eighty-one wounded.

Because of his courage, Price refused to accept Mulligan's sword of surrender. In turn, the colonel refused parole. With his wife, Marian, who had traveled to Lexington to be with her husband, Mulligan remained a prisoner until October 30, 1861, when he was exchanged for Confederate General D. M. Frost.

Marian Nugent Mulligan's war efforts went further than raising money for the Brigade and following her husband into conflict situations. Largely through her efforts, in September 1861 Mother Francis Monholland sent twenty Irish-born Sisters of Mercy to nurse wounded members of the Twenty-Third Illinois Infantry. When Confederate forces blocked off the Missouri River and damaged their steamer transport, preventing them from reaching Lexington

and the Brigade, the nuns established a field hospital in Jefferson City. As a student at Saint Xavier Academy, Marian Nugent had come in close contact with Chicago's "walking nuns." These indomitable women, known throughout the city for their educational, charitable, and hospital work, soon earned another title, "angels of the battlefield."

Despite defeat and surrender at Lexington, the Chicago area gave Mulligan a hero's welcome. On November 8, 1861, the St. Louis, Alton, and Chicago Railroad sent a special train to meet the Mulligan family in Joliet, where thousands waited along the platform. According to the *Chicago Evening Journal*, "The roofs of the cars, of the depot and other adjacent buildings were thronged with male and female spectators, the female population of Joliet exhibiting an astonishing degree of agility in climbing." After a brief speech, the hero of Lexington boarded the Chicago-bound train. According to another account, "At Lockport and Athens huge bonfires were burning, and the crowds cheered lustily as the train swept by." Despite the late hour, thousands of Chicago men, women, and children welcomed Mulligan back with a torchlight procession that "turned night into day." Although the *Tribune* continued to disparage Irish Catholics, it had to admit that: "Probably no man ever received such a spontaneous and triumphant welcome to this city or was ever greeted by such a vast assemblage. . . . His gallantry upon the field of action, and his well-directed and indomitable efforts in the cause of Freedom merited the respect and honors, if not the worship, which were showered upon him."[15]

Prominent Irish Catholics such as William J. Onahan and Philip Conley planned to honor Mulligan with a public banquet, but he "earnestly decline[d] it." Instead he devoted his energies to reassembling the Irish Brigade, a task involving another trip to the nation's capital. After securing official permission to continue recruiting, Mulligan and his wife visited New York where he reviewed the "Fighting Irish" Sixty-Ninth Infantry and lectured at Cooper's Union on December 17, 1861. That same day the mayor approved a resolution extending "the hospitalities of the city of New York" to Colonel Mulligan, "the gallant defender of the Stars and Stripes at Lexington." According to the *New York Times,* Mulligan "gave a thrilling description" of the nine-day siege of Lexington and his entire narrative "abounded in passages of eloquence, of humor and of patriotism, rarely equaled." Proceeds from his Cooper Union lecture were sent to Ireland to aid victims of hunger and poverty.[16]

After his return to Chicago, Mulligan received a new assignment, commander of Camp Douglas on the city's South Side. Named after Senator Douglas and located close to his grave, the camp had opened in September 1861 as a training ground for Union soldiers. Eleven months later it became a prisoner of war camp for Confederate captives. According to historian Harold Smith, "Mulligan did all he could to improve conditions, giving particular attention to medical care and food." Yet critics painted him as an inadequate and indifferent administrator when he left Camp Douglas to return to the ravages of war. For the next two years, notes Smith, the Irish Brigade waged "guerrilla warfare at its worst, raids, ambushes, and night fighting against some of the most skilled partisan irregulars of the Confederacy."[17]

In July 1865 the much depleted Brigade was mustered out in Richmond, Virginia. Battlefield fatalities, serious wounds, disease, and physical impairments had reduced it to about one-third of its original members.[18] Of the losses, Mulligan's death was the most difficult to bear. According to War Department records, Confederate bullets struck him from his horse during the Second Battle of Kernstown, July 24, 1864.

Ordering attempted rescuers to save the regiment's flag instead of attending to his needs, Mulligan was captured by rebel forces. When Marian Nugent Mulligan, in nearby Cumberland, Maryland, heard that her husband had been seriously wounded, she left their infant daughters under the care of others and rushed to the battlefield. Not only was she too late, she also learned that her nineteen-year old brother, Lieutenant James Nugent, had lost his life in an attempt to rescue the colonel. Mulligan may have died as a Confederate prisoner, but his captors gallantly surrendered the body to his grieving widow.

Chicago Mourns a Hero

When Mrs. Mulligan brought her husband's body back to Chicago she found the entire city in mourning for its popular Irish-American hero. On Sunday evening, July 31, 1864, huge crowds accompanied the casket from the train station to Bryan Hall where Mulligan was to lie in state. It was an event unlike any that Chicago ever had seen, a grieve-the-death but celebrate-the-life funeral that Irish Catholics have traditionally given their chieftains from the time of Daniel O'Connell in 1847 to that of John F. and Robert F. Kennedy in the 1960s and Mayor Richard J. Daley in 1976.

All day Monday, August 1, 1864, thousands waited in long lines to pay their last respects to the colonel of the Irish Brigade. Union flags "entwined with black and white crepe" hung above the main entrance. Inside Bryan Hall mourners could read Mulligan's dying words, "Lay me down and save the flag," as well as his famous reply when General Price asked for the Brigade's surrender at Lexington: "If you want us, come and take us."[19]

On the morning of the funeral, men, women, and children jammed suburban trains and city railway cars and, according to the *Tribune,*

Camp Douglas, training ground for Union soldiers and notorious Confederate prisoner of war compound. (Courtesy, Special Collections and Preservation Division, the Chicago Public Library)

"buggies, carriages, wagons and vehicles of every description were pressed into service by their eager owners, while multitudes swelled the throng by arriving on foot from every point of the compass." The mayor, the entire city council, judges, and officers of the army and navy, joined pallbearers and members of the funeral arrangements committee and marched in a body from the Tremont Hotel to Bryan Hall where they were met by various military and parish societies, all in ceremonial dress. The Light Guard Band played a dirge after which Mulligan's body was placed in a funeral car drawn by "six fine black horses furnished by the United States Express Company."[20]

Conspicuously absent from the procession were local branch members of the Fenian brotherhood. According to Civil War historian William L. Burton, Colonel Mulligan had "cleverly managed to convince the clergy that he was not a Fenian, while giving ardent support to the Fenian cause." Bishop James Duggan's early 1864 condemnation of the Fenians caused quite a stir both in Ireland and America. When arrangements for Mulligan's funeral were published, Chicago Fenians found themselves in last place, behind all other civic and religious societies. Therefore, they withdrew from the funeral cortege. In a letter to the *Tribune,* Fenian leader Major Michael Scanlan paid tribute to the Brigade colonel and nationalist comrade, praising his courage and virtue, but said, implying the machinations of Duggan and other clerics, that their designated funeral procession position was an insult to revolutionary Irish Republicanism.[21]

When the cortege arrived at Saint Mary's Cathedral at Madison and Wabash, the assembled clergy chanted the office for the dead and Reverend Thaddeus Butler, chaplain of the

Irish Brigade, sang the High Mass. According to the *Tribune,* a unique feature of the funeral ceremony was the Light Guard Band's performance of "Mulligan's Requiem," arranged from the Oratorio of Elijah. In an eloquent and stirring eulogy, Reverend John J. McMullen, D.D., president of Saint Mary of the Lake University, praised his boyhood friend Mulligan as an American patriot and a devout Catholic, whose "profession and practice of religion were pleasures to him, rather than a duty."[22]

After Mass, a long line of Chicago's most prominent citizens, as well as religious and secular organizations and ordinary citizens on foot marched behind the carriage carrying the casket. From Saint Mary's Cathedral, the procession headed north along Michigan Avenue to Lake Street, west to Wells Street and then north to the railroad depot at Kinzie Street where a train waited to transport Mulligan's body for burial in Evanston's Calvary Cemetery. As the funeral procession moved slowly through the streets, the bells of city hall and the city's churches tolled a solemn requiem for Chicago's most beloved Civil War hero.

It was especially fitting that Reverend Denis Dunne, D.D., rather than Bishop Duggan, gave the final absolution and benediction

Marian Nugent Mulligan and her daughters, Marian, Allie, and Adele, gathered around the portrait of the late Colonel Mulligan. (Courtesy, Chicago Historical Society, ICHi–17702)

at Mulligan's funeral. Dunne was one of the most imposing, popular, powerful, and productive priests in the city. Not only was he vicar general of the diocese, the most important member of the bishop's council, but since 1854 Dunne had been pastor of Saint Patrick's, the mother parish of the Chicago Irish. In addition to supervising the construction of Saint Patrick's Church, Dunne had established in 1857 the first chapter of the Saint Vincent de Paul Society to relieve the suffering of the poor.

Born on February 10, 1824 in Stradbally, Queen's County (now County Laoighis), Ireland, Dunne emigrated with his parents to Canada. His father and uncles were ship carpenters and they found ready employment in the Cunard shipyards, and a measure of prosperity in Chatham, New Brunswick. After completing primary school, Denis enrolled in the classical course at Saint Andrew's College, Charlottetown, Prince Edward Island, the only Catholic educational institution in the Maritime provinces. About 1845, Chicago's first bishop toured the eastern United States and Canada seeking candidates for the priesthood to serve his growing diocese. Intrigued by Bishop Quarter's description of Chicago, young Denis decided to enter the Quebec City seminary to prepare for ordination. Around the same time, his father died and the family business suffered a further setback when the Cunard shipyards went bankrupt.

By 1845 Denis's brothers had found employment as ship carpenters in Chicago, and it was through their influence that the rest of the family moved from New Brunswick to Chicago. According to Dunne historian, Len Hilts, the family built a boat that could navigate the Welland Canal and set out in the spring of 1848 for Quebec. Denis met them with the sad news that Bishop Quarter had died and they would have to travel to the cathedral in Detroit for his ordination—a journey through fifty-three more locks.[23]

Denis Dunne's first Chicago appointment was to the faculty of Saint Mary of the Lake University, close to the present-day site of Holy Name Cathedral. He then served as parish priest in the bustling lead mining town of Galena, and later in Ottawa, at the western end of the Illinois and Michigan Canal. In the fall of 1854 Dunne returned to Chicago as pastor of Saint Patrick's, succeeding Reverend Patrick McLaughlin who had died in a cholera epidemic. His relatives settled nearby, purchasing homes on Adams Street, directly across from the church. Indeed, Dunne was the patriarch of what became an important Chicago family, prominent in religious and secular life. One of his nephews, Patrick Riordan, became the esteemed archbishop of San Francisco. Another, Finley Peter Dunne, wrote the famous "Mr. Dooley" essays that captured the essence of the Chicago Irish at the turn of the century.[24]

Saint Patrick's Irish Legion

Like so many Irish Catholic immigrants, Dunne was a fervent American patriot. He encouraged Irish-American Catholics to enlist in the army in order to preserve the Union and to demonstrate their love of country. Although Illinois had raised the necessary quotas without resorting to a draft, Dunne believed that many Irish had been reluctant to serve in the Union army because of the lack of Catholic chaplains in a number of the regiments. To rectify this situation, he decided to form a legion from his parish.[25]

On August 8, 1862, Father Dunne presided over a meeting at Saint Patrick's school that

✢ ✢ ✢

The Mulligan monument in Calvary Cemetery, Evanston. The colonel rests a few feet away; Denis Dunne's grave is also close by. (Courtesy, The New World)

62

included prominent laymen, including Alder-men Redmond Sheridan and James Conlan. Participants endorsed plans for an Irish Legion and a resolution that viewed "with contempt, abhorrence and detestation those unfortunate Irishmen who have sought, or who are are now seeking, the protection of the blood-stained felon flag of Great Britain, to escape their duty to the United States; and that such men deserve, if not hanging, at least to be put out of the country."[26] By unanimous vote, the men named Dunne pro-tem colonel of the Irish Legion.

In its account of the meeting, the *Chicago Times* acknowledged the bravery and patrio-tism of Irish immigrants and noted that thou-sands of Irish Catholics had already rushed to the rescue of their adopted country, leaving "peaceful avocations" to bring "terror and dis-may" to the Confederate foe. However, early organization of the Legion had its rough spots. Father Dunne successfully lobbied for the appointment of Timothy O'Meara, a New Yorker, over William Snowhook, a Mexican War veteran who had strong backing from Chicago Republicans, as Legion colonel. O'Meara, a heavy drinker, had frequent conflicts with his officers, but in combat proved a brave soldier.[27]

On September 22, 1862, the War Department mustered in the Irish Legion as the Ninetieth Illinois Infantry Regiment and assigned it to guard Confederate prisoners at Camp Douglas. In a week's time Legionnaires were on their way south. They served under General Grant during the Mississippi campaign, participating in many battles, including the siege of Vicks-burg, and marched with General William Tecumseh Sherman through Georgia and the Carolinas. Casualties were high, particularly on November 25, 1863, at Missionary Ridge where the Ninetieth Illinois suffered 143 killed, wounded, and missing. During the engagement O'Meara lost his life and Lieutenant Colonel

Owen Stewart was seriously wounded. He recovered to take command of the Legion.

In the course of the war, the Ninetieth Illi-nois suffered some three hundred combat casu-alties. Considering the primitive conditions of medicine and health care in the 1860s, wounds imposed a greater risk than in later wars. Many of the Legion succumbed to a variety of illnesses. Such diseases as diptheria, cholera, smallpox, tuberculosis, and dysentery (often the product of contaminated food) could be more frightening than the dangers of combat. In a May 1863 letter to his wife from "hot as hell" Lafayette, Tennessee, Captain Peter Casey expressed fear of hospitalization. He worried that he might become sick before too long and "if a man gets into the [hospital there] is a poor chance for him." But if he did fall ill, Casey instructed his wife that she should come to headquarters where five ladies, all "the wives of officers" were staying.[28]

When President Lincoln signed the Emanci-pation Proclamation in January 1863 to keep Britain and France neutral in the War between the States, and to appease the abolitionist wing of his own party, he dampened Irish-American Catholic—as well as lower-class urban and rural—enthusiasm for the Union cause. The most obvious indication of reaction to the free-ing of African-American slaves was the July 1863 New York Draft Riot, where a largely Irish mob, protesting a law that would permit the rich to buy their way out of military service, killed eleven African Americans and burned down a black orphanage. Although German and Anglo-Americans also participated in anticon-scription demonstrations in Boston, Mas-sachusetts; Pottsville, Pennsylvania; Troy, New York; Milwaukee, Wisconsin; and Dubuque, Iowa, newspapers stressed the heavy involve-ment of Irish Catholics. The press also reported physical and verbal harassment of African

Americans in Chicago and many rural areas of the North.[29]

In August 1863 the *Chicago Tribune* singled out Irish Catholics who "resist the draft, mob or murder conscription officers, get up bloody riots, vote en masse for the worst Copperheads and rebel sympathizers. . . ." And the newspaper warned that, "The conduct of the Irish toward this beneficent country in the hour of its direst peril is not only ungrateful and wicked but absolutely suicidal to the Irish if they succeed in overthrowing it."[30] Moreover, the *Tribune* reprinted Daniel O'Connell's appeal of twenty years past to Irish Catholics in the United States to remember their own experience with British oppression.

During his 1843 agitation to repeal the Union that linked Ireland with Britain, Daniel O'Connell, liberator of Irish Catholics in the United Kingdom and a key player in the successful effort to end slavery in the British Empire, pleaded with Irish Catholics in the United States to take a place in the vanguard of abolitionism. He said that their own historical experience as victims of British colonialism should encourage them to empathize with the plight of African-American slaves and that the principles of their religion, Irish nationalism, and the American Declaration of Independence should make them advocates of the liberty and equality of all people regardless of religion, race, or nationality. Many Irish-American Catholics responded to the advice of the founding father of modern Irish nationalism by telling him not to interfere in American affairs and by reducing their financial contributions to the Loyal National Repeal Association, O'Connell's organizational instrument of agitation.[31]

The ineffectiveness of O'Connell's counsel can be read in Captain Peter Casey's correspondence to his wife. Although Casey's command of the written language was poor, he evoked the day-to-day miseries of a soldier, one who did not consider liberating African Americans the motive for his sacrifice. "I was officer of the day yesterday and I have to be in the saddle nearly twenty-fore hours And I am sick sore and downharted," he told his wife, adding, "I wish every dam abolishinest in Chicago felt as I do this morning they would be careful how they have rushed the country into war."[32]

When War Department officials announced a September 1864 draft, Alderman John Comiskey led the opposition. Although his name is more closely associated today with the baseball team founded by his son, Charles, "Honest John" was an ardent American patriot who had helped launch both Mulligan's Irish Brigade and Father Dunne's Irish Legion. But the draft lottery, he believed, was a capitalist plot to make money while working-class soldiers died on the battlefield. Comiskey argued that the lottery permitted the rich to avoid the war by purchasing substitutes, and he insisted that if the poor had to do the fighting, they should be rewarded with substantial bonuses for their service.[33]

Negative reactions to the Emancipation Proclamation and the abuse of African Americans in Chicago and elsewhere fueled Copperhead efforts to end the war on favorable terms for the South. Once again, the press highlighted Irish involvement, such as Charles Walsh's November 1864 unsuccessful scheme to free Camp Douglas Confederate prisoners. Antiwar activities and draft-dodging infuriated *Tribune* editorial writers. They denounced Irish Catholics as disloyal and ungrateful. Irish behavior was not the result of "inherent cowardice or hatred of freedom," the *Tribune* noted, "for they are a fighting, pugnacious race, and passionately fond of the enjoyment of the largest liberty compatible with public safety." Warning that it would take years for Irish

Catholics to live down the stigma of disloyalty, the *Tribune* called on "every intelligent Irishman to use his influence with his more illiterate countrymen, to open their eyes and instruct them in the obligations of patriotism and good citizenship."[34]

When the Democratic Party held its national convention in a hastily constructed auditorium on Michigan Avenue in August 1864, delegates selected General George McClellan as their candidate. Early in the campaign a war-weary electorate threatened to make the election close, but after General Sherman took Atlanta and General Philip Sheridan cleared out the Shenandoah, Abraham Lincoln's political fortunes soared. He easily won re-election in November 1864 but lost the Irish-Catholic urban vote by a large margin—Lincoln carried Chicago by less than two thousand votes, 14,388 to McClellan's 12,691.[35]

Finally, the manpower and economic superiority of the North triumphed. On April 9, 1865, General Robert E. Lee surrendered to General Grant at Appomattox. Five days later, John Wilkes Booth assassinated Lincoln. The public mourning that followed made life uncomfortable for Irish Catholics and other Democrats who had opposed the martyred president's war policies and his Emancipation Proclamation. But for returning veterans there was only praise. Chicago welcomed them back "bronzed and battletorn, begrimmed with the smoke of a hundred conflicts—toughened by thousands of miles of marching." On June 12, 1865, at the doors of Saint Patrick's rectory, Father Dunne received three cheers from Irish Legion veterans. But it was a sad as well as a happy occasion for the priest and his parishioners: 980 legionnaires had left Camp Douglas for Mississippi, but only 221 returned to Chicago for discharge. Forty-one of the survivors were too crippled to carry a weapon.[36]

The next day, Chicagoans feted the Irish Legion as they marched through the city streets carrying their regimental colors, "one of which was literally torn to shreds." When they reached the board of trade, Governor Richard Yates paid tribute to the memory of Colonel Mulligan as well as to the "thousands of humble men, now sleeping in nameless graves far down in Chattanooga." The *Tribune* reminded its readers that the "gallant old 90th regiment—the Irish Legion—[was] one of the oldest regiments in the field, having entered Sherman's army at Vicksburg."[37]

Thanks to the impressive record of courage and sacrifice compiled by the Irish Brigade and the Irish Legion, Chicago's Irish challenged conventional wisdom about the loyalty of Catholic immigrants. But only three years after Chicago welcomed home the Ninetieth Regiment, the voice of nativism emerged as shrill as ever. An *Evening Post* editorial of September 9, 1868, complained of the large Irish population in the city's jail, reform schools, hospitals, and charitable institutions. "Scratch a convict or pauper," said the *Post,* "and the chances are that you tickle the skin of an Irish Catholic, an Irish Catholic made a criminal or a pauper by the priest and politician who have deceived him and kept him in ignorance, in a word, a savage, as he was born."

These were offensive words, particularly to the ears of Father Denis Dunne. As vicar general of the diocese, he had worked tirelessly to build and sustain churches, schools, and charitable institutions throughout northern Illinois. During the 1850s he had supervised the completion of Saint Patrick's Church and Holy Name Cathedral while establishing Chicago's first chapter of the Saint Vincent de Paul Society that did so much to aid the poor. In addition to taking the lead in organizing the Irish Legion, he had opened an industrial school for the orphaned sons of Civil War veterans. Instead of receiving the praise and cooperation of his bishop, Duggan attempted to have the state revoke the school's charter.[38]

Dunne and other prominent Chicago priests were deeply concerned by the bishop's frequent absences from the diocese and his erratic, arbitrary, and irresponsible administrative conduct. For example, without warning in 1866, Duggan closed Saint Mary of the Lake University and transferred Reverend John McMullen to a poor Irish parish just south of Saint Patrick's. After considerable thought, Dunne joined with McMullen, Reverend James McGovern, and Joseph P. Roles in informing Rome about the disorganized state of the diocese. Retribution was swift. On his return from Europe in 1868, Duggan stripped Dunne of his vicar generalship and banished him from Saint Patrick's. The forty-five-year old priest took refuge in the home of his brother Edward, directly across the street from the church he built. Although Duggan eventually was removed from Chicago and committed to a St. Louis sanitarium, Dunne did not live long enough to see his name vindicated.[39]

Passing of a Patriot Priest

On December 23, 1868, three years and six months after receiving and acknowledging the

admiration and respect of the Irish Legion, Dunne, disgraced and impoverished, died of heart failure. To add insult to injury, Duggan tried to extract a deathbed confession from the gravely ill priest. But Dunne refused to recant and died "with the censure of the Bishop upon his back. . ."[40] Despite Duggan's enmity, Dunne retained the loyalty of his fellow priests and the overwhelming majority of the laity. For five days after his death, Chicago newspapers detailed Dunne's career and his courage in confronting episcopal opposition. The *Tribune,* which feasted on anti-Catholicism, admitted that "few men were more beloved by our citizens at large than the deceased. Not only was he an ornament to the Catholic Church, but to the clergy as a body." Indeed, the *Tribune* went so far as to proclaim that: "Men of all denominations feel that in the death of Dr. Dunne the city has sustained an irreparable loss."

Maintaining an old Irish tradition of honoring dead heroes with public processions, prominent Chicago Catholics met with members of Dunne's family to plan his funeral.[41] They also crafted a series of resolutions refuting charges

✛ ✛ ✛

Reverend Denis Dunne, Saint Patrick's patriot pastor (1824–68). (Courtesy, The New World)

against their priest and published them in the Chicago daily newspapers. On Christmas Day 1868, for example, readers of the *Chicago Times* learned that the "poor have lost a sincere friend, the orphans a father, his parishioners a dear and loving pastor, the community at large a most devoted citizen." Equally important, "by his spotless life," Denis Dunne had proved himself "a model worthy of imitation by all."

Like Mulligan's four years earlier, the Dunne funeral was a massive display of affection as well as grief, uniting Catholics from Chicago's North, South, and West Sides. So great were the crowds who came to Saint Patrick's to pay their last respects that parishioners requested his burial be postponed a day. With Christmas decorations still in place, Saint Patrick's was "brilliantly illuminated, and handsomely draped" for the December 26 requiem Mass. More than fifty priests joined thousands of mourners who crammed every inch and cranny of the church to hear Reverend Stephen J. Barrett's eulogy to Dunne, "And ye are of the salt of the earth."

In its account of the funeral Mass, the *Tribune* noted that Bishop Duggan's absence "was much commented upon and in many instances called forth angry imprecations on the head of that functionary. Especially was this feeling noticeable among the clergy, who openly expressed their dissatisfaction and characterized the action as a disgrace to the church in view of [Father Dunne's high position]." On Sunday, December 27, 1868, Colonel Owen Stewart and members of the Irish Legion joined with Irish Brigade veterans and those of other

regiments to march in a body from Wall's Hall at the southeast corner of Halsted and Adams to Saint Patrick's where they formed a military escort for the funeral procession. According to the *Chicago Times,* the streets in front of the church were "completely blockaded" by thousands of spectators who waited to pay their respects.

Inside the church he had built, Father Dunne's body lay in a coffin of "solid rosewood, without ornament or device,—emblematic of the character and life of the deceased." When pallbearers began their descent down the steps of the church, "a solemn and impressive stillness pervaded the vast assemblage, and as by a common impulse, every hat was lifted." Sixty carriages waited outside to carry the mayor and aldermen, the Sisters of Charity of Saint Vincent de Paul, friends and relatives, and members of the clergy to the railway depot on Kinzie Street. For nearly two hours, the procession moved slowly through the city. Thousands of Chicagoans crowded sidewalks along the line of march, and many homes and businesses flew flags at half-mast in respect for the dead priest. Another powerful sign of Dunne's importance and influence was the donation of three trains by the Chicago and Northwestern Railroad to transport mourners to Evanston's Calvary Cemetery. Sixty-three cars followed each other so closely and moved so slowly that "at a distance they seemed as only one immense and continuous line." Following a graveside service, the founding father of the Irish Legion was laid to rest in the Dunne family plot near the remains of the colonel of the Irish Brigade.

Mr. Dooley Reconsidered
Community Memory,
Journalism, and the Oral Tradition

Charles Fanning

A Boyhood in Old Saint Pat's

Think of a boy born on the Near West Side of Chicago two years after the end of the Civil War. His parents are Irish Catholic immigrants, and they live at 136 West Adams Street, a stone's throw from their church—Saint Patrick's. Theirs may have been the first marriage performed in the new building, for it took place on December 29, 1856, three days after the church was dedicated. The pastor who married them, Reverend Denis Dunne, is a force in Chicago Catholicism, named vicar general of the diocese in 1855, and soon to raise an Irish Civil War regiment known as the Ninetieth Illinois Infantry. He is also the boy's uncle.[1]

Imagine the conversation, the stories that the boy, Peter Dunne, must have heard and overheard throughout his childhood in the 1870s from his parents and six brothers and sisters and their other relatives, friends, and neighbors at the crossroads of West Adams and Desplaines. There were memories of Ireland, of the Great Hunger, of the hard crossings in the coffin ships. There were first impressions of the New World, stories of early disappointments and later modest successes. By way of his Uncle Denis, there were first-hand accounts of the Civil War, in which so many Chicagoans had fought. Because the boy's father was sympa-

thetic to "the cause," there were tales of the minor victories and major defeats in the movement to free Ireland from British rule, including the tragic Rising of 1798, the bizarre 1866 Fenian "invasions" of Canada by Civil War veterans, and the Chicago-based Dynamite Campaign in London in the early 1880s. There were also reports of resurgent Irish nationalism under a charismatic young leader named Charles Stewart Parnell, who would come to Chicago in February 1880, when the boy was twelve. Perhaps Peter's father took him along to McCormick's Hall to see the great man. As he moved through his teens, the boy would have charted the roller coaster of Parnellism and the cause in the 1880s, for the political connections between Ireland and Chicago remained strong. Indeed, on November 29, 1890, less than two weeks after the verdict against Mrs. Katherine O'Shea and Parnell in the divorce trial that was to ruin "the Chief," an Irish nationalist delegation, including influential parliamentary party members John Dillon and William O'Brien, addressed a mass meeting of eight thousand in Chicago's Battery D Armory. Among "those on the platform" was the same boy, a rising young journalist now known (having reversed his two given names) as Finley Peter Dunne. Moreover, Dunne had recently been credited with breaking open the notorious

Chicago Evening Post, *1880s*. (Courtesy, Special Collections and Preservation Division, the Chicago Public Library)

1889 Cronin murder case, a thick tangle of Irish nationalist intrigue the upshot of which was the conviction of the detective who had been in charge of the investigation.[2]

A graduate of Scammon Elementary School and West Division High School, young Peter had been an early and easy talker, and was encouraged in reading and the life of the mind by his mother, Ellen Finley Dunne, a lover of Dickens, Scott, and Thackeray, and his older sister Amelia, who began a teaching career in the Chicago public schools in 1880.[3] Quick, observant, street-smart, the boy soaked in the sights, smells, and especially the speech of the Irish West Side, and from there the expansive world of greater Chicago. He was a born jour-

nalist, alert to the vivid turn of phrase that captures the essence of fact and the rhythm of life, grasping the pith of a story, event, or idea, and following the resultant shock waves pulsing out—personal, familial, political, cultural. In June 1884, right out of high school and sixteen years old, Peter Dunne took a job as an office boy and cub reporter for the *Chicago Telegram*. Eight years and five increasingly responsible jobs later, he was editorial chairman at the *Chicago Evening Post*.[4]

Enter Mr. Dooley

It was there, at the ripe old age of twenty-six, that Dunne created the voice of Mr. Martin J.

Dooley, an aging immigrant saloonkeeper on Archer Avenue. In the *Post* of Saturday, October 7, 1893, the inaugural column opened with John McKenna, a genial South Side politician, entering Dooley's place and greeting his old friend. Here are Mr. Dooley's first words:

> "Hello, Jawnny," replied Mr. Dooley, as if they had parted only the evening before. "How's thricks? I don't mind, Jawnny, if I do. 'Tis duller here than a Ray-publican primary in the fourth ward, th' night. Sure, ye're like a ray iv sunlight, ye are that. There's been no company in these pa-arts since Dominick Riley's big gossoon was took up be th' polis——no, not the Riley that lived down be th' gas-house; he's moved over in th' fifth wa-ard—may th' divil go with him: 'twas him bruk that there mirror with a brick for an' because I said Carey, th' informer, was a Limerick man. This here's Pat Riley, th' big, strappin' kid iv Dominick Riley, that lived beyant th' rollin' mills. He was th' 'ell's own hand f'r sport."[5]

The news here is that we are suddenly in a real neighborhood, where people are placed by family, geography, and reputation, and we are listening to a real voice, that of an immigrant Irish Chicagoan in 1893. Almost immediately, these weekly 750-word monologues (delivered to John McKenna or long-suffering millworker Malachi Hennessy) became a Saturday-evening Chicago tradition. The last in a series of dialect experiments for his creator, Mr. Dooley succeeded "Colonel Malachi McNeery," a fictional downtown Chicago barkeep whom Dunne had invented to provide weekly commentary in the *Evening Post* during the world's fair of 1893. Dunne had modeled the colonel on a friend of his, Jim McGarry, whose Dearborn Street

saloon was a gathering spot for newspapermen and visiting celebrities, including boxer John L. Sullivan and actor James O'Neill. In contrast to the McGarry/McNeery Loop location, Dunne placed Mr. Dooley's barroom on "Archey Road" in the South Side, Irish working-class community known then as now as Bridgeport.[6] The shift is significant: from a central and cosmopolitan watering hole to an outlying neighborhood institution where a regular clientele of Irish millworkers and draymen find solace and companionship. To create this sort of place, Dunne surely looked to the childhood community where he came to consciousness, on the equally Irish, somewhat better off Near West Side, around West Adams and Desplaines in Saint Patrick's parish.

✛ ✛ ✛

Young Finley Peter Dunne. (Courtesy, Author's collection)

Between 1893 and 1900, some three hundred Dooley pieces appeared in Chicago newspapers. Taken together, they form a coherent body of work, in which a vivid, detailed world comes into existence—a self-contained immigrant/ethnic culture with its own customs, ceremonies, "sacred sites," social pecking order, heroes, villains, and victims. The Chicago Dooley pieces constitute the most solidly realized ethnic neighborhood in nineteenth-century American literature. With the full faith of the literary realist, Dunne embraces the common man as proper subject and creates sympathetic, dignified, even heroic characters, plausibly grounded in a few city blocks of apartments, saloons, factories, and churches. The result of Dunne's labor is the great nineteenth-century Irish-American novel—in weekly installments. He also provides, piece by piece, a ringing answer to Mr. Dooley's criticism of the historical profession: "Historyans is like doctors. They are always lookin' f'r symptoms. Those iv them that writes about their own times examines th' tongue an' feels th' pulse an' makes a wrong dygnosis. Th' other kind iv histhry is a post-mortem examination. It tells ye what a country died iv. But I'd like to know what it lived iv."

Finally, all of these historical and literary riches are transmitted through the vernacular voice of an aging Irish immigrant. Dunne's use of dialect is a major breakthrough. Until Mr. Dooley began speaking, the brogue had been used pervasively in nineteenth-century drama, fiction, and journalism to portray the stereotypical "stage Irishman," a demeaning comic caricature of ignorance, belligerence, and garrulity, the purpose of which was mockery of supposed Irishness. But Mr. Dooley's brogue smashes the stereotypes for good and all. When he is being funny, he provokes laughter not because he knows so little, but because he knows so much. He is witty, satirical, cutting, and he exposes

delusions rather than reinforcing them. Moreover, Mr. Dooley is funny in only half the Chicago pieces. He is just as often utterly serious, treating such subjects as starvation in Ireland and Chicago, wanton murder and grim retribution in the urban underworld, and heroic sacrifices by Bridgeport firemen in their tinderbox neighborhood, "consthructed f'r poor people out iv nice varnished pine an' cotton waste." Throughout the 1890s, Mr. Dooley gave Chicagoans weekly examples of the potential for serious fiction of common speech and everyday life.[7]

Community Memory and Community Mores

It is striking how fully formed Dunne's conception was from the outset. In the first six weeks, he wrote prototypical pieces defining the two most precious and lasting contributions of the Chicago Dooley columns. First, Mr. Dooley is the custodian of urban, ethnic community memory stretching back to pre-Famine Ireland, in stories about Christmas visiting, crossroads dances, and being graduated "be th' toe iv th' hidge schoolmasther's boot." Harshest of all are the still vivid images of "our parish over beyant, whin th' potatoes was all kilt be the frost an' th' oats rotted with th' dhrivin' rain. . . . Musha, but 'tis a sound to dhrive ye'er heart cold whin a woman sobs an' th' young wans cries, an' both because there's no bread in th' house." He also preserves stories of the wrenching, turbulent crossing to America, the shattered dream of gold in the streets, the rough-and-tumble of life along the Illinois and Michigan Canal, and military service in the Union and Fenian armies. Second, Mr. Dooley is the historian of the community mores of Irish Chicago in the 1890s, in stories of stoic, exploited millworkers and day laborers, failed politicians who lose their money, successful ones who forget their friends, lace-curtain social climbers with pianos in the parlor, and voluble "pathriots" committed-—rhetorically-—to Irish freedom. He provides telling vignettes from the quotidian passing scene of the sufferings of the poor, the embarrassments and compromises accompanying the slow rise to middle-class respectability, and the painful gulf that opens between immigrant parents and their American children.[8]

Appearing on November 4, 1893, the earliest piece of community memory was a powerful, generalizing meditation on the paradox of Irish failure at home and success abroad as immigrants, all the way back to the "Wild Geese" of the seventeenth century. Irish freedom had been in the news all year, as a Home Rule bill made its way through the British House of Commons, and was passed on September 1. Prompted specifically by the reputed Irish background and newsworthiness of Austrian premier Count Taafe ("a good ol' Meath name in th' days gone by"), Mr. Dooley recites a litany of Irishmen who are admired everywhere except at home: soldiers (Pat McMahon, "th' Frinchman, that beat Looey Napoleon," O'Donnell, the Spanish duke, Sheridan and Kearney in the United States), writers (Charles Lever, Oliver Goldsmith, William Carleton), and orators (Edmund Burke and Chicago's own "Macchew P." Brady). He then remarks that "there's Mac's an' O's in ivry capital in Europe atin' off silver plates whin their relations is staggerin' under th' creels iv turf in th' Connaught bogs," and continues with a perspective and eloquence fitting for a man of Mr. Dooley's years, but impressively precocious for his creator:

> "Wirra, 'tis hard. Ye'd sa-ay off hand, 'Why don't they do as much for their own counthry?' Light-spoken are thim that suggests th' like iv that. 'Tis asier said than done. Ye can't grow flowers in a granite block, Jawn dear, much less whin th' first shoot'd be thrampled under foot without pity. 'Tis aisy f'r us over here, with our bellies full, to talk iv th' cowardice iv th' Irish; but what would ye have wan man iv thim do again a rig'ment? 'Tis little fightin' th' lad will want that will have to be up before sunrise to keep th' smoke curlin' fr'm th' chimbley or to patch th' rush roof to keep out th' March rain. No, faith, Jawn, there's no soil in Ireland f'r th' greatness iv th' race; an' there has been none since th' wild geese wint across th' say to France, hangin' like flies to th' side iv th' Fr-rinch ship. 'Tis on'y f'r women an' childher now, an' thim that can't get away. Will th' good days ever come again? says ye. Who knows! Who knows!"[9]

With similar alacrity, on November 25, 1893, Dunne established the prototype of his many compassionate renderings of Irish-American urban daily life with a piece in which Mr. Dooley comes to the aid of the little Grady girl, who has been sent out in a snowstorm to get beer for her profligate father. The context here was the onset of the "Black Winter" of 1893–94, when the depression that had hit the rest of the country during the summer caught up to Chicago in the wake of the temporary prosperity brought by the world's fair. Not coincidentally, the *Evening Post* was running a series on "The Children of the Poor" around this same time.[10] Again, Dunne surprises with his immediate sureness of touch. The piece opens with a vivid descriptive paragraph:

> Up in Archey road the streetcar wheels squeaked along the tracks and the men coming down from the rolling-mills hit themselves on their big chests and wiped their noses on their leather gloves with a peculiar back-handed stroke at which they are most adept. The little girls coming out of the bakeshops with loaves done up in brown paper under their arms had

2800 block of Archer Avenue in Bridgeport, 1885. (Courtesy, Chicago Historical Society, ICHi–09283)

to keep a tight clutch on their thin shawls lest those garments should be caught up by the bitter wind blowing from Brighton Park way and carried down to the gashouse. The frost was so thick on the windows of Mr. Martin Dooley's shop that you could just see the crownless harp on the McCormick's Hall Parnell meeting sheet above it, and you could not see any of the pyramid of Medford rum bottles founded contemporaneously with that celebrated meeting.

So much of the everyday Irish-American scene is caught here: working men defined by a gesture, the threadbare quality of city life reflected in Bridgeport's children, a hint of nos-

talgia for Ireland and Parnell. Atypical for the Dooley series, this deliberate composition of place shows us Dunne imagining his way into the neighborhood.

Mr. Dooley's friend John McKenna enters, and the two exchange jokes about the bitterly cold weather, which reminds Dooley of a cautionary tale about the danger of wanting to know just how cold it is. A man named Denny "that kep' th' block below Finucane's" bought a thermometer, and went out so often in his shirt sleeves to check the temperature that "wan day he tuk noomony in th' lungs an' died." At this point, "a rattle at the door and a short cry" announce the appearance of "something that looked like a rather large parcel of rags, but on close inspection turned out to be a very small girl carrying a very big can." Mr. Dooley identifies her as "Grady's kid—Grady, th' villain, th' black-hearted thafe, to send th' poor choild out to her death," and he orders McKenna to "go over an' fetch that can iv milk. Musha, musha, ye poor dear. Naw, naw, don't wipe ye'er nose on me apron, ye unmannerly crather. Give me a towl, Jawn, fr'm in under th' shilf where thim Angyostooria bitthers stands." Soon, in a graphic image, the Grady girl is "laving her

purple nose in the warm milk," and Mr. Dooley is narrating "the history of her father in forcible language." The piece ends with Dooley closing up early, taking five dollars from the cash drawer, and marching off, with McKenna and the little girl in tow, "to lick Grady."

Also in these first weeks came vignettes of a legislative battle between Bridgeport Alderman Billy O'Brien and Mayor Carter Harrison about the placement of a garbage dump (October 21), a Dooley recollection of the great Chicago Fire of 1871 (October 14), and, on December 23, a

Bridgeport saloon of Michael McAuley, 3107 South Halsted Street. (Courtesy, Chicago Historical Society, Ryerson Collection)

memory of Christmas in Ireland from Mr. Dooley's childhood before the Famine, when "th' lads that'd been away 'd come thrampin' in fr'm Gawd knows where, big lads far fr'm home in Cork an' Limerick an' th' city iv Dublin—come thrampin' home stick in hand to ate their Christmas dinner with th' ol' folks."

Holidays and Everydays

Yearly holidays and commemorative events were often the catalyst for Dooley pieces that chronicle Irish and Chicago customs, from Christmas, Thanksgiving, and the Fourth of July, to Orange parades on July 12, the United Irish Societies' "freedom picnics" on August 15, and, naturally, Saint Patrick's Day. For example, the first two Memorial Days of Mr. Dooley's talking career inspired pieces about Irish Chicagoans in the Civil War. In the first of these (June 2, 1894), Dooley recalls hearing the news of the firing on Fort Sumter, and he goes on to narrate his cousin Mick's attempts to avoid the draft, and the "free fight up an' down Archey road because Dan Dorgan said Shur'-dan [Sheridan] was a betther gin'ral thin Thomas Francis Meagher. Thim was th' only two afther Mulligan was kilt that th' Ar-rchey road cared f'r." (The reference here is to Colonel James Mulligan, leader of Chicago's Irish Brigade. In his second Memorial Day piece, Dunne has Dooley retell the local legend of Mulligan's having died "down somewhere in Kentucky; an' th' las' wurruds he was heard to utter was, 'Lay me down, boys, an' save th' flag.'") The moving center of the first piece, however, is the face of ordinary, unheroic grief that Mr. Dooley puts on the occasion:

"But I've made it a rule niver to go out on Dec'ration Day. It turns the hear-rt in me gray f'r to see th' women marchin' to Calv'ry with their veils over their heads an' thim little pots

iv gyraniums in their hands. Th' sojers has thim that'll fire salutes over their graves an' la-ads to talk about thim, but there's none but th' widdy f'r to break her hear-rt above th' poor soul that died afther his hands had tur-rned to leather fr'm handlin' a pick."

The second Memorial Day piece (June 1, 1895) grew from the dedication at Oakwoods Cemetery of a monument to the Confederate dead. Here Mr. Dooley relates a heated exchange from the previous Thursday evening, Memorial Day itself. A real hero of the war, millworker Pat Doherty, who "inlisted three times" and came home with "enough lead to stock a plumber in his stomach an' his legs," hasn't marched in the parade: "I can get hot enough runnin' a wheelbarrow without makin' a monkey iv mesilf dancin' around the sthreets behind a band." Nor has he gone out to decorate the graves: "I hadn't th' price," says he, but "th' women wint out with a gyranium to put over Sarsfield, the first born." Again, the moving, sympathetic perspective. Just then, Morgan O'Toole, a blowhard political hack, breezes in and declares the new Confederate monument "a disgrace to th' mim'ries iv thim devoted dead who died f'r their counthry." This is too much for Pat Doherty, who exposes O'Toole as a draft-dodger and goes on to give a withering depiction of the reality of the war:

"Doherty was movin' up to him. 'What rig'-ment?' says he. 'What's that?' says O'Toole. 'Did ye inlist in th' army, brave man?' says Pat. 'I swore him over age,' says I. 'Was ye dhrafted in?' says th' little man. 'No,' says O'Toole. 'Him an' me was in th' same cellar,' says I. 'Did ye iver hear iv Ree-saca, 'r Vicksburg, 'r Lookout Mountain?' th' little man wint on. 'Did anny man iver shoot at ye with annything but a siltzer bottle? Did ye iver have to lay on ye'er stummick with ye'er nose burrid in th' Lord knows what while things was whistlin' over ye that, if they iver stopped whistlin', 'd make ye'er backbone look like a broom? Did ye iver see a man that ye'd slept with th' night befure cough, an' go out with his hooks ahead iv his face? Did ye iver have to wipe ye'er most intimate frinds off ye'er clothes, whin ye wint home at night? Where was he durin' th' war?' he says. 'He was dhrivin' a grocery wagon f'r Philip Reidy,' says I. 'An' what's he makin' th' roar about?' says th' little man. 'He don't want anny wan to get onto him,' says I."

O'Toole slinks out, and the piece ends with Doherty remembering the singing voice of a fellow soldier: "There was a man in our mess—a Wicklow man be th' name iv Dwyer—that had th' best come-all-ye I iver heerd. It wint like this."

With much less advance notice than was provided by holidays, Dunne also wrote Dooley pieces in response to late-breaking news. When four Chicago firemen died in a Friday morning blaze, the Saturday *Post* contained Mr. Dooley's recollection of the tragic hubris of fireman Mike Clancy, the most admired man in Bridgeport, who feels himself slowing down and vows to quit after one more "rale good ol' hot wan."

> "An' he did, Jawn. Th' day th' Carpenter Brothers' box factory burnt. 'Twas wan iv thim big, fine-lookin' buildings that pious men built out iv celluloid an' plasther iv Paris. An' Clancy was wan iv th' men undher whin th' wall fell. I seen thim bringin' him home; an' th' little woman met him at th' dure, rumplin' her apron in her hands."[11]

In another piece about firemen, Mr. Dooley puts us inside Saint Patrick's Church, as he describes one of the most famous parishioners in the 1890s—Chicago fire chief Denis Swenie. It's a memory from the time, as Dooley admits, when "I lived down be Saint Pathrick's," and "I used to see him there at high mass, with a long black coat to his back." With impeccable timing, "ivry Sunday about th' gospel ye'd see th' little dhriver come tear-rin' down th' aisle with his hat in his hand. Thin ivry wan'd lave his devotions an' give an' eye an' an ear. Ye cud ha-ardly hould th' althar byes, an' avin the soggarth [priest] himsilf'd take a squint over his shoulder. . . . 'What box?' ye'd hear th' chafe say. 'Twinty-sicond an' Loomis,' an' they was off. Thin ye'd look around an' all th' la-ads that stood up near th' dure where they could ate peanuts was gone. Divvle th' soul could stop thim."

A Chicago Parish in Ordinary Time

Other pieces give us rare and colorful pictures of the activities that centered around a late nineteenth-century urban parish, to which Dunne's childhood experience of Saint Patrick's surely contributed. The annual parish fair at "Saint Honoria's" in 1895 features "Roddy's Hibernyun Band playin' on th' cor-rner," a shooting gallery, booths selling everything from rosaries to oyster stew, and a raffle for a doll, a rocking chair, and "a picture iv th' pope done by Mary Ann O'Donoghue." Other parish productions include a "temperance saloon" that lasts only one night, as the patrons have "dhrunk thimsilves into chollery morbus with coold limonade," a genealogy lecture in the school hall that erupts into a brawl over whose ancestors were kings and whose only dukes, and the staging of *The Doomed Markey* by the "Saint Patrick's Stock Company" with Denny Hogan in the title role. For this, Dunne surely drew on the experiences of his sister Amelia, who wrote and directed plays for the Chicago public schools.[12] One lively piece describes the parochial school graduation of "Hennessy's youngest," which includes a recitation of Robert Emmet's speech from the dock, a flute solo of "Kathleen Mavourneen," and a moralizing play

1853 wedding photo of Martha Tower and Denis Swenie. (Courtesy, Chicago Historical Society, ICHi–12629)

in which devil and angel fight for the soul of Tommy Casey.

Several pieces depict the involvement of a compassionate clergy in the lives of poor and ailing parishioners. In December 1897 Mr. Dooley notes that Father Kelly has "spint all th' money that he ought to be usin' to buy a warm coat f'r his back, spint it on th' poor, an' he dipt into th' Easther colliction that ought to 've gone to pay inthrest on th' church morgedge. It'll be a smooth talk he'll have to give his grace th'

+ + +

Painting of fire marshal Denis J. Swenie, romanticized at the height of his career in 1899 by F. L. Van Ness. (Courtesy, Chicago Historical Society, ICHi–12627)

archbishop this year." A year earlier, Dooley recalls the hard winter of 1874, when "th' nights came cold, an' bechune relievin' th' sick an' givin' extremunction to th' dyin' an' comfortin' th' widows an' orphans th' little priest was sore pressed fr'm week's end to week's end. They was smallpox in wan part iv th' wa-ard an' diphtheria in another an' bechune th' two there was starvation an' cold an' not enough blankets on th' bed." And he reaches back even further to commemorate the corporal works of mercy of "the little soggarth that died along in sixty-sivin iv nursin' th' chollery patients. Pax vobiscum." Here Dunne was likely drawing on extended community memory, as Father Patrick McLaughlin, the pastor of Saint Patrick's before Denis Dunne, had died of cholera in July 1854. Moreover, there

79

had been an outbreak in Chicago in the late 1860s. This was the third major American cholera epidemic in the nineteenth century, and it had begun in the East in 1866. Many Irish died, and in some circles immigrants were blamed for having caused the disease. It's possible that the cholera touched Finley Peter Dunne's own family. His sister Ellen had died on October 12, 1866, aged fifteen months, and his twin brother John died in infancy. The boys had been born on July 10, 1867.[13]

Oral Tradition, Journalism, and the Genius of Finley Peter Dunne

Writing this essay for the 150th anniversary of Saint Patrick's parish has got me thinking anew about just how exceptional Dunne's Chicago Dooley pieces are. These brief essays, written under deadline and often for specific occasions, are of extraordinary quality. Over the thirty years since I began reading them, I've often wondered how to explain the great gift of this young journalist, his ability to create the illusion of a speaking voice grounded in place that still rings true across the hundred years since it first appeared. It seems to me now that the answer lies in the coming together in these newspaper pieces of oral tradition and the written word. These are, after all, transcribed renderings of imagined conversational speech, much of it inspired by stories that had been told to the young Peter Dunne.

All oral narrative, from pre-Homeric Greece to modern Africa, has been defined by communication theorist Walter J. Ong as a set of episodic variations on conventional themes and formulas, held together by a single living voice. Moreover, Ong sees the storytelling event as at once both private and public: "Basically, the singer is remembering in a curiously public way—remembering not a memorized text, for there is no such thing, nor any verbatim succession of words, but the themes and formulas that

he has heard other singers sing. He remembers these always differently, as rhapsodized or stitched together in his own way on this particular occasion for this particular audience."[14] All of this is very different from conventional print narrative, which Ong describes as a linear selection of events, tightly plotted according to the pyramid of rising action, climax, and dénouement, and with the narrator's voice usually diffused among several characters.

The great story writer Frank O'Connor provides a specifically Irish context for the distinction between orality and literacy when he recalls that within his own lifetime written stories still had leisurely, discursive, ritual beginnings taken directly from oral tradition; for example: "By the hokies, there was a man in this place one time by the name of Ned Sullivan, and a queer thing happened him late one night and he coming up the Valley Road from Durlas." O'Connor goes on to explain that "in its earlier phases, storytelling, like poetry and drama, was a public art, though unimportant beside them because of its lack of a rigorous technique." Against this "public art," O'Connor contrasts the modern short story, "a private art intended to satisfy the standards of the individual, solitary, critical reader."[15] Later on, O'Connor asserts the potential literary richness of such a transitional period: "When an oral tradition like [that of the Irish] comes into contact with a written tradition—preferably one that is not too highly developed—it may produce literature of the highest quality, autonomous and primary in the way of Greek and Hebrew literature."[16] Thus, O'Connor describes the fruitful period of transition from storytelling to story writing in Ireland in the early years of this century. Of course, this is also Mr. Dooley's time frame, and these thoughts can help us understand Finley Peter Dunne's genius as well, for it is as a speaking voice delivered through the medium of print that he has preserved the cultural memory and mores of Irish Chicago.

Charlotte Dunne, Amelia Dunne Hookway, and Finley Peter Dunne, c. 1910. (Courtesy, Len Hilts)

In the first place, Dunne was a great talker who hated to write. Stories are legion of both his sparkling, erudite conversation and the pains he often took to avoid setting pen to paper.[17] We know that he wrote the Dooley pieces in longhand, late on Friday nights for the Saturday *Post*, more often than not with a copy boy hovering at his elbow. The pieces were tossed off—one quick go—with almost no revision and very few lined-out phrases. (I've seen some of the manuscripts.) Thus, the Chicago Dooley pieces combine virtually spontaneous composition and a minimal sense of *writtenness*. Indeed, in a 1907 essay on the nature of literary inspiration, Dunne could be describing oral rather than written narrative when he declares that "the final measure of [literary] genius" is "the act of improvising," which, with "lightness and certainty, . . . penetrate[s] the most remote and secret caverns of the mind and produce[s] the long-buried and half-forgotten treasure."[18] Moreover, as in the oral tradition, these Dooley pieces utilize a set of formal conventions: the entry of a patron into the saloon, ensuing episodic narratives, often introduced by a familiar phrase ("I see by th' papers," or "D'ye mind th' Clancys that lived over be Halsted sthreet"), and a sharp, epigrammatic closing pronouncement. Also, the pieces contain aspects of both private and public utterance: private because a dialect voice speaks at first from and to a specific ethnic audience; public because the work appears in that most democratic dispenser of information and opinion, a daily newspaper.

And finally, the Dooley pieces are like oral storytelling in their seemingly ephemeral nature. Few American journalists in 1893 would have believed that their cheap and ubiquitous product could end up as anything other than wrapping for fish and chicken bones. (There were some thirty daily papers in Chicago alone.) Dunne's own inability to see

lasting value in his early pieces comes through in letters written in 1899 to the publisher of his first two Dooley collections, to whom he gave free rein to "read proof on this whole mass . . . and correct unavoidable inconsistencies. I suspect there are duplicates. Cut out anything you wish." Dunne also confided to this publisher that "I sometimes feel that I ought to have chucked Dooley long ago, and begun on something new."[19] In any event, some of the credit for keeping Mr. Dooley alive goes to Dunne's sister Amelia, who wrote Irish and other dialects into some of her plays for the public schools and encouraged her brother to "keep it up" as well.[20] The literary situation changed dramatically for Dunne in 1898, when the popularity of Mr. Dooley's satiric perspective on the Spanish-American War led to national syndication and the publication of the first book of selected columns, *Mr. Dooley in Peace and in War*.[21] From this point on, a Dooley piece was very much a *printed* text.

In sum, the Chicago Dooley pieces constitute a rare and marvelous hybrid form. An early Dooley piece *is* closer to talk than writing. This body of work is truly transitional in Frank O'Connor's terms, bridging the gap between storytelling and printed short fiction to create, from fall 1893 through the end of 1897, an astonishing four-year window into the world of nineteenth-century Irish Chicago. This was a great achievement for Dunne and an even greater gift to those who were living in that immigrant/ethnic world. Telling stories maintains ties with one's origins, past, and shaping worldview—crucially important ties when the place from which these have sprung lies an ocean away. For immigrants and their children from a home culture with a strong oral tradition like that of the Irish, storytelling keeps a community intact and alive.

From our end of the twentieth century, there's a retrospective, piercing sense of urgency here, for the decade of the 1890s was virtually the last time when such a preserving endeavor was possible for Irish Americans from the great post-Famine migration. At midcentury, Harvard scholar John V. Kelleher recalled his own early search for authentic materials from which to construct an Irish-American novel: "My father used to tell me I would never get what I was looking for. What I needed was the talk in the kitchens at night, when the old country friends came visiting. 'If you had the record of one night's talk, you'd have it all. . . . That talk vanished before the talkers. After the turn of the century it all died out; and especially after that you never heard them going off into Irish when they wanted to talk above the young folk's heads.' "22

It is a great blessing that we do have some of that talk, thanks to the genius of Finley Peter Dunne and to the genius loci of his home parish, Saint Patrick's. The Chicago Dooley pieces illustrate the truth of the creed of Patrick Kavanagh, whose own poetry is rooted in the small farms and fields of his native County Monaghan: "Parochialism is universal; it deals with the fundamentals."23 The last corroborating word on the miracle of Mr. Dooley should be by rights that of an admirer to whom these pieces spoke directly. Signed "E. M. L.," the following poem appeared just below that Saturday's Dooley piece in the *Chicago Evening Post* of January 26, 1895. Fittingly, the writer thanks Dunne for having put his own world into words—spoken words, that is—for the praise is all in terms of oral utterance: blarneyin', shpakin', banther, sayin's, speechin'. "Ho, talk save us!" as James Joyce says in *Finnegans Wake*.

Dooley Darlin'

Yerrah, Dooley darlin', sure 'tis you've the blarneyin',
The scorchin', witty and the tindher tongue.

With McKinna shpakin' you can stop the achin'
Of my poor ould heart, faix it makes me young.

It brings me back to my own Tip'rary—
The fun so rousin', the wit so keen,
So dhroll an' sparklin', so sly an' sooth'rin'
Like a colleen's banther on an Irish green!

'Tis a long and dhrairy, aye! a lonesome wairy
Spell o' years I've spint since I sailed away,
Since I crossed the ocean through my loy'l devotion
To the furled flag that will wave some day.

Thrue, fate was kind, but my heart was hungry
For christenin's frolics and weddin's fun,
The cross-roads dance and the patth'rn's coortin'—
Och! If I'd give them all I'd be never done.

They have these things here, too, but sure they don't cheer you.
'Tis mane to say it, but their fun is tame;
An' the divil a story, but those that bore ye,
Have I heard to stir me till Dooley came!

I'm here I know, but I'm back in Munsther
When the paper comes an' Mollie reads.
The Tip'rary touch! 'Tis there, Mavourneen,
In brave Dooley's sayin's, in brave Dooley's deeds.

Ah! there's more than fun, sure, for there's sermons spun, sure,
By you Dooley, darlin', straight from your sowl;
An' 'twixt sayin's witty there are sthrains of pity,
An' scorn as bitther as a Saxon's scowl.

There's been tellin' sthrokes in Dooley's speechin'—
Didn't Pullman squirm at things he said?
And others thank him for thoughts as tindher
As a mother's glances at her baby's bed.

6

Celtic Revived
The Artistry of Thomas O'Shaughnessy

Timothy Barton

The year 1956 was an auspicious one for Saint Patrick's parish and the Chicago Irish. Not only did it mark the centennial of the dedication of the church at Adams and Desplaines but also the revival of the annual Saint Patrick's Day parade downtown after a lapse of more than fifty years. But in an odd counterpoint to such a joyous year in the life of Saint Patrick's Church, Thomas A. O'Shaughnessy died in relative obscurity in February 1956. At the turn of the century, he had been one of Chicago's most celebrated artists, a tireless promoter of Irish culture. It was O'Shaughnessy's unique vision that transformed Saint Patrick's from a dark building in a declining neighborhood into a masterpiece of Irish ecclesiastical art and restored the church to its central place in the life of the city. Although eight decades have passed since Thomas O'Shaughnessy bestowed his gifts on Saint Patrick's, they still have the power to move and inspire.

Portrait of the Artist

Thomas Augustin O'Shaughnessy was born in 1870 in central Missouri, the son of James O'Shaughnessy and Catherine Mulholland O'Shaughnessy. His interest in art, he once said, began at thirteen when he studied under Sister Ledwina at the Loretto Academy in Kansas City. It was there that O'Shaughnessy was introduced to early Christian art and the works of Saint Bride in the fifth century, as well as the notion that art and religion could be amiable partners in the devotional life of the church. He later attended Saint Joseph's College (1886–88) and the Academy of Fine Arts in Kansas City (1889–94).

In 1893 O'Shaughnessy visited Chicago with his family to attend the World's Columbian Exposition. For its spectacle and impact no single event affected the American consciousness more than the world's fair. Its classically inspired architecture, along with the voluminous number and breadth of exhibits, made it a monument to art and science that showcased America's prowess on the world stage.

Two Irish exhibits would have captured O'Shaughnessy's interests. The Irish Village and the Irish Industries Association Village were both situated on the Midway Plaisance, which was the more informal collection of ethnic exhibits, cafes, and carnival amusements. Perhaps the most important influences on the young O'Shaughnessy were the reproductions of the medieval Irish antiquities, such as the Ardagh Chalice, Bell of Saint Patrick, Cross of Cong, and the "Tara" Brooch. All of this work, fabricated by the renowned metalsmith Edmond Johnson, was instrumental in the development of the Celtic Revival aesthetic movement. Moreover, the display of these works in Chicago is considered an important event in the birth of the Celtic crafts movement in the United States.[1]

O'Shaughnessy must have been invigorated by what he saw. Following graduation, he packed his bags and moved to Chicago, following his brother James who had found work at one of the city's newspapers. Thomas O'Shaughnessy, too, was employed in journalism, working as an illustrator for the *Chicago Daily News.*

To continue his study of fine arts, O'Shaughnessy enrolled at the School of the Art Institute (1894–1900). There he studied with Louis Millet, a renowned stained glass and stencil artist who collaborated with architect Louis Sullivan on the decoration of many prominent buildings.

In 1900, at the prompting of Millet, O'Shaughnessy traveled to Europe. His visits to Paris and Dublin were especially important to his artistic and cultural sensibilities. O'Shaughnessy enrolled at the Willets School in Dublin, although his studies went beyond that formal academic setting. His research focused on history as well as art, and he spent hours in monasteries and libraries poring over ancient texts with their illuminated pages. It was probably during this period that O'Shaughnessy met the famous Czech graphic artist Alphonse Mucha, whose work influenced the younger artist.

By 1902 O'Shaughnessy had completed his education and was poised to make his mark in his adopted city. Ironically, the reputation he first built was in civic affairs and not in the religious art that today forms the nucleus of his fame. If O'Shaughnessy's name was known, it might have been for the two dozen drawings he exhibited in a group show with other artists, including the prominent *Chicago Tribune* cartoonist, John T. McCutcheon. Many Chicagoans would have remembered his illustration of the

1903 Iroquois Theater fire for the *Chicago Daily News*, an image so powerful it was printed by competing dailies. Still others would have been familiar with the ornate certificate O'Shaughnessy designed for the Irish Fellowship Club's 1910 guest of honor—President William Howard Taft.[2]

O'Shaughnessy received the widest civic recognition at the time for his efforts to make Christopher Columbus's discovery of America a holiday.[3] His love of history and the effect that the Columbian Exposition had on him probably were the sources of O'Shaughnessy's ardor on behalf of Columbus. It was the year after the fair when organizers announced that the replica ships of Columbus's voyage would be destroyed. O'Shaughnessy vehemently protested, but went one step further than other outraged citizens: he proposed to refurbish them.

O'Shaughnessy was the prime mover in two large historical pageants that reenacted Columbus's discovery of America—complete with the reproductions of the *Nina,* the *Pinta,* and the *Santa Maria*—held in Jackson Park in 1910 and Grant Park the following year. Reports of a quarter million people attending the 1911 spectacle underscore the enthusiasm for O'Shaughnessy's efforts. The popularity of the pageant prompted the *Tribune* to pressure Mayor Carter Harrison for a legal holiday to commemorate Columbus. Consequently, on October 12, 1911, Chicago became the first major city in the United States to officially celebrate Columbus Day. The mayor's proclamation thanked Thomas A. O'Shaughnessy, "the Chicago artist, for his unselfish public service

✛ ✛ ✛

Artist Thomas A. O'Shaughnessy transformed Chicago's oldest church into a masterpiece of Celtic Revival art between 1912 and 1922. (Courtesy, Joseph J. O'Shaughnessy)

Solemn High Mass, Saint Patrick's Day, 1941. O'Shaughnessy's design extended to every facet of the church decor, from windows to stencils to light fixtures. (Courtesy, Chicago Historical Society, ICHi–26674)

in conceiving, planning, and carrying out with such distinguished success this first worthy celebration of the anniversary of Columbus landing in the New World."[4]

Most of O'Shaughnessy's zeal, however, was reserved for things Irish. He took it upon himself to educate the general public about Irish art and decoration, history, and culture. Whether making floats for parades to disseminate information about Ireland, or designing the costumes for a celebration of Irish culture at Orchestra Hall, O'Shaughnessy always stood at the ready to be chief promoter of Ireland at civic gatherings and events. At his disposal in this crusade were his considerable artistic talents and great command of Irish art and religious history.[5]

In 1911 the Reverend William McNamee became pastor of Saint Patrick's, inheriting a parish that had changed dramatically since its founding nearly sixty-five years earlier. Saint Patrick's was in a declining neighborhood, attendance at masses was dwindling, and the church itself had grown somewhat worse for wear.

If McNamee perused the newspapers of the time, he would have read of the exploits of the indefatigable O'Shaughnessy. Though no historical record exists of the exact nature of their first meeting, by 1912 McNamee and O'Shaughnessy were partners. McNamee sought to revitalize a parish, O'Shaughnessy to use his talents to promote Irish art and culture. These two men joined forces on one project: the rebirth of Saint Patrick's Church.

Saint Patrick's role at the center of Chicago's Irish-Catholic community was established with the completion of its substantial edifice in 1856. The church was comparable in size to those of the First Baptist, First Congregational, First Methodist, and other prominent congregations, located farther east along Washington Street. Construction began in 1852 to replace the frame church built in 1846 at Randolph and Desplaines Streets. Although the cornerstone

was laid in 1853, an epidemic delayed construction. The walls were only about eight feet high when the pastor, Reverend Patrick J. McLaughlin died, from cholera, in 1854. Reverend Denis Dunne succeeded McLaughlin and, by summer 1856, the church (with the exception of its distinctive spires) was completed enough for services. It was dedicated on Christmas day.

With its Milwaukee cream-colored brick and octagonal towers, Saint Patrick's was an imposing structure amidst the smaller dwellings of the Near West Side. Moreover, its Romanesque revival style of design distinguished it from other classical- or Gothic-inspired ecclesiastical architecture in Chicago. The rebirth of the style—which was based on medieval German designs—is widely credited to architect Richard Upjohn's Church of the Pilgrim in Brooklyn (1844–46), but James Renwick's design of the Smithsonian Institution (1848–49) is the most prominent example.

The architects of Saint Patrick's, Asher Carter (1805–77) and Augustus Bauer (1827–94), were well established in Chicago and familiar with the Romanesque style. Carter had worked for Renwick in New York before being sent to Chicago to supervise construction of Renwick's Second Presbyterian Church (1849), then located at Wabash and Washington Streets and said to have been "the first public building of any pretension in the city." The German-born Bauer had emigrated after the failure of that country's 1848–49 democratic revolution. Carter and Bauer formed their partnership in 1855. They had a thriving practice; in one year they were credited with designs for thirty-two houses, one church, thirteen commercial structures, and eight out-of-town projects.[6]

With the *au courant* style of Saint Patrick's, the parish may well have meant to demonstrate the new-found stature of Catholics in Chicago. Other attributes of the style would also have appealed to the fledgling parish. An architect at the time described the style as having "an eminent degree of the qualities now so important. These appear to be first, economy; secondly, the rapidity of execution; thirdly, strict simplicity combined with high capability of ornament; fourthly, durability; fifthly, beauty."[7] The broad, unadorned wall surfaces of Saint Patrick's, detailed with simple brick corbels at the top, are hallmarks of the style. So, too, was the high-peaked central gable that graced the facade (it was removed sometime after 1920, but rebuilt in 1993).

Saint Patrick's was more restrained than the Gothic-inspired architecture of other local denominations. In planning the church during a period of intolerance toward Catholics, the parish may also have had in mind the observations of a contemporary critic on the Romanesque revival style who remarked, "its entire expression is less ostentatious, and if political character may be ascribed to Architecture, more republican."[8] The style reflected a stately, but tastefully restrained, demeanor.

Although completed in 1856, any kind of elaborate treatment of the interior appears to have been postponed until the early 1870s. The alterations of the interior are described in one account:

> the cold and cheerless interior of the church was enlivened by a new set of stations and frescoed in a beautiful manner, the sanctuaries were fitted up with elaborately carved altars, the pews upholstered, a gallery built for both the people and the choir, and the latter supplied with an organ of large dimensions and power in keeping with the size of the church— all at an additional cost of about $25,000.[9]

In addition to the altars, the work presumably included the ornately carved, black walnut altar railing, as well as the pulpit and the plaster canopy over it. This woodwork, including statues, has been attributed to the Buscher family. Anthony Buscher and his nephew, Sebastian, sculpted many of the wood features still intact today at Holy Family Church.[10]

In 1885, perhaps in an effort to reassert its primacy among Catholic parishes, Saint Patrick's undertook the completion of its steeples. The noted architectural firm of Willett and Pashley, whose other commitments included the reconstruction of Holy Name Cathedral and the archbishop's new mansion on North State Parkway, oversaw the work. Through the years, the Gothic and Byzantine spires (symbolizing the Roman and Eastern churches) have given Saint Patrick's its distinctive silhouette.

The landscape overlooked by the towers changed dramatically over the next two decades. Frame residences gave way to the larger brick buildings used for light industry and warehousing. By the time Reverend William J. McNamee was appointed as pastor in 1911, the church had become a distant memory to Chicago's Irish Catholics, and its congregation had diminished severely.

Imprisoned Light

If the Romanesque architecture of Saint Patrick's gave aesthetic credentials to Chicago Irish-Catholics, it was Thomas O'Shaughnessy who revived the glory of Irish artistry with his Celtic-inspired decoration. From the outset, he and Father McNamee intended nothing short of the full-scale revival of the church.

The first step toward their goal was the installation of the bronze Gaelic-design cross on the exterior, at the corner, in 1912. Accounts of its dedication underscored the enthusiasm for McNamee's plan:

> With the reopening of St. Patrick's Church, for years a deserted parish, Chicago now has the

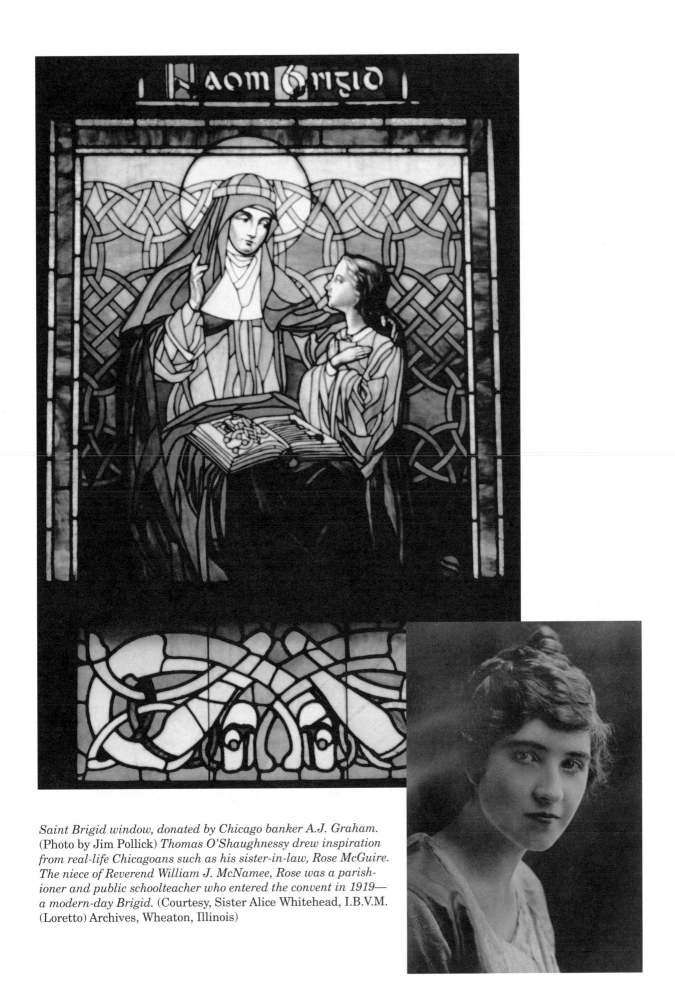

*Saint Brigid window, donated by Chicago banker A.J. Graham.
(Photo by Jim Pollick)* Thomas O'Shaughnessy drew inspiration
from real-life Chicagoans such as his sister-in-law, Rose McGuire.
The niece of Reverend William J. McNamee, Rose was a parish-
ioner and public schoolteacher who entered the convent in 1919—
a modern-day Brigid. (Courtesy, Sister Alice Whitehead, I.B.V.M.
(Loretto) Archives, Wheaton, Illinois)

Thomas A. O'Shaughnessy dedicated the great Faith window on the east wall of Old Saint Patrick's Church to the memory of Terence MacSwiney, the Lord Mayor of Cork, who died after a 74-day hunger strike in London's Brixton prison in 1920. A martyr for Irish independence, MacSwiney predicted that "it is not they who can inflict the most, but they who can endure the most, who will conquer." (Courtesy, The New World)

only real American example of an all-Celtic church and the edifice is looked upon with hopeful ambition by its conservors as the nucleus of a Celtic revival.

Probably the most interesting single piece entering into the embellishment of the church is the great bronze cross that adorns the outer wall, the tracings of which were taken from the widely known chalice of Ardagh by Thomas A. O'Shaughnessy. . . .

For more than forty years, St. Patrick's parish was one of the largest and most prosperous in Chicago. But in recent years, as the business district expanded, the church was robbed of its congregation until Father W. J. McNamee came from Joliet to take charge of the church. Thousands of Chicagoans attended the masses at the church in the morning and viewed with wonder the remodeled edifice.[11]

Although this description implies that the redecoration was complete, the work, in fact, evolved over the next ten years. In 1915 O'Shaughnessy oversaw the installation of the glass mosaic shrine of Saint Patrick. But the major focus was the creation of new windows.[12]

It is not known when O'Shaughnessy began to work on glass-making on a full-time basis. Some accounts state that he made his first art glass windows when he was fifteen, aided by his grandfather, James Mulholland. Although his first major installation was the memorial windows for the Elks Temple in New Orleans (circa 1910), Saint Patrick's windows represented O'Shaughnessy's best known work in Chicago. One of the fullest descriptions of the innovative quality of glass appeared in the *Chicago Citizen,* the city's weekly Irish-American newspaper:

The process by which the glass for these windows has been made is a new one. The direct light of the sun, even at mid-day, fails to weaken the decorative quality of the windows, while in half light of early morning and the late evening, the windows are unusually luminous. . . . They are not only interesting during the day when the light is admitted through them, but at night when the church is lighted from within, the windows lose none of their decorative value and harmonize perfectly with the pearl-like tones in which the church interior is decorated.[13]

O'Shaughnessy's spirit illuminates Saint Patrick's. Opening the doors of the church reveals a room bathed in luminescence. Before observing the details of the windows the viewer is aware of the sanctuary's radiant glow—of light that is intensified, rather than absorbed, as with most stained glass. In comparison with traditional ecclesiastical windows, which are dark and rich in tone, O'Shaughnessy's glass casts brilliant pastel hues in blues, rose, cream, greens, and oranges.

The evocative qualities of Saint Patrick's windows rely as much on the quality of the glass as they do on the actual imagery. O'Shaughnessy claimed that the manufacturing process was based on the ancient method for "pot glass," which produced glass with an opal-like translucence. The first use of this colored glass was for vessels, made around 7,000 B.C. Ancient glass was opaque; colored opalescent glass was created by adding metal oxides to the molten glass, which was cooked in clay pots. Various oxides produced a range of luminous colors. The fusion of color in the glass and the resulting jewel-like luster makes it appear as if the color is literally imprisoned in light.

Opalescent glass was introduced into American glass-making by John LaFarge and Louis Comfort Tiffany in the 1870s. The striking mosaic-like window compositions in deep translucent colors gave a new expressive quality to glass. "By itself," according to decorative arts expert Sharon Darling, "opalescent glass was somewhat porcelain-like in appearance, but, against the light, and at certain angles, it had much of the fire and changing hue of opal."[14] O'Shaughnessy may have seen Tiffany's windows when they were exhibited in Chicago at the 1893 World's Columbian Exposition.[15] Another important artist in opalescent glass was O'Shaughnessy's teacher, Louis Millet. Windows by Millet, and his partner George Louis Healy, were prominent in Chicago, probably most notably in the Auditorium Building.

When O'Shaughnessy began his work on Saint Patrick's he made aesthetic commitments that set this work apart from other ecclesiastical glass. In 1912 opalescent glass had fallen into disfavor as architectural tastes began to follow the Gothic revival and traditional stained glass. O'Shaughnessy realized, however, that compared with traditional, nineteenth-century stained glass windows, the color quality of opalescent glass was more pure and radiant. Moreover, the fact that color was in the glass itself, rather than painted on it, gave his windows the character of mosaics, such that their designs are as brilliant at night as they are during the day. What distinguishes O'Shaughnessy's windows further is their serene pastel coloring. He uses a color palette similar to other contemporaries, but his colors are much more muted. Instead of the deep, assertive shades traditionally employed, O'Shaughnessy chose creamy tones that give the windows a more intimate feeling and create a serene cast within the church itself.

O'Shaughnessy oversaw various facets of the production of his windows, from their design and assembly to the manufacture of the glass. The glass itself was fabricated in Kokomo, Indiana, using sand from Ottawa, Illinois. O'Shaughnessy extolled the qualities of Illinois' finest white sand for glass-making, finding it every bit as comparable to sand imported from Europe.

Working like a painter with a palette of colors, O'Shaughnessy maintained a stockpile of glass in some two thousand tints, in a spectrum of resilient pastels: sapphire blue, deep orange, purple, emerald green, pale yellow. However, unlike the artist painting on canvas, glass is only part of window making; the joining of the pieces is every bit as vital. Again, O'Shaughnessy broke ranks with most of his contemporaries, who used lead for cames (the I-shaped metal channels joining glass). Instead of lead or zinc, he used an alloy of copper and tin, "making it possible to employ in places lines of joining as slender as a pen stroke which are more enduring than the broad lead lines of the mediaeval [sic] school of window making." The result was framing that, in the words of one stained-glass expert:

> is a piece of art in itself . . . framing [which] does not interfere with but becomes a part of and reinforces his design. Instead of using glass as a transparent painter's canvas he treated glass more like a water color artist. While there are maybe 100 different colors in each window, there are at least two to four different mixes of that color.[16]

Celtic Inspiration

The technical virtuosity of O'Shaughnessy's work notwithstanding, the windows of Saint Patrick's are most widely appreciated for their Celtic artistry. From the founding of Catholicism in Ireland in the third century, and the particular historic organization of its church around individual religious communities, the Irish have had a strong devotion to their native saints. The cultural theme for Saint Patrick's windows could not have been any more obvious.

The *Book of Kells*, the ninth-century illuminated manuscript, was the inspiration for O'Shaughnessy's work. He viewed this world-famous treasure at Trinity College in Dublin in 1900, sketching its pages for weeks. O'Shaughnessy was likely one of the last to enjoy such

*In 1996 workers uncovered and recreated the complex and rhythmic patterns of
O'Shaughnessy's stencils, inspired by the ninth century* Book of Kells. (Photo by Erin Jaeb.
Courtesy, Old Saint Patrick's Church)

extensive access. One can imagine him using all his reputed Irish pluck to obtain permission. His gumption paid off, as the folio proved to be the most significant influence for his artistic vocabulary. There are few artworks that define a culture as well as this medieval masterpiece, for it illustrates not only Ireland's embrace of Christian liturgy but also its even more ancient devotion to complex symbolism. The folio is central to Irish art and is universally praised for its artistry. Marilyn Stokstad argues that the exuberance and exaggeration of the *Book of Kells*

> demonstrate the quality of the Irish imagination—flowing freely but within the clear bounds of intellectual control—which could create a fantastically real dream world as precise and as brilliant in line and color as gold filigree or millefiore enamel, and as plausible as any visual images of the sensate world.[17]

The spirals and whorls that have come to be associated with Irish art are present in the volume, but so too are images of animals—serpents with human or bird heads, an otter catching a fish, a rat gnawing on a wafer—all of these rendered as ethereal interlaced borders around the major figures of Christ, the angels, the apostles, or other Christian personages. The pages are boldly colored in an array of yellows, blues, greens, reds, and browns. In its merging of the rich pre-Christian era with the newfound liturgy, the manuscript is regarded as the supreme achievement of Celtic art.

Saint Patrick's windows carry on this Irish religious tradition, telling stories of Irish saints, as well as history and politics, using all of the rich color, complex format, and ecclesiastical imagery of the *Book of Kells*. The twelve sanctuary windows are a reliquary of Irish Christianity, depicting various Irish saints:

Saint Patrick arriving at Tara; Saint Columba, the sixth-century poet who was exiled and, as a missionary, established an important center of learning in northern Italy; and Saint Attracta, the founder of Irish convents, accepting the veil from Saint Patrick. Others depicted are Saint Brigid, Saint Finbar, Saint Colman, Saint Columbanus, Saint Senan, Saint Brendan, and Saints Carthage and Comgall. Allegorical representations of the evangelists Matthew, Mark, Luke, and John—winged images of a human, lion, eagle, and oxen—make up the design of the glass canopy over the altar, completed in 1913.[18]

On May Day 1916 O'Shaughnessy married Brigid McGuire, managing editor of the *Chicago Citizen* newspaper and Father McNamee's niece. O'Shaughnessy's close association with the church made his work here that much more special, so personal touches are not surprising. The female model, for example, for the window depicting Saint Brigid—the educator and arts patron whose prayers, according to legend, caused angels to supervise the designs of the *Book of Kells*—was O'Shaughnessy's sister-in-law. As it turned out, the choice was fitting. Rose McGuire was a Chicago public school teacher who entered the Ladies of Loretto in 1919 and became an administrator and one of its most respected educators.[19] Noteworthy as well is the Saint Brendan window, which bears a distinct resemblance to O'Shaughnessy himself.

Although Saint Patrick's windows are principally ecclesiastical in their themes, they also have social and historical overtones. Many of the scenes depict secular activities. Saint Brendan, who, in the fifth century, claimed to have crossed the Atlantic Ocean bringing Christianity to the Western hemisphere, is shown being greeted by Native Americans. Others are depicted as artists, teachers, and soldiers. The window of Brian Boru carries political associations, as it was not until his kingship in the eleventh century that Irish clans achieved a semblance of political unity.

O'Shaughnessy's political sympathies are exhibited in the MacSwiney Window, a work of complex liturgical symbolism as well as strong overtones of Irish nationalism, executed at an important point in Ireland's campaign for independence. The window was dedicated "to the glory of God and to the honor of Terence Mac-Swiney and of those men and women dead and living who have served and who have suffered for the freedom of Ireland" in November 1920, a month after the death of MacSwiney, Lord Mayor of Cork. His seventy-four day hunger strike in London's Brixton prison focused international attention on the Irish war for independence.[20]

The window is huge in scale, twenty-five-feet tall, and it dominates the east wall. Colored primarily in the green, white, and orange of the Irish Republic, it is a rich portrait of what a contemporary account describes as the "story of Ireland, from the glorious, happy past to the tragic, glorious present."[21] The circular portion at the top represents the Trinity, with the eye of God at the center. Below it is a Celtic cross divided into nine panels. The largest panel, at the axis of the cross, shows a radiant Virgin Mary amidst a halo of stars. The remaining sections depict Irish saints in their historical roles as philosophers, geographers, teachers, and missionaries. Centered in the semicircle at the base is the soul of Terence MacSwiney entering heaven, between the red flames of trial and persecution. At the sides of the window, from top to bottom, are angels of Faith (in white), Hope (green), and Charity (orange).

The flowing design and the radiance of the MacSwiney Window demonstrate O'Shaughnessy's mastery of stained-glass technique. Its fluidity and rich symbolism and color make the window a powerful work of iconography, compa-rable to the best work in the stained glass medium. The window was O'Shaughnessy's last for the church, a poignant climax to his long association with Saint Patrick's.

Throughout the MacSwiney and other windows, the major figures are set off by a colorful embroidery of Celtic knotwork, serpentine dragons, and other symbols used in the *Kells* folio. It is easy to appreciate O'Shaughnessy's fascination with Celtic ornament. By the time he traveled to Dublin, O'Shaughnessy was more than likely familiar with the Celtic Revival campaign in Ireland. It was a multidisciplinary arts movement asserting national identity, based on Ireland's rich cultural heritage. In the visual arts, ancient ornaments offered an exciting decorative vocabulary. The variety of historic patterns—spirals, intertwined ribbon work, abstract animal ornament, scrolls, plaitwork, and knots—was endless. In addition to their strong cultural meanings, the motifs were striking for their lissome lines, which were similar to the then-popular art nouveau style.

But the windows were only the first step in the church's rejuvenation. Although overlooked by later generations, "frescoes" were an important aspect of religious architecture. Along with stained glass, hand-carved statues and the complex woodwork of altars, wall decoration was part of the profuse tapestry of church design at the beginning of the twentieth century. As they have from the onset of Christianity, the fine arts enhanced the religious experience, giving church-goers an atmosphere conducive to contemplation.

O'Shaughnessy's multicolored stencils on the church's walls and ceilings do not draw from overt religious themes, but they have all of the mystic qualities of traditional Irish symbolism.[22] The stencil pattern at the window level is comprised of winding ribbons in white, blue, orange, and yellow, terminating in an abstract dragon and bird's beak. At the base of the pilasters on the side walls is a pattern of intertwined, geometric fret work. Braided crosses, recalling the patterns of medieval Irish crosses, are the central design in the ceiling coffers at the sides of the church.

What is striking about O'Shaughnessy's scheme, as seen in an old photograph, is that it did not compete with the historic character of the architecture and woodwork but enhanced the traditional fabric of the church. The church walls were painted a shade of pinkish-orange. In contrast to the lighter color of the walls, the pilasters were painted a darker gray, reinforcing their structural role. The stencil bands at the ceiling cove and near the tops of the windows articulated the architecture, breaking up the expanses of wall. They ran around the church to the front, framing the side altars and culminating in the broad arch over the altar.

The stencil work was completed in 1922 (although recent investigation has revealed that portions of the stenciling in the balcony were never finished), in time for the celebration of the parish's seventy-fifth anniversary Mass on March 17. Satisfied with his work, O'Shaughnessy commented on its uniqueness: "Only the Japanese and the Celts tried to express in lines instead of in mass."[23] The abstract and lineal character of Celtic design was unusual for church art, which typically favored more figurative work or designs based on traditional ecclesiastical symbols. Visually, the fluid and overlapping stencil patterns convey an unusual sense of depth and movement, in contrast to traditional religious motifs.

O'Shaughnessy's stylistic treatment of the glass and stencil designs was informed by progressive artistic movements. One influence for his work at Saint Patrick's was Louis Sullivan's stencil design and color schemes. Both O'Shaughnessy and Sullivan employed intricate

interlace patterns, reminiscent of the Celtic ornament in Owen Jones's *The Grammar of Ornament*, an important decorative arts reference in the late nineteenth century. Some of Sullivan's work, particularly that in selected stencil designs at the Auditorium Theater and for the Transportation Building at the World's Columbian Exposition, has even been interpreted as Celtic in inspiration.[24] The original color scheme for Saint Patrick's is similar to that of the Old Chicago Stock Exchange Trading Room (now preserved at the Art Institute of Chicago). The similarities are not unusual, as O'Shaughnessy's former teacher, Louis Millet, consulted with Sullivan on the Stock Exchange project.

The art nouveau style was another important influence. The flat, two-dimensional character of the stained-glass figures at Saint Patrick's is consistent with the nouveau approach. O'Shaughnessy was a friend of one of the masters of the movement, Alphonse Mucha, whose posters of Sarah Bernhardt were some of the most celebrated examples of the art nouveau. Mucha designed posters as narrow panels, with full-length figures. The compositions were simplified into a few basic forms but employed complicated and intricate patterns to ornament the surface. In the same way, O'Shaughnessy focused his compositions on one or two basic figures and ornamented the remainder of the window with a profusion of color and interlace.

O'Shaughnessy's work at Saint Patrick's, in its proficient use of historic Irish imagery and revival of Irish stained-glass making, is an important, if heretofore overlooked, contribution to the Celtic Revival. The best known works in Ireland are art glass windows by Harry Clarke, Wilhemina Geddes, An Tùr Gloine (the Tower of Glass); embroidery by the Dun Emer Guild; and the decorative painting of Sister Concepta Lynch in the Dominican Convent at Dunlaoghaire. Because most Celtic

By 1950 O'Shaughnessy's distinctive wall designs had been replaced, but his translucent stained glass windows still bathed Old Saint Patrick's with brilliant light. (Courtesy, Old Saint Patrick's Church)

Revival was in the form of jewelry or small art objects, the scope of O'Shaughnessy's designs at Saint Patrick's make the church a significant contribution to the movement.

It would be easy to characterize O'Shaughnessy's work as that of a fervent nationalist, yet he was anything but a one-dimensional artist. He was widely respected for his glass-making skills and artistry. Some of his prominent window installations include Saint Procopious Abbey, Lisle (1916); Saint Luke's Church, River Forest (1919); Saint Catherine's Church, Spring Lake, New Jersey (1922); Cathedral of the Immaculate Conception, Springfield, Illinois (1928–29); and Saint Stephen's Episcopal Church, Chicago (1933). In 1925 he was the spokesman for the American delegation at the International Exposition of Modern and Industrial Art in Paris. For the International Eucharistic Congress, held in Chicago in 1926, O'Shaughnessy designed the poster. In 1930 he was made an officer in the French Academy of Art. By 1933 his artistic experiences in Chicago had come full circle with his extensive involvement in the Century of Progress exposition. He produced the art glass windows for the Illinois Host House and the window he made for the Hall of Religion was accorded the place of honor. But most fitting was his role as artistic director for the Irish Village Exhibit. Its layout of half-timbered, thatched-roof huts, detailed with Celtic ornament, recalled the village he had seen forty years before in Jackson Park.

At the time when other churches were using traditional ecclesiastical references and symbols, O'Shaughnessy's work offered an alternative vision. His decoration evoked the heritage and experience that had a special meaning to its parishioners, but that transcended cultural boundaries. Through color and design, the decoration communicated the mysticism of the medieval church.

O'Shaughnessy's theology is as sound today as it was at the beginning of the century. Saint Patrick's still provides a theology steeped not only in Christian and cultural symbols but in luminescence and color. Thomas O'Shaughnessy's work at Saint Patrick's is a testimony to the spiritually evocative power of light and design. The renowned twentieth-century architect Louis Kahn once said that the sun never knew how wonderful it was until it shone on the wall of a building. Kahn probably never saw Saint Patrick's, but if he had he would have appreciated the ethereal quality of its radiant interior.

The first time I was ever in Saint Patrick's Church was for a memorial mass in 1975. My mother and I attended a mass for deceased members of the International Brotherhood of Electrical Workers. My father, Edward Ignatius Barton, an IBEW member, died in 1974 and so, naturally, we were invited.

These days, I focus on the stenciling and other details of the church. But back in 1975, all I saw was light. Growing up Catholic in a Catholic neighborhood and going to Catholic schools, I was used to dark, mysterious places. Niches and statues. Shadows. Saint Patrick's was awash in light, and it was all from the windows and through the colored glass—entirely the work of the sun. If the International Brotherhood noted the lack of electric lighting fixtures, they didn't mention it.

Several years later, I would end up working at the City of Chicago's Landmarks Commission and learn to look at buildings in an intellectual way. But in 1975, sitting in a pew next to my mother and memorializing the brotherhood, my take was all emotional.

I was thankful for Saint Patrick's Church then in a way I will never be again. Was I thinking about my father that day? There wasn't a moment I wasn't thinking about him being gone. But the church—in a sense—somehow, strangely, didn't rub it in. Instead of sitting in a dark and melancholy sanctuary, I was in a light and airy space that exuded hope.

Of course, I didn't know O'Shaughnessy's name at the time and wouldn't until much later. But now I think he built into his designs for Saint Patrick's prescriptions that work for all, not just us Irish.

To wit: Look beyond complexity to simplicity. If you study the stencils at Saint Pat's, you will see what I mean. Also, keep your head up. (I like to imagine that O'Shaughnessy, too, spent hours in a schoolroom gazing out the windows.)

And last, but not least, if churches must be the repository of so much sadness, if we must go there to try to remember the face of a loved one, then they should not be the deepest, darkest part of the woods, but an open clearing where the light will penetrate.

Saint Patrick's Daughter

Amelia Dunne Hookway and Chicago's Public Schools

Janet Nolan

In October 1908 Mark Twain wrote to Chicago school principal Amelia Dunne Hookway praising her for the Howland School's production of his play, *The Prince and the Pauper*. America's most famous writer minced no words about the significance of what Hookway had accomplished. Twain assured "Dear Mrs. Hookway" that her work with Chicago school students "supports & reaffirms what I have so often & so strenuously said in public: that a children's theater is easily the most valuable adjunct that any educational institution for the young can have, & that no otherwise good school is complete without it." The reason was simple: "its lessons are not taught wearily by book & by dreary [homily], but by visible and enthusing <u>action</u> . . . " Children's theater, he continued, "is the only teacher of morals & conduct & high ideals that never bores the pupil, but always leaves him sorry when the lesson is over." Indeed, Twain insisted, children's theater is "one of the very, <u>very</u> great inventions of the twentieth century."

As president of the New York Children's Theater, Twain was also pleased to learn that the Howland schoolchildren created all "the construction work, stage-decorations, etc. That is our way, too." Moreover, he agreed wholeheartedly with Hookway's belief that plays "made a year out of the past live for the children" as no

history book ever could. Not only is drama the best history teacher, Twain contended, the children also carry the lesson from school to home "& infect the family with it" when they reenact their parts. "And the family are glad & proud . . . glad to learn, glad to be lifted to planes high above their dreary workaday lives."[1]

Hookway answered Twain in May 1909, prefacing her reply with an explanation of why it had taken so long to send the promised pictures from *The Prince and the Pauper*. "Two days after he had finished one set of photographs for our school gallery, our photographer—who is of the wagon-on-prairie variety—disappeared." Only when he "literally pitched his tent in our vicinity . . . a fortnight ago," did she gain possession of the pictures. "[N]early every boy in the Howland [School] made a personal trip to my office to inform me" that the itinerant photographer had returned to their Lawndale neighborhood, "for all had known of my great desire to get the pictures to you."

Amelia Dunne Hookway's correspondence with America's most famous writer did not remain a private affair. She shared Twain's letter with the drama critic of the *Chicago Record-Herald,* who featured it in his Sunday review "Dramatics at Howland School" on May 23, 1909. But Amelia believed that Twain's conviction about the value of children's theater deserved an even wider audience than a Chicago newspaper could offer. "I only wish [your letter] could be printed in every 'Graded Course' all over the United States," she told Twain. "It must do something for dramatics in the schools. I am a very proud and happy woman because you thus wrote to me," Hookway concluded, adding that *The Prince and the Pauper* "will stay with us for many years."[2]

Twain's abiding admiration for Hookway is evident in yet another letter to her. "If I were going to begin life over again," the seventy-three-year-old writer confided, "I would have a children's theater and watch it, and work for it, and see it grow and blossom and bear its rich moral and intellectual fruitage; and I should get more pleasure and a saner and healthier profit out of my vocation than I should ever be able to get out of any other . . . Yes, you are easily the most fortunate of women, I think."[3] The world famous American man of letters had decided that the importance of the work of women like Amelia Dunne Hookway of Chicago was indispensable to the health of the nation.

Others supported Twain's opinion. In a lengthy feature story in May 1909, drama critic James O'Donnell Bennett singled out the Howland School at Sixteenth and Spaulding Avenue. "Perhaps no other school in the country, and certainly no other in Chicago, has so successfully developed the work of guiding and training the dramatic instinct that is the heritage of every normal child as has [the] Howland School. . . . All these plays," he reminded his *Chicago Record-Herald* readers, "were composed by Mrs. Hookway, principal of the school (and a sister of Peter Dunne we may add), and were prepared for the stage by her and the teachers who work with her, among them Miss Crowley and Miss McGrath." Echoing Twain, Bennett concluded that "in all this, Mrs. Hookway and her associates are doing a work that is as important as any of the work that is done in the classrooms of Howland School."[4]

A Daughter of Saint Patrick's

The recipient of such praise, Amelia Dunne Hookway, the eldest sister of "Mr. Dooley" creator Peter Finley Dunne, was born on April 24, 1858, just across West Adams Street from Saint Patrick's, the oldest church in Chicago and the center of a then-thriving Irish-American community. She was the first of seven children born to Irish immigrant parents who had met and married in Chicago.

Amelia was also the first of the large Dunne brood to enter Saint Patrick's parish grade school. The girls' school, dating from 1852, was opened by Irish-born Sisters of Mercy, who were succeeded by the Sisters of Loretto eleven years later. After the Great Chicago Fire, which miraculously spared the parish, the Daughters of Charity of Saint Vincent de Paul took charge of the school, increasing enrollments from 250 to 400 between 1871 and 1874. Successful female graduates of the parochial grade school could then enter the prestigious four year Saint Patrick's Girls' High School, which the Daughters conducted around the corner from the church on West Adams Street. Nearby on Desplaines Street, the Christian Brothers operated Saint Patrick's Academy for Boys.

In its early years, the girls' high school prepared students like Amelia for teaching careers by offering courses in English, Latin, mathematics, science, and social studies. After the turn of the century, the high school was closed and replaced by a two-year commercial course offering secretarial and accounting classes. The high school was reopened in 1925, and accredited in 1930 by the Chicago Normal School.[5] Once again, Saint Patrick's Girls' High School was providing teacher training to young women from Chicago and its suburbs. Throughout its

✛ ✛ ✛

Howland School players, The Prince and the Pauper, *1908.* (Courtesy, Len Hilts)

history, the school's curriculum emphasized preparation for jobs in the educational and business institutions of the city rather than in the home.

The girls' high school was something of an oasis in the urban neighborhood surrounding Saint Patrick's. Situated in a tree-filled garden, the school provided an intellectual haven for daughters of the local Irish Catholic lower middle class. Its curriculum was rigorous, and only the relatively well-off could afford the fees associated with advanced education. Since the Dunnes were fairly prosperous by Irish-American standards of the day, however, Amelia enrolled in the high school. The education she received at Saint Patrick's allowed her to become a self-supporting professional after graduation.

The gratitude of Saint Patrick's students was clear even a half a century after they had left the school. In the 1950 Saint Patrick's alumnae notes, "Leaves from Our Alma Mater," for example, the retired schoolteacher Katie Callaghan Dillon acknowledged her debt. "[I] have reason to be proud of the training I received as a student at Saint Patrick High School . . . ," she recalled. "[W]ith the foundation I received here, I later taught shorthand and typewriting in the Chicago public schools."[6] The "Leaves" also recognized other early graduates of the school such as Annie Byrne who became a music teacher in the Chicago public schools and Bessie Powell Hayes who taught school in the nearby suburb of Oak Park. The booklet also reminded its readers of the career of Amelia Dunne Hookway, the principal of the Howland School.

The Dunnes' encouragement of scholastic achievement in their daughter was typical of Irish-American families in the late nineteenth and early twentieth centuries. Mothers, as much as fathers, were the engineers of an often female-centered intellectual ambition. Ellen Finley Dunne was no exception. She encouraged her children to read Irish and English literature, filling her household with the works of Dickens and Thackeray as well as the children's magazines *Youth's Companion* and *St. Nicholas.* Of all the Dunne children,

Amelia's alma mater. (Courtesy, Daughters of Charity Archives, Mater Dei Provincialate, Evansville, Indiana)

✦ ✦ ✦

Amelia Dunne.
(Courtesy, Len Hilts)

Amelia and Peter especially enjoyed their mother's library, even creating lifelong nicknames for each other derived from a favorite story they had read there as children.[7]

Amelia's long association with the Chicago public schools began in June 1880 when she was elected an assistant teacher in the Scammon School where her brother Peter had been enrolled. During the late 1870s Amelia struck up a friendship with Ella Flagg Young, former principal of the Scammon School and later Chicago's first female superintendent. With Young's support, Amelia convinced her father to send the precocious Peter Finley to high school, a career path taken by none of the other brothers in the family, and for good reason. In the 1880s Chicago's high schools offered a rigorous curriculum focusing on the classics and foreign languages. Called "the crown of our public school system" by then superintendent George

Katherine Dunne Flood, Amelia's schoolteacher sister. (Courtesy, Len Hilts)

Howland, the city's high schools were a "Citizens' College" taking great pride in their "thorough and intelligent instruction."[8] Although Peter proved to be an unmotivated student at West Division High School, without his sister Amelia's influence he might never have enrolled, becoming, instead, a carpenter like his brothers, and leaving Mr. Dooley unborn.[9]

Indeed, although Saint Patrick's, like the public schools, offered a first-rate secondary education for boys, young men in the parish were less willing than their sisters to delay their entrance into the labor market since males without the benefits of advanced education could find well-paid work more easily than females. For instance, as we have seen, Peter alone among his brothers went on to high school, and he enrolled only at the insistence of his sister Amelia. The Dunne sisters, on the other hand, were all high school graduates. In fact, the imbalance in the educational aspirations of young men and women in the parish became so noticeable by 1881 that the Christian Brothers inaugurated a three-year commercial course aimed at preparing males for jobs in the front offices of the city's businesses. Crucial support for this endeavor came primarily from the Society of Patrons, a group that featured prominent Catholic business leaders, including furniture magnate John M. Smyth and meatpacker Michael Cudahy. Later, the public schools would adopt many of the same tactics pioneered by Saint Patrick's Academy to lure young men into high school classes.

Ambitious girls needed no such inducements to tempt them into high school classrooms, however, since many of the better jobs open to women required a four-year high school education.[10] In fact, three of the Dunne sisters—Amelia, Kate, and Mary—became teachers in the Chicago public schools, a pattern that became increasingly common in Irish-American households by the 1890s. Equally significant, the Dunne family's upward mobility was

directly linked to the daughters' occupation. Not long after Kate joined Amelia on the faculty of the Scammon School in 1882, for instance, the entire family moved out of the deteriorating neighborhood around Saint Patrick's to a new home on Laflin Street. They continued to move farther west in the city, following in the wake of Amelia's steady rise from classroom teacher at the Scammon School to head assistant at the Central Park School at Walnut Street and Kedzie Avenue.

After their mother's premature death from tuberculosis in 1884, Amelia became the centerpiece of the family and a mother substitute for her younger siblings, particularly Peter and Charlotte. When their father died in 1889, several of the adult Dunne children continued to live together and pool their resources, like many other Irish-American families in Chicago. No doubt Amelia, Kate, and Mary's salaries as schoolteachers, along with Peter Finley's newspaper earnings, helped pay the rent on their new Warren Boulevard address. Multiple paychecks also made it possible to send their younger sister Charlotte to the prestigious Mount Saint Joseph Academy in Dubuque, Iowa.

As a rising star in the Chicago school system, Amelia was the family's chief breadwinner, especially after she was named principal of the George Howland School in 1896 at an annual salary of $1,700. Another chapter in her life began in 1901 when she married Canadian immigrant William Hookway, and moved into the apartment above his drugstore at Harrison Street and Independence Boulevard. A landmark on the West Side for generations, the Hookway Drugstore building soon became a favorite gathering place for younger generations of Dunnes.

At the time of her death from typhoid and meningitis at the age of fifty-six in November 1914, Amelia Dunne Hookway was lauded not only as the sister of the internationally famous writer now known as Finley Peter Dunne, but also in her own right. In fact, *The New World* remembered her as "one of the city's best known Catholic educators, . . . a recognized literary authority . . . , [and author of] several plays."[11] The *Chicago Tribune* also noted her talents, acknowledging that "some of her Irish dialect is said to be as clever as that which brought fame to her brother's 'Mr. Dooley'."[12] Finley Peter Dunne himself was no less forthcoming about Amelia's impact on his career. He remembered her urging him to "keep it up" when he first began writing, and he insisted that his sister was "responsible for the continuation of the Dooley series," when he once thought of abandoning it.[13]

Nevertheless, despite her key role in shaping not only her brother's but her family's destiny, Amelia has been eclipsed by her brother's fame. Even on the day before her death a newspaper headline proclaimed, "Finley Peter Dunne at Bedside of Sister Mrs. Amelia Hookway . . . [Who] Is Dying." Only on second thought did the article let its readers know that it was Amelia who "encouraged [her] brother to write 'Mr. Dooley' stories . . ."[14] Although her long career as a teacher and principal was formally recognized in 1928 with the opening of the Amelia Dunne Hookway School at Eighty-First and LaSalle Streets, later generations have forgotten the pioneering contributions of this remarkable woman.

Amelia Dunne Hookway's career aptly illustrates both the importance of Irish-American women in the upward mobility of their families and the need to recover their history. Unlike their brothers who mostly remained in the working class in the early years of this century, more and more Irish-American women joined the ranks of the lower middle class, often, like Amelia, as teachers in the public schools of large American cities. In fact, many Irish-American daughters entered white collar work at least a generation before their brothers.

Encouraged by their mothers, the daughters of Irish America became professionals in numbers equalled by no other second generation immigrant group at the turn of the century.[15]

Irish Roots

The high visibility of Irish-American girls such as Amelia in high schools like Saint Patrick's had deep Irish roots. In fact, the atypical patterns of Irish-American women's lives in the late nineteenth and early twentieth centuries resulted from the unusual contours of their mothers' immigration from Ireland. Unlike most other European female immigrants, the majority of the young women leaving Ireland in those years were unmarried and traveling independently of husbands or fathers.[16] Consequently, once they arrived in America, Irish women needed to find paid work immediately in order to survive. As a result, Irish women in the United States had the highest female employment rates of all immigrant groups.[17] Most of these women became domestic servants or took other unskilled, low-paying jobs.

Typically, Irish-born women retired from the American workforce after marriage, but they did not change their expectations about the importance of women's paid work.[18] While they dissuaded their daughters from entering domestic service, they encouraged them to go to school in order to secure better jobs.[19] This encouragement caused Irish Americans in general to achieve some of the highest school attendance levels of any immigrant group by the early twentieth century. In addition, Irish-American girls rivaled and often surpassed their brothers in educational achievement, especially at the higher grade levels.[20]

Economic necessity was not the only reason that mothers in turn-of-the-century Irish America encouraged their daughters to go to school, however. Their own Irish schooldays had also provided a model for female educational success. By the time of their emigration, Irish women had already spent at least a few years in the national schools of Ireland, one of the first free public school systems in the world. The hundreds of thousands of Irish women arriving in America in the late nineteenth and early twentieth centuries were already able to read and write in English, thanks to their Irish educations, and they already had first-hand experience with life in the classroom. In addition, attendance in the national schools had given girls a new female role model: the educated woman teacher. Here, for the first time, girls brought up on earthbound farms in rural Ireland met young women who had achieved their status not by birth or marriage, but by diligence in school, a diligence schoolgirls could imitate. The memory of these female professionals provided a powerful new possibility to generations of rural Irish girls, even if most of them were destined for low wages in American cities.[21]

Mobile Irish Americans; Amelia in flowered hat at right. (Courtesy, Len Hilts)

The impact of this new possibility on the lives of the daughters of Irish immigrant mothers is shown in census statistics that reveal the rapid mobility of second-generation Irish women in America. While slightly more than 70 percent of Irish-born women in the United States in 1900 were domestic servants, for example, only one quarter of second generation Irish-American women in that year had taken service jobs. The participation of women in the professions also paints a striking picture of the impact of education on female generational mobility in Irish America at the turn of the century. In 1900 only 3.3 percent of Irish-born women in the country were professionals, but more than 14 percent of American-born Irish women were counted as professionals by census takers.[22] These startling numbers show the results of high levels of Irish-American female school attendance and the impact of that attendance on Irish-American women's occupational mobility. Much of this mobility stemmed no doubt from the influence of Irish-born mothers encouraging their American-born daughters to go to school.

Amelia Dunne Hookway's life is representative of the lives of many Irish-American female professionals counted by the census takers. These women often began their educational careers in parochial grade schools and Catholic high schools, like Hookway's Saint Patrick's, eventually becoming teachers in public elementary schools. By the turn of this century, they dominated the ranks of urban public school teachers in cities with large Irish-American populations. In 1908, for example, the majority of the graduates of Chicago's Normal School had Irish last names and by 1910, at least one third of all teachers in Chicago's public schools were Catholics.[23] The heavily Irish-American faculty of Hookway's own Howland School was typical of the ethnic composition of teachers in all the city's public elementary schools in the early years of this century.[24]

Classroom, Saint Patrick's High School for Girls, 1931. (Courtesy, Brother Konrad Diebold, F.S.C., Saint Patrick High School)

Backlash

The entrance of so many Irish Americans into public school teaching did not go unnoticed by contemporary critics. In fact, the abundance of Irish-American teachers in the elementary schools of America's largest cities fueled an anti-Catholic and anti-Irish backlash. Under the guise of "good government" reforms, Protestant civic leaders began to devise various methods to stem the tide of Catholic school graduates into the teaching ranks of the public schools. One such critic, University of Chicago professor George S. Counts, summed up the fears of his time and class. Insisting that fully 70 to 80 percent of Chicago's teachers "look to the Vatican for guidance" and that the "teacher supply is being contaminated" because Catholics have "invaded the student body of the Chicago Normal College, the source of practically all new teachers in the elementary schools," Counts traced the origins of this invasion to the "organized efforts of teachers in Catholic high schools."[25]

Although the compulsory reading of passages from the King James Bible and other overtly anti-Catholic curriculum issues in the public schools had been settled by the turn of the century, the perceived divide between Catholic education and Protestant values remained intact. As a result, in cities throughout the United States where large numbers of Catholic school graduates were winning teaching jobs, Protestant-dominated school boards began to search for ways to keep Catholics out of the public school teaching ranks.

After the turn of the century, eligibility for teaching appointments in Chicago became firmly attached to a post-high school training period at the Normal School in the city's Englewood neighborhood. In 1903, for example, the Chicago Board of Education enacted new rules preventing graduates of Catholic high schools from becoming eligible for teaching jobs until they had worked elsewhere for a period of two to four years. Only Normal School graduates could expect immediate employment in the city's public schools. Over the years several unsuccessful attempts were made to impose strict numerical quotas on the the number of Catholic school graduates eligible for admission to Chicago Normal. Despite these roadblocks, however, James Sanders tells us, as early as 1902, two-thirds of the Normal School's entering class came from three Catholic high schools on the South Side of Chicago. By 1908 the overwhelming majority of Normal School graduates were Irish Americans.[26] The move to stem the tide of Irish-American women into public school teaching had failed, just as Counts had feared.

The roots of the cultural struggle between Protestant-dominated school boards and Irish-American teachers over the souls of the public schools dated back to the settlement of Chicago in the 1830s. Here again Saint Patrick's School offers a telling illustration of this conflict. Public education in Chicago was originally an offshoot of Protestant clerical efforts. While such an education was clearly denominational to modern eyes, most contemporaries in the early days of Chicago accepted a Protestant worldview as natural and did not question its hegemony. This acceptance was challenged, however, with the arrival of large numbers of Irish immigrants beginning in the 1840s. Since the new Irish Chicagoans were Catholics for the most part, and since priests and nuns followed closely in their wake, the city's Protestant-dominated public schools came under harsh scrutiny by the Catholic community almost immediately.

The early years of Irish settlement in Chicago also coincided with the virulently anti-Catholic, anti-immigrant (in those days, the terms were largely synonymous) nativist political movements that clouded much of ante-bellum American politics. The mass migration of alien Irish into the city alarmed the local elite, and the public school curriculum was fashioned into a frontline defense against the papist paupers who had descended in their midst. As a result, the public schools required daily readings from the King James Bible, and school texts extolled Protestant virtues as "American," while denigrating Catholic culture as alien and probably seditious. In the face of such hostility, Catholic leaders throughout the city urged parents to withdraw their children from the public schools and enroll them instead in parochial schools.[27] The first Saint Patrick's school, opened in 1850 by an Irish schoolmaster named O'Connell, was a modest affair limited to boys. But change came swiftly. In 1852 the parish opened a school for girls. By the turn of the twentieth century, Chicago's parochial school system had grown into the largest in the United States, and Saint Patrick's and other like-minded schools had educated thousands of the city's growing Catholic population.[28] Not only had such institutions played a crucial role in laying the foundation for Catholic education in Chicago, their success in developing commercial courses later, ironically, was emulated by the public schools.

The entry of so many graduates of Catholic schools into the public schools as teachers beginning in the 1880s and 1890s was a remarkable event in light of the history of public education in Chicago. For the first time Catholics were entering the system in large numbers not as students, but as teachers. Since Protestant cultural values held sway in Chicago's public classrooms (partly as a result of Catholic self-segregation into separate schools), anxieties reemerged that Irish-American teachers would convert the public schools into adjuncts of the flourishing parochial school system. Some feared that the Protestant "American" voice in education would be lost and a "Hibernicization" of the city's schools would result.

The noted educational authority Lotus D. Coffman of Columbia University Teachers' College agreed. In 1911 he wrote that since teachers "mediated between the child and the outside world," it was "very important to know what the teacher's motives, background, and values" were. "The kind of people we get in teaching," he reminded his readers, "necessarily affects the kind of teaching we get." He went on to warn that the teaching force in large cities was being recruited from a "group of the least favored and cultured . . . in other words, the intellectual possessions of the race are [being] left to a class of people who by social and economic station, as well as by training, are not eminently fitted for their transmission." He concluded with the alarm that, "The classes with the least are contributing the largest percentages of teachers," and this imbalance made the growing "problem of teachers who are not thoroughly Americanized" even graver.[29] Since more and more Irish-American women were entering the ranks of big city teaching in the early years of this century, Coffman's targets are clear.

These fears, while not entirely unfounded, were mostly unrealized, despite the rapid influx of Catholic-school-educated Irish-American women into teaching jobs in Chicago's public elementary schools. Even though most of these young women came from Irish Catholic families similar to Amelia Dunne Hookway's, they were Americanized themselves and felt no conflict with the dominant values of public education, especially once the more egregious of the anti-Catholic biases had been eliminated.[30] The young women teaching in the city's public schools were quite content to separate church and state despite the dark forebodings of the Protestant educational establishment. What they were not content to do, on the other hand, was submit to what they thought were unfair labor practices. As a result, they demanded greater control over their financial lives and sought influence over curriculum matters. It was in these areas that the struggle for control of the public schools in Chicago now lay.

Beginning in 1897, teacher activists Margaret Haley and Catherine Goggin, themselves daughters of Irish-born mothers, helped elementary school teachers in Chicago band together to form the Chicago Teachers' Federation (CTF), the first teachers' union in the United States.[31] Contesting the new restrictions placed on their access to teaching jobs, as well as the ceilings on their salaries and pensions, CTF members demanded and won full pension rights in 1900, allowing Chicago's elementary teachers to make teaching a lifetime career for the first time. Largely because of the CTF's efforts, Chicago elementary school teachers also saw their annual pensions double from $400 to $800 between 1900 and 1920, despite a well-orchestrated effort on the part of school administrators to eliminate the pension altogether in those years. In addition, CTF self-help increased starting salaries for elementary school teachers almost twofold from $650 to $1200 in the two decades after 1900.[32]

Another major arena in the struggle between teachers and administrators centered on the issue of teacher control in curriculum matters. Teachers' councils were designed to provide a forum for teachers to discuss curriculum changes and textbook selection. Based on the belief that the women in the classroom were better qualified to decide on these matters than were the businessmen sitting on the school board, the teachers' council movement was a bold move for professional autonomy. Advocates believed that teachers' councils would democratize education and prevent classroom teachers from being reduced to hired hands obedient to top-down decision making by "progressives" on the school board. As CTF leader and former teacher Margaret Haley saw it, there were "[t]wo ideals . . . struggling for supremacy in American life today: one the industrial ideal . . . which subordinates the worker to the product . . . ; the other, the ideal of democracy,

the ideal of the educators, which places humanity first. . . ."[33] Haley and her heavily Irish-American supporters in the CTF insisted that teachers' councils were a key step in preventing the "deskilling" of the teacher and in advancing democracy in the classroom.

Yet another school board effort to curtail teacher autonomy involved the selection of school principals. Before the years of the heaviest influx of Catholic school graduates into public school teaching after 1900, principals were promoted from the ranks of classroom teachers. These veterans were viewed as the "principal teacher" in the school, a professional among other professionals. The career of Amelia Dunne Hookway followed this path. Starting as a classroom teacher at the Scammon School, she moved up through the ranks, gaining the principalship of the Howland School in 1896 on the strength of her talent and experience. Although she supervised a faculty of close to forty teachers in a school with almost 1800 pupils,[34] she never forgot her teaching responsibilites, including her children's theater that Mark Twain so admired. Nevertheless, despite the dedication and success of Irish-American school principals like Amelia Dunne Hookway, just as more and more Irish-American teachers were gaining the necessary experience for promotion to principal, the school board began its successful campaign to hire outside "experts" as principals. Principals were no longer promoted from the ranks of female teachers and they had ceased to be colleagues. Now they were managers. Thus, an important avenue of professional mobility was closed to the women staffing the schoolrooms of the city.[35] In those same years, teachers' councils were eliminated, and members of the CTF lost their jobs by school board decree.

In the decade after Amelia Dunne Hookway's death in November 1914, the "golden age" of promise for Irish-American women teaching in the public schools of Chicago began to wane. By the 1920s, despite significant gains in salaries and pensions and higher standards of teacher training, more and more Irish-American women in the Chicago public schools saw former avenues of job mobility closed to them as professional bureaucrats replaced talented teachers in supervisory positions. Normal School graduates now remained in the classroom while male graduates of new university departments of education gained administrative positions, along with the higher salaries and greater autonomy that went with these jobs. "Payless paydays" became increasingly common in the lives of Chicago's teachers as the city's tax base declined in the face of corporate tax loopholes. By the 1930s married women were forced to give up their jobs in the classroom, as depression unemployment brought more and more men into teaching.[36]

Legacy

Nevertheless, Amelia Dunne Hookway's generation of Irish-American women forged a new path in the history of education and the Irish in Chicago. Daughters of Irish-born mothers achieved the highest educational levels available to women of their time and social class. They used their educations to better the lives of not only their own families but also of their city. They set a precedent for women's achievement followed by those who came after them. They democratized the public schools, developed a public voice for ethnic professional women, and introduced hundreds of thousands of students from all walks of life to the pleasures of education. Mark Twain's admiration for the work of women like Amelia Dunne Hookway in America's public schools was well placed indeed.

After Hookway's death in 1914, Ella Flagg Young eulogized her former colleague. "Mrs. Hookway," Young wrote, "achieved marvelous results in arousing a sense of personal dignity and responsibility in the [Howland School] children through literature and drama. [She] wrote several dramas, one illustrating the story of Columbus . . . The play stirred deeply not only the children, who were thrilled with patriotic emotion, but also parents, foreign and native born."[37] A daughter of Saint Patrick's had indeed enriched the lives of the Chicago schoolchildren placed under her care.

The Rebirth of an Urban Church

Reverend John J. Wall

A few years before I was appointed pastor at Old Saint Pat's in 1983, I took a summer trip to Ireland. I left Chicago with a pocketful of names and addresses, determined to look up distant relatives and friends. Arriving in the small town of Skibbereen, I was instructed to "ask at the local" for directions to the home of a cousin I had never met. I left the pub and followed a road far out into the country until I came to the crossroads, beyond which the cousin's farm was to be seen. I managed that, but discovered at the crossroads that there was no farm in sight. Assuming I was to proceed along the same road I continued on and before long met an elderly gentleman dressed in the characteristic tweed jacket and cap of Irish sheepherders. I greeted the man and asked if the road I had taken "was the way to the Cudahy place." He paused, looked me over from head to toe, and then fumbled with lighting his pipe while seeming to consider his answer with care. Finally, blowing out his match and taking a deep drag on his pipe, he answered me with what I have come to understand was typical Irish indirectness. "Why wouldn't it be?" was all he said as he kicked the nearest sheep and went on his way.

My experience at the crossroads in Skibbereen served me well when I began to explain to family and friends why I wanted to be pastor of Old Saint Patrick's. Of all the parishes in Chicago, why this one? Of course the old brick church just west of downtown was crowded every Saint Patrick's Day, friends pointed out, but what about the rest of the year? And the neighborhood—wasn't it still Skid Row? They were right about the deserted streets and the grimy buildings and empty pews, but that was only the half of it, as the Irish would say. Something else existed at the crossroads at Adams and Desplaines, something not visible to the naked eye. It was holy ground.

The decisions we make in life often are fraught with uncertainty. The directions we choose to pursue seldom guarantee our arrival at a desired destination. But of all the decisions I have ever made, the one to pursue the pastorate at Old Saint Pat's was one of the clearest. I never felt so certain about anything in my life as I did about the future of Old Saint Patrick's. Every time I would see its steeples from the Kennedy Expressway I couldn't help but think about the potential of a church located so close to the heart of downtown. Some of the same factors that had contributed to the parish's decline were now creating the potential for new growth. The crumbling tenements of Madison Street's Skid Row had fallen to the wrecker's ball. In their place had risen new giants of the West Side—the Sears Tower and the Social Security Administration Building with its "bat column" sculpture, for example. Ironically, the expressways that had isolated Saint Patrick's from its neighborhood in the late 1940s and 1950s were now bringing thousands of cars practically to the front door of the church. The time was right, I believed, for the mother parish of the Chicago Irish to take on a new identity as a metropolitan church and spiritual center.

My choice of Saint Patrick's was deliberate. Coming of age in the 1960s I had watched with fascination the way so many significant individuals had drawn energy from symbolic places: John F. Kennedy launched his presidential campaign from the steps of historic Faneuil Hall on Boston's waterfront; Dr. Martin Luther King Jr. brought the 1963 March on Washington to the steps of the Lincoln Memorial for his memorable "I Have a Dream Speech." Saint Patrick's was just such a place. Not only had the church escaped destruction in the Great Fire of 1871, but thanks to the genius of Finley Peter Dunne, the parish lived on in literature. In the 1890s, Dunne drew upon his boyhood experiences at Saint Patrick's for his "Mr. Dooley" columns that were published in newspapers across the country. Little did I know when I read about Finley Peter Dunne that I would one day follow in the footsteps of his uncle Denis, who completed Saint Patrick's Church just two years after the cholera epidemic of 1854. Right from the beginning, Saint Patrick's had left its mark on the city. And I believed with all my heart that it could happen again.

When I submitted a proposal for redeveloping Old Saint Patrick's into a metropolitan church "center" serving young adults and ministering to the urban workforce, some among my family and friends wondered about the potential that I spoke of with such certainty. But for me, I saw a place of great history that once again stood at a fortuitous crossroads of urban life. When they asked me if I really thought this was the way to go in my life, I had only one answer: "Why wouldn't it be?"

Nearly fourteen years have passed, but I can still remember making a midnight visit to the church at the end of my first day as pastor. Sitting alone in the darkness and silence of the city's oldest building, surrounded on all sides by plaster statues, I began to think of the men, women, and children who had filled the pews and gathered at the table of the Lord for nearly a century and a half: the communion of saints. If I harbored any doubts about Saint Patrick's being holy ground, they had vanished by the time I turned out the lights.

As I reflect on the history of the rebirth of Old Saint Patrick's, dozens of events, scores of stories, and hundreds of names and faces pass through my mind. Never could I do justice to the many individuals who have provided the lifeblood and spirit of this parish. But on the occasion of Saint Patrick's 150th anniversary I would like to step back a bit and acknowledge some of the "crossroads" moments that capture the remarkable revitalization of Saint Patrick's parish.

An Inside-Out Church

When Joseph Cardinal Bernardin named me pastor of Saint Patrick's Church on August 1, 1983, there were four "registered" members. As a result, during those first few months I did what hundreds of parish priests had done in Chicago since the 1830s: I walked the neighborhood, getting the feel of the place. In my wanderings I saw plenty of people who were the last vestiges of Skid Row that rapidly was to give way to a different kind of life on Chicago's West Side. On a bright autumn morning, I noticed one man in particular: he was wearing his jacket inside out. The image continued to haunt me long after my walk ended, and in the next few weeks I began to understand why. It came to symbolize the dream that was taking shape within and around me, the dream of Saint Patrick's as a dying church turned "inside-out" by its efforts to understand and respond to the world.

At my installation as pastor not long after, I described that dream as having three key components. The first was that Saint Pat's might become a vital center for the laity, dedicated to the Christian mission each individual brings to his or her investments in work and civic responsibilities. The hope was that, through careful listening and creative responses, we might be able to develop models of ministry to the Christian in the marketplace that other parishes might use.

Second, I spoke of creating a major center for young adults who were searching for ways to be more meaningfully connected to the Catholic Christian community. At that time Reverend John Cusick was part-time director of Young Adult Ministry for the Archdiocese of Chicago. If there is one person who has shared the dream of Old Saint Patrick's from the beginning it is John. His passionate commitment to young adults and his powerful gift of preaching were now brought to Old Saint Pat's as he began a monthly young adult liturgy here and prepared to move the office of Young Adult Ministry to Saint Pat's when he was named full-time director in 1985.

The third key dimension of the dream I articulated was that Saint Pat's might continue as a creative link to our roots and our heritage, as we together forged the future of our faith, our culture, and our society. While this last component, in hindsight, seems less clearly defined than the earlier two, it reflected that sense of appreciation for the historical significance of this place, as well as the potential for making connections that, like those between work and faith and those between young adults and church, often seemed to be overlooked.

The common denominator among these three dimensions was that Saint Pat's would be a church in service to those engaged with life, wherever that life investment found them. If, often, the Catholic experience is one of parochialism, Old Saint Patrick's might break new ground by reaching out to those who yearned deeply for an understanding of their rich experiences of life but had failed to find answers within their experiences of church.

To become this "inside-out" church, it was clear, would demand that we not wait for people to come to us, but rather reach out in new ways to invite people who for one reason or another were not feeling included by the Church. For example, one "truth" that often seems to guide the Church's ministry to young adults is that the cycle of life dictates that sometime during the period of late adolescence or young adulthood a person will drift away from the Church—or lose the appreciation of what the Church has to offer. A large part of Old Saint Pat's success in the past decade has resulted from a refusal to believe in the "life-cycle" theory as the only truth about young adult church involvement.

Is it possible that young adults' minimal participation might be due to the Church's failure to meet their needs rather than their "aberrant" lifestyles? Inherent in that seemingly obvious possibility was the genius behind the success Father Cusick had experienced revitalizing the Archdiocesan Office of Young Adult Ministry. Joining the work of that ministry to Old Saint Patrick's—with its central location and proximity to the workplace of so many young adults—seemed a natural marriage.

So, too, did tapping into people's hunger for a deeper sense of meaning within their daily work. Throughout my ministry as a priest, I have witnessed the profound sense of responsibility men and women bring to their vocations in the world. Because of its strategic location on the fringe of Chicago's Loop business district, Saint Pat's seemed to stand out as a place where the vocation of the Christian layperson in and to the world could be supported and reinforced.

But if those groups were to be the focus of this reborn, urban church, Old Saint Pat's would have to find a way to gather them together. The strategy adopted was simple: create programs of high quality and genuine substance that would give people reason to come to Old Saint Pat's, and once they were here, ensure that they encountered the kind of hospitality that would make their experience enjoyable and encourage them to return with others.

To this day, but beginning with my first few weeks as pastor, I have tried consciously to say "yes" to as many requests or invitations that came our way. Whether it was a trade union interested in using the parish hall, a suburban parish looking to host a meeting for its members who worked downtown, or a group of young adults wanting to rent the gym for a basketball league, I always tried to remember the story of Sarah and Abraham from the Hebrew Testament and the lesson that when you welcome the stranger you can encounter the divine. Wherever I went in Chicago I collected names and addresses, adding them to the mailing lists of the long-time supporters of Reverend Stephen J. O'Donnell, who served as pastor from 1960 to 1983. I also pirated lists from the Young Irish Fellowship Club, the Young Adult Ministry Office, and the Vocations Office of the Archdiocese of Chicago. Gradually, we found we had a pool of potentially interested individuals that was more than sufficient to fill the pews of the church when they were invited to participate in my installation as pastor on October 9, 1983.

But if we were to experience a continuation of those numbers beyond that single event, it was clear that our approach to "marketing" Old Saint Pat's would have to break away from the traditional church pattern into a more secular model. My sister, Mary Kay Wall, fresh from running several political campaigns and tuned in to Chicago's professional young adult and business communities, took charge.

Rather than attempt to create programs that young adults would be enticed to attend—a seemingly daunting challenge given the competition for their time and attention in a city like Chicago—the decision was made to invite groups that already had vibrant young adult membership to make use of the facilities at Old Saint Pat's. One of the earliest—and most important connections—was with the Young Irish Fellowship Club, an offshoot of the group founded in 1902 by prominent Irish Americans in Chicago. In the mid-1980s the young men and women of the club were seeking an alternative to restaurants and bars for their monthly board meetings. We offered them free space at Old Saint Patrick's and before long, young adults were streaming into the neighborhood and through our doors. When the Young Irish Fellowship Club used our social hall or gym for parties or fund-raisers they began to feel an affinity for the place that extended them hospitality.

The monthly liturgies sponsored by the Young Adult Ministry Office also brought large numbers of young adults to Saint Pat's. Consequently, many of those young adults returned for Mass on other Sundays as well, bringing along friends or family members. From that latter group's faithful attendance grew our gradual awareness that Saint Pat's might meet the needs of a broader, adult family constituency.

Various young adult organizations ranging from the Notre Dame Club of Chicago and other college alumni groups began to inquire about meeting at Old Saint Patrick's. Whenever possible, the answer was "yes!" Each group infused life into the previously empty streets around Adams and Desplaines; there always seemed to be young men and women who felt a special connection to the church and its mission. Increasingly, young men and women came to the parish for a meeting or party and returned with friends, a chain-migration in reverse for Chicago's oldest Irish parish.

If the key strategy in beginning to create a sense of identification with Saint Pat's for young adults was the "incorporation" of other successful organizations that already met their needs for socialization and networking, the

At the time Presidential Towers were constructed in the early 1980s, Old Saint Patrick's claimed only four registered parishioners. (Photo by Bob Thall. Courtesy, Commission on Chicago Landmarks)

"The World's Largest Block Party," established in 1985, has become a Chicago tradition, transforming the streets around Old Saint Patrick's. (Photo by Jim Pollick. Courtesy, Old Saint Patrick's Church)

✛ ✛ ✛

strategy for tapping into people's secular life experience was the concept of an "urban forum." It began, simply enough, from a series of kitchen conversations with small groups of men and women who were attempting to integrate Christian values with their experiences of work and family. Building on the suggestions of such respected Chicagoans as Ed Marciniak, Dan Cantwell, and Russ Barta, Saint Patrick's hosted well-known individuals who were willing to reflect publicly on their own efforts to lead ethical and meaningful lives. The first forum in the spring of 1984 featured Sharon Gist Gilliam, budget director, City of Chicago; Mary Laney, NBC news anchor; Illinois Attorney General Neil Hartigan; James J. O'Connor, president and CEO of Commonwealth Edison; and Andrew M. Greeley, Chicago's well-known priest-scholar.

The forum was an immediate success, drawing hundreds of interested individuals to each session of the five-part series. While the quality of the programs contributed to the success of the fall forum, so too did its structure: participants could walk over to Saint Patrick's after work, enjoy a light supper followed by a presentation and questions, and still head home at a reasonable hour. The urban forums taught us valuable lessons about the necessary combination of quality, hospitality, and sensitivity to the needs of the participants. As in our outreach to young adults, it was clear that this group would readily respond if approached in a new way. The first forum led to a second gathering that discussed the responsibility of the business community toward urban poverty. From that program the seeds of Old Saint Pat's Community Outreach Group were planted.

In 1987 we launched the Crossroads Center for Faith and Work under the direction of John Fontana. Driven by his strong entrepreneurial style and high energy, small groups soon began focusing on specific issues relating to professional life. Lawyers, nurses, human resource executives, and others came to Saint Patrick's to explore the meaning of their daily work. Concurrently, Eileen Durkin joined the staff as director of community formation to coordinate the development of programs to meet the needs of the expanding membership and to greatly enrich the quality of our liturgies and feasts.

It was clear that something was happening, something new and exciting and different. A dying church was being revitalized, turned "inside-out" by its efforts to understand and respond to the world. This image took on new meaning for me as I celebrated mass. In most churches after the sun sets the windows are dark and gloomy. Not so at Saint Pat's. Shortly after the turn of the century, Thomas A. O'Shaughnessy revived the ancient tradition of using metal oxides to imprison color in opaque glass. As a result, Saint Patrick's windows are visible both inside and outside the church, depending on which side has the greater light. One evening I looked around and realized that the luminescent windows are a powerful symbol of the mission of Saint Patrick's. With the slightest illumination from daylight or street lamp, O'Shaughnessy's gentle colors sparkle for the eye, and their stories of faith and work are illuminated. The luminescent quality of Saint Pat's windows is a powerful symbol to me that the work of the church ought not to be self-centered or self-contained. It is when we turn "inside-out" as church and engage the work of the world that our faith most illuminates human experience.

Reclaiming an Urban Ritual

It was May 2, 1985. A group of fifteen or twenty people sat down and made a decision. On Friday night, July 26, Saint Patrick's would host a party for the entire metropolitan area of Chicago. Drawing on their own vivid memories of block parties in the city's neighborhoods, the group decided to reclaim this urban ritual for Saint Patrick's. Melanie O'Brien suggested we call the event "The World's Largest Block Party." (This group was not short on ambition!)

In less than three months, the name and the idea became a reality. Five thousand people gathered on a hot July night, transforming the West Loop from a forgotten backwater of the city into a place of high celebration. Although none of us consciously realized it at the time, the

block party evoked an even older tradition of the crossroads dances in Ireland. All we knew in the summer of 1985 was that a small band of people had for one night infused life into the city. Amazingly, in three years' time the event grew from five to fifteen thousand people. And it continues to be one of Chicago's premier summer celebrations, the place to be for young adults.

To this day, "The World's Largest Block Party" remains an exercise of the imagination. To walk the streets around Saint Patrick's in the weeks before the event is to see a decidedly nondescript urban landscape on the far west edge of downtown. Even now, when much of the neighborhood has greatly improved, the setting for the party still lacks the grace and grandeur of Chicago's lakefront and parks. But the thousands of people who have gathered on the streets and sidewalks around Saint Patrick's Church every summer since 1985 see things differently. Thanks to a legion of volunteers who generate life and vitality, civility and goodness, the ordinary landscape is suddenly transformed into quite a magical place.

On a scale much grander than even its hyperbolic founders ever imagined, "The World's Largest Block Party" embodies the spirit of hospitality that has become a hallmark of Saint Patrick's Church. I'm not sure when this value was "institutionalized" in the parish, but clearly it occurred long before the first block party in 1985. I remember seeing it in the actions of my own family and friends who gathered at Saint Patrick's in the early years of my pastorate. Instinctively, they reached out to anyone they hadn't met before, offering smiles and warm words of welcome. I also remember that when we gathered to brainstorm ideas for Old Saint Patrick's the evening almost always began or ended with a meal. The hospitality continued through the late night chore of cleaning up the dishes. Before long I began to see a pattern: young men and women would leave an event at

Students join Reverend Robert E. McLaughlin (left), *pastor of Holy Name Cathedral, and Reverend John J. Wall* (right), *pastor of Old Saint Patrick's, at the opening of the north campus of Frances Xavier Warde School, September 1994. The school unites the past and present—the Sisters of Mercy, the first nuns in Chicago, taught at Old Saint Patrick's in 1846.* (Courtesy, Old Saint Patrick's Church)

Saint Patrick's only to return the next time with a friend or two in tow, broadening the early circles of support. And while I don't remember exactly when it happened first, I cannot recall a liturgy in my time here that didn't begin with the greeting of strangers or newcomers by those who already felt more "at home."

When Monsignor Dan Cantwell came to live and work at Old Saint Patrick's in 1984, the legendary Catholic Action leader began to mark this place in highly symbolic ways. In fact he hadn't even finished unpacking his belongings when he took a sledgehammer to the plasterboard walls that had subdivided the once beautiful rectory parlors into tiny offices.

When the dust cleared, we realized that Dan Cantwell was reclaiming Saint Patrick's legacy of hospitality.

His commitment to opening up the experience of the church was even more dramatic. On Christmas Eve, the seventy-year-old priest set to work with his crowbar, removing the communion rail from the steps of the sanctuary. The fact that there was now a hole in the carpeting—with Christmas Mass just hours away—bothered him not at all. Gone was another barrier that had separated the congregation from the Lord's table. Dan Cantwell died in the winter of 1996 but his example of hospitality and inclusivity lives on. Perhaps one of the

Reverend John J. Wall, pastor of Old Saint Patrick's, blesses the new cross for Chicago's landmark church, 1993. (Photo by Patrick Kavanaugh. Courtesy, Old Saint Patrick's Church)

most practical manifestations of that belief at Saint Patrick's has to do with membership.

When I arrived in 1983, you could count on one hand the number of registered parishioners. At most only a small group of men and women attended liturgy on Sunday and during the week. While the Near West Side was on the verge of regaining its identity as a residential and commercial neighborhood, even Presidential Towers had yet to break ground. It was clear that if the pews of Saint Patrick's were to be filled, it would be by people who lived far from the traditional boundaries of the parish.

Reaching out to twenty-and-thirty-year olds made a lot of sense, I knew, but it was unclear whether young people would be eager to assume the responsibilities of formal membership during a period of life that might be transitional in many ways. The staff recognized early on that any Catholic who chose to participate at Saint Patrick's would be either unattached to church, or already involved in a local parish. To ask unattached Catholics to commit to registering, with its traditional meaning of affiliation and financial support, seemed destined for failure. (Even in neighborhood parishes, the tradition of "getting your envelopes" was on the wane by the 1980s.) The staff also recognized that young adults might not want to sever all connections with their old parish, especially since attending Saint Patrick's would involve a fair amount of travel.

The wisdom that emerged from early conversations and meetings was to invite people to a new way of being connected to church. Rather than expect each interested individual to conform to an exclusive category of membership, we discussed possible relationships. For example, a person could join Saint Patrick's as a "member" who considered this to be his or her primary church. A Catholic registered at another parish who wished to worship regularly at Saint Patrick's could become an "asso-

Workman Bill Sattler restores Old Saint Patrick's central gable in a dramatic cross-raising ceremony, 1993. (Photo by Patrick Kavanaugh. Courtesy, Old Saint Patrick's Church)

✛ ✛ ✛

ciate." Other ways of belonging ranged from "participant" to "weekday member" to "friend" and, finally, for those searching to discover a place for themselves within Saint Patrick's community, "candidate." The flexibility and accessibility of joining in this way was a concrete expression of the hospitality we sought to extend. While the categories have been refined and reduced in number today, the approach still guides our sense of membership. Rather than lead to a congregation of half-hearted commitments, it has enabled us to grow well beyond the numbers anyone ever imagined, whether counting the people in church on Sunday morning, the thousands who have participated in our quality programs, or the tens of thousands who have gathered for the block party over the years.

The Rebirth of an Urban School

One crisp fall morning a few years ago, I walked the long way around from the rectory on Adams Street to the church's offices on Desplaines. When I approached the gate outside the courtyard building leading to the old school I was taken off guard by a sight I had never seen in the decade I had lived at Old

Saint Pat's: a red, toddler-sized two-wheel bike. Indeed I would venture to guess it had been a generation or more since children rode their bicycles around this part of the neighborhood. Chained to a streetlight opposite the courtyard gate, the bike clearly belonged to one of the newest members to call Old Saint Pat's home. I gave silent credit to a resourceful parent who had turned a bike ride to school into special time shared with a child. And as I passed into our offices, I began to think about our latest venture that had become a reality: the reopening of Old Saint Patrick's School.

When I began my work on the Near West Side in 1983, the parish's schools were only a memory. The Christian Brothers' Academy for Boys had moved to the Northwest Side of

Celebrating the 150th anniversary of Old Saint Patrick's on March 17, 1996, are Reverend John J. Wall, pastor, Mary Ellen O'Toole, parade queen, Mayor Richard M. Daley and his wife Maggie, and Most Reverend Edwin M. Conway. (Photo by Jim Pollick. Courtesy, Old Saint Patrick's Church)

Chicago in the early 1950s. Although Saint Patrick's grammar school closed in 1967, the Daughters of Charity continued to staff the High School for Girls until 1970. Considering that Saint Patrick's had very few members, let alone young families in the 1980s, we didn't think the parish needed to develop programs for children. In fact, whenever the topic surfaced, it raised red flags all around the conference table.

Reverend David Murphy, a Carmelite priest who had joined our staff in 1989, expressed the insight shared by many at Saint Patrick's: "If we try to be all things to all people, we'll be nothing for anyone." There seemed to be a consensus that plenty of other Chicago parishes served the needs of children through schools and Christian doctrine programs. Our commitment, after all, was to serve the spiritual needs of adults and to help them make the connections between human experience and faith.

But it wasn't long before the issue of children resurfaced again, this time from another perspective. We began to hear, over and over, the dilemma that faced working parents: how could they provide a quality education for their children that was also convenient to their offices downtown? Our research revealed that although there were few options for parents of young children, the situation was changing rapidly. Several businesses had begun to develop day-care programs for children of employees, and it would be only a matter of time until these boys and girls reached school age. Parents, as well as the corporate community, expressed interest and support for a downtown school.

While we were aware that parishes often view schools as a way to attract new members or serve an existing population, Old Saint Patrick's charted a different course. Consistent with everything else we were attempting to do, the school was experimental in nature, beginning with a preschool and kindergarten in a store-

front location. Gradually, more grades were added as news of our endeavor spread. What set us apart from other private schools, however, was our commitment to provide an education not just for the affluent but for children of every race, religion, and socio-economic group in Chicago. Our original design committee for the school, ably led by Maggie Daley, the city's First Lady, and later our school board, has consistently worked to create an inclusive educational experience that is reflective of our best dreams for Chicago. By design and by mission, 30 percent of the students in our school must come from families who require some form of financial aid. To accomplish this we needed to find funding that went beyond the resources of parents, to develop a curriculum of the highest caliber, and to structure a program of religious education that would meet the needs of Catholic as well as non-Catholic students. And if that wasn't enough of a tall order, we also added another condition: that the school be structured in such a way that it wouldn't compromise Old Saint Patrick's mission to the adult experience of faith.

The dream of this model urban school could not have been realized without finding the right person to act as principal. Sister Mary Ellen Caron, R.S.M., a brilliant young educator and administrator with a deep love for children and a passion for justice, accepted the leadership role. She skillfully wove together faculty and students, parents and board, donors, architects, and construction workers and opened the first new school in the archdiocese of Chicago in more than twenty-five years. From its first day on September 7, 1989, Chicago's newest Catholic school has succeeded beyond our wildest hopes. Indeed, enrollment continued to grow so rapidly that before long, the school expanded to the North Side, thanks to a joint venture with Holy Name Cathedral. Renamed Frances Xavier Warde School after the American founder of the Sisters of Mercy, the two

campuses offer a high-quality education to students from preschool through eighth grade.

Frances Xavier Warde School is one of the most profound contributions Saint Patrick's has made to the fabric of urban life. It is also one of the clearest examples of the way in which our response to issues is mission-driven rather than membership-driven. To this day, the majority of parents whose children attend the Warde School are not members of Old Saint Patrick's, although a significant number of families have joined the parish after first sending their children to our school. Whenever I think about that red two-wheeler parked in front of Old Saint Patrick's, I am reminded that there are many ways an urban church can contribute to the work of the laity in the world. And sometimes, like the success of the Frances Xavier Warde School, they catch us by surprise.

Reclaiming Sacred Space

Another "crossroads" moment occurred in the summer of 1993 as part of the restoration of Saint Patrick's Church, the sacred symbol of our historic presence and ongoing mission. Following the renovation of the social hall down in the basement, workers installed a new roof and began to replace the ornamental stonework that had been removed from the cornice of the church years ago. The final stage in the project was the replacement of the Celtic cross that had stood for more than a century at the apex of the roof. While it would be years before the interior restoration was completed, we viewed the crossraising as an opportunity to celebrate the dramatic progress we had made.

Ordinarily an undertaking of this nature would have been scheduled for a weekday. Not only did the project involve a huge crane, but for safety reasons, the steps of the church had to be cordoned off. But this was sacred space, we argued, and it deserved a Sunday celebration. What better time than between the two major masses on September 15, 1993. As the 9:45 a.m. mass concluded, worshipers gathered outside behind a protective tape. Those arriving early for the 11:45 a.m. Mass encountered a considerable crowd as well as blocked entrances and had little choice but to join in.

Dressed in my vestments, I donned a hard hat and climbed into the back of the crane where I led a brief prayer service. We all peered skyward as the replacement cross was raised into position. And then it happened. It was just a gesture, and it took only a moment, but I will never forget it.

There were several workers stationed at various spots on the roof of the church waiting to guide the cross over the parapet of the roof and then affix it to its foundation. One of them, I suppose the foreman, began to give directions to the crane operator over a two-way radio. But as the cross hovered just over the side of the roof, and the workers cradled it in their arms to lower it into place, my attention was drawn to the foreman. He removed his helmet, set down his radio, and bowed his head. Then, making the sign of the cross, he resumed his gear and finished the job. The foreman's gesture proclaimed more powerfully than any words could that the place we call Saint Patrick's is holy ground.

For the past decade thousands of Chicagoans have been involved in the restoration of Old Saint Patrick's Church. I am convinced that the motivation for their generosity is not to create a museum to the past. Rather, it is to honor the persistent reality that this church continues to be holy ground where living, vibrant people gather, striving to live out a vision of life that is personally and socially transforming. Larry

Booth, the principal architect for our restoration project, recently said, "There's a magic to this place. The building has embedded itself in the consciousness and memories of so many people and families in Chicago. It's not only the oldest building in Chicago, it is probably the most loved."

At another moment of rebirth when Thomas O'Shaughnessy designed stained glass windows and stencils for Saint Patrick's between 1912 and 1922, he breathed new life into Chicago's oldest house of worship. He also challenged contemporary ideas about sacred art and opened his generation and ours to an appreciation of Celtic art and spirituality that had been lost to the world for centuries. His windows and stencils invite us to experience the religious imagination of the Celts and to explore with him their core spiritual insight: that all of life is holy—not just part of it—for wherever you stand is holy ground.

Epilogue

The preceding stories and reflections have been my attempt to capture some of the underlying values that have shaped the rebirth of Old Saint Patrick's and to identify some of the successful strategies that will be the current generation's contribution to the ongoing legacy of this historic church. As expressed in Saint Pat's mission statement, we have tried to create a dynamic experience of church that is driven by our clear commitment to the work of the laity in the world. Our programmatic focus on the adult experiences of work, family, and citizenship; our trademark style of hospitality in every program we offer or liturgy we celebrate; our unique appreciation of the necessity of marketing; our creative approaches to fundraising; and the quality and breadth of our programs and staff—all in some way mark Old Saint Pat's as unique. We are a metropolitan church center rather than a local parish. The membership comes together to pursue the mission of this particular church rather than to be served by it.

But in the end, there is really one basic insight that is at the heart of all that we do. It is the same vision that is celebrated in Thomas O'Shaughnessy's art. It is the insight that spirituality is not one component of life, to be appreciated by some and ignored by others, but rather the dimension of meaning in life that all men and women constantly seek.

We acknowledge that for many, "church" can be an intimidating experience. Finding a role for "church" or a specific church to belong to may not be at the top of everyone's "to do" list on this or any other day. But we believe if this church we call Old Saint Pat's can keep its mission clear, we can serve that deeper call that all men and women experience repeatedly in every dimension of life: the call to make sense of who we are, where we are going, and what we are called to do along the way.

In the end we know that Old Saint Pat's will be judged by the degree to which we can offer an experience, a program, a place that genuinely touches what is deepest in people's experience and that helps energize their spirits to live their lives in a fully committed way. Conscious of the sacred and historic past of this place, we seek to continue to serve the people of Chicago from this crossroads of urban life. Four goals are clear as we celebrate our sesquicentennial.

The first is the continuing development of the Crossroads Center concept, with its multidimensional response to the issues of faith and work, faith and culture, faith and family, and faith and adult spirituality. In choosing this direction, we seek to position Old Saint Pat's as an innovative metropolitan "center" rather than a traditional, member-focused parish. In everything we do, it is the intent of our membership to reach beyond our own borders and

boundaries to empower individuals and groups to better do the important work of the world.

Our second goal is to attend to the ongoing development of Old Saint Pat's "campus." Even as the work of church restoration proceeds, we know that other decisions regarding building and property must be made today, if twenty-five years from now we still wish to have the capacity to fulfill our mission. Generating energy around the necessary fund-raising events, remaining creative and innovative, and developing new connections to fuel our continued growth will be a focus of much of our activity in the years to come.

A third important goal involves developing an approach to administration and governance that is consistent with our unique mission and constituencies. Assuring ownership of the mission that has evolved is critical for the continuation of that mission. Assuring continuity in governance beyond the term of the current pastor also is necessary for the long-term impact of Old Saint Pat's.

Finally, we look forward to completing the restoration of Old Saint Patrick's, the sacred symbol of our historic presence and ongoing service. In this effort we have been supported by hundreds of friends and benefactors who have recognized the significance of this historic church and the artistic genius of Thomas O'Shaughnessy. My hope is that the restored church will truly be a source of inspiration to all who enter it.

Although we have accomplished much at Saint Patrick's in a relatively short time, I have come to understand that the phenomenon of the "new" Saint Patrick's is really not so new after all. Somehow, in the bricks and mortar of these old buildings and in the bone and blood of the generations who have sought God in their midst, the spirit of creativity and innovation has flowed freely. As we mark the 150th anniversary of Old Saint Patrick's we also honor those who have gone before us. Thanks to the vision, commitment, and dedication of thousands of Chicagoans across the generations, Saint Patrick's looks forward to a new century of ministry at the crossroads of the city. This is indeed an enchanted, holy place.

Notes

Introduction

1. I extend heartfelt thanks to Charles Fanning and Suellen Hoy for their critical contributions to this introduction.
2. Samuel L. Clemens, *Life on the Mississippi* (New York: Dodd, Mead, and Company, 1968), 400. Special thanks to Walter Nugent, Andrew V. Tackes Professor of American History at the University of Notre Dame, for pointing out Mark Twain's apt comment.
3. Quoted in "Saint Patrick's Academy, Chicago." Undated article in Saint Patrick High School Archives.
4. See nobel laureate Seamus Heaney's marvelous essay, "The Sense of Place," *Preoccupations: Selected Prose, 1968–1978* (New York: Farrar, Straus, Giroux, 1980), 139.

Chapter 1. Saint Patrick's Day at Saint Patrick's Church

1. This article appears to be a reprint, with modifications, of one that appeared in the *Chicago Tribune,* March 18, 1896.
2. I want to thank John E. Corrigan, who discovered Jimmy Lane's story in the *Chicago Times-Herald*, March 18, 1896. He also called my attention to John Kelley's reminiscences on the demise of the Saint Patrick's Day parade in the *Chicago Tribune*, March 16, 1913. I would not have been able to interpret who marched in the parade through the years without his descriptions of various Irish-American

organizations in Chicago found in *Irish American Voluntary Organizations*, ed., Michael F. Funchion (Westport, Conn.: Greenwood Press, 1983). For additional information on James Lane, see *Chicago Daily News*, September 23, 1897, and Alfred T. Andreas, *History of Chicago*, 3 vols. (Chicago: A. T. Andreas Co., 1884–86) 3: 398. Following Reverend Lane up the aisle of the church in 1996 were members of the Dunne and O'Shaughnessy families whose ancestors were intimately associated with the history of Old Saint Patrick's Church.
3. See Ellen Skerrett, "Chicago's Irish and 'Brick and Mortar' Catholicism: A Reappraisal," *U. S. Catholic Historian* 14, no. 2 (spring 1996), 53–71.
4. Playwright Brian Friel describes this characteristic of Irish (and Ugandan) festivities in *Dancing at Lughnasa* (London: Faber and Faber Limited, 1990), 48.
5. Right Reverend James O. Van de Velde, "Panegyric on Saint Patrick," (Chicago: Western Tablet, 1852), 10.
6. *The New World*, March 2, 1912, quoted in Reverend Monsignor Harry C. Koenig, ed., *A History of the Parishes of the Archdiocese of Chicago*, 2 vols. (Chicago: Archdiocese of Chicago, 1980) 1: 756.
7. Frank Brown entered first grade at Saint Patrick's school in 1917. He later became a distinguished professor of economics at De Paul University.
8. Among the sources I consulted on Saint Patrick's Day festivities elsewhere were Michael Cottrell, "Saint Patrick's Day Parades in Nineteenth-Century Toronto:

A Study of Immigrant Adjustment and Elite Control," *Histoire Sociale–Social History*, 25: 49 (May 1992), 57–73; Timothy J. Meagher, " 'Why Should We Care for a Little Trouble or a Walk through the Mud': Saint Patrick's and Columbus Day Parades in Worcester, Massachusetts, 1845–1915," *New England Quarterly*, 58: 1 (March 1985), 5–26; Kenneth Moss, "Saint Patrick's Day Celebrations and the Formation of Irish-American Identity, 1845–75," *Journal of Social History*, 29: 1 (fall 1995), 125–48; Charles J. O'Fahey, "Reflections on the Saint Patrick's Day Orations of John Ireland," *Ethnicity*, vol. 2 (1975), 244–57; and Robert Jerome Smith, "Festivals and Calendar Customs," in *Irish History and Culture*, ed., Harold Orel (Lawrence, Kans: University of Kansas Press, 1976), 129–45.

9. See Emmet Larkin, "The Devotional Revolution in Ireland," *The Historical Dimensions of Catholicism* (Washington, D.C.: Catholic University of America Press, 1984).

10. These "sister societies" included Saint George's (English), Saint Andrew's (Scottish), Saint David's (Welsh), and Saint Nicholas' (Dutch).

11. See *Chicago Tribune*, August 20, 1882, which includes a reprint of an article in the *Chicago Democrat*, Tuesday, March 21, 1843, and Andreas, 1: 153.

12. Details from Bishop Quarter's episcopal journal, reprinted in James J. McGovern, ed., *Souvenir of the Silver Jubilee in the Episcopacy of His Grace, the Most Reverend Patrick Augustine Feehan, Archbishop of Chicago* (Chicago: Privately printed, 1891), 85–87.

13. *Western Tablet*, March 20, 1852.

14. In 1879 the Saint Patrick's Society was still toasting guests from "sister societies" of Saint Andrew's, Saint George's, and the Germania Maennerchor (*Chicago Tribune*,

March 18). Founded in 1865 by Onahan, the Saint Patrick's Society was not a parish-based organization but rather drew its members from throughout the city.

15. *Western Tablet*, March 26, 1853.

16. *Western Tablet*, March 25, 1854.

17. *Chicago Times*, March 17–18, 1865, and *Chicago Tribune*, March 18, 1878.

18. In 1896, for example, Irish clergymen sang and performed before a crowd of two thousand at the People's Institute to raise funds for the new Saint Charles Borromeo Church. *Chicago Tribune*, March 17, 1858; March 18, 1879; and March 18, 1896.

19. *Evening Journal*, February 23, 1864.

20. *Evening Journal*, March 17, 1866, and *Chicago Times*, March 19, 1867.

21. *Chicago Tribune*, March 16, 1913.

22. As quoted in Charles Fanning, *Finley Peter Dunne and Mr. Dooley, The Chicago Years* (Lexington, Ky.: University Press of Kentucky, 1978), 146.

23. Fanning, 166–70; *Chicago Tribune*, March 18, 1877; and *Chicago Evening Post*, March 16, 18, 1893.

24. *Chicago Tribune*, March 18, 1902.

25. *Chicago Evening Post*, March 21, 1896.

26. *Chicago Tribune*, March 17, 1912.

27. *Chicago Tribune*, March 18, 1902.

28. *Chicago Tribune*, March 18, 1903.

29. Patricia Kelleher, "Gender Shapes Ethnicity: Ireland's Gender Systems and Chicago's Irish Americans," (Ph.D. diss., University of Wisconsin-Madison, 1995).

30. In addition to *The New World*, March 2, 1912, articles describing the era of Father McNamee include the *Chicago American*, March 17, 1915; *Chicago Tribune*, March 18, 1922; and the *Chicago Herald and Examiner*, March 18, 1926.

31. Koenig, 1: 757.

32. *The New World*, February 12, 1954.

33. Virginia McHugh LeFevour, "Saint

Patrick's, 123 Years and More to Come," *Chicago's 24th Annual Saint Patrick's Day Parade* (Chicago: Saint Patrick's Day Parade Committee, March 17, 1979), 92–93, and Steve Neal, "Old Saint Pat's Rich in Celebration's Lore," *Chicago Sun-Times*, March 17, 1991.

34. *Chicago Tribune*, March 17, 1912, and *Chicago Evening Post*, March 21, 1896.

Chapter 2. Creating Sacred Space in an Early Chicago Neighborhood

I am deeply grateful to Len and Kay Hilts for sharing their meticulous research on the Dunne family and Old Saint Patrick's and allowing me to borrow priceless family photographs for reproduction in this book. And I want to extend a special thanks to Suellen Hoy, Tim Barton, and Charlie Fanning for their generosity in reading versions of my chapter and offering insightful comments and perspective based on their own remarkable scholarship.

1. Ellen Skerrett, "Chicago's Irish and 'Brick and Mortar' Catholicism: A Reappraisal," *U.S. Catholic Historian* 14, no. 2 (spring 1996), 53–71.

2. I owe an enormous debt to the National Endowment for the Humanities, which awarded me a Youthgrant in 1974–75 to research Irish Catholic parishes in Chicago.

3. *Chicago Weekly Times*, January 8, 1857. For the significance of Milwaukee brick, see Brenda Fowler, "What's Doing in Milwaukee," *New York Times*, June 4, 1995.

4. *The New World*, March 2, 1912.

5. W. B. Ogden to Edwin Crowell, August 31, 1840, *Ogden Letter Books*, 2: 494, Chicago Historical Society; *Daily Chicago American*, August 5, 1840, cited by Bessie L. Pierce, *A History of Chicago*, 3 vols. (New York: Alfred A. Knopf, 1937–57), 1: n.73, 377.

6. In his pioneering research on Irish Catholicism, Emmet Larkin coined the term *devotional revolution* to describe the dramatic changes in popular practice that occurred during the episcopacy of Cardinal Paul Cullen (1852–76). See especially, *The Historical Dimensions of Irish Catholicism* (Washington, D.C.: Catholic University of America Press, 1984).

7. Excerpts from Bishop Quarter's episcopal journal, quoted in James J. McGovern, *Souvenir of the Silver Jubilee in the Episcopacy of His Grace, the Most Reverend Patrick Augustine Feehan, Archbishop of Chicago, 1890* (Chicago: Privately printed, 1891), 64, 69; *Chicago Daily Democrat*, October 15, 1845.

8. Desmond J. Keenan, *The Catholic Church in Nineteenth-Century Ireland: A Sociological Study* (Totowa, N. J.: Barnes and Noble Books, 1983), 116.

9. "A Day in an Irish Town," *The Illustrated London News*, July 28, 1849.

10. *The New World*, January 20, 27, 1906; *Chicago Citizen*, January 27, 1906.

11. In January 1849 Denis Dunne received a poignant letter from his oldest brother, Michael, congratulating him on his new parish assignment in Galena, Illinois. After relating family news in Chicago, Michael Dunne reminded Denis that the move from New Brunswick "was not done altogether for your sake alone" but rather for the entire family and "above all . . . for the glory and honour of almighty God . . ." Len Hilts, "The Dunnes of New Brunswick and Chicago," unpublished manuscript, 1996.

12. *Daily Chicago Journal*, May 21, 23, 1853.

13. Thanks to Nancy Sandleback, assistant archivist, Archdiocese of Chicago, for going

above and beyond the call in obtaining a readable copy of *Western Tablet*, May 28, 1853. Bishop Van de Velde's remarks are quoted in McGovern, 177.

14. *Weekly Chicago Democrat*, August 26, 1854.

15. *Chicago Daily Journal*, March 19, 1857; *Chicago Times*, December 27, 1868.

16. According to Dunne family historian Len Hilts, Father Dunne assumed personal responsibility for funds to complete Saint Patrick's Church when Bishop Duggan reneged on his promise to pay for alterations. After Denis's death, his brothers paid the debt in full. Hilts notes that the Dunne enclave around Saint Patrick's included the family of Peter at 109 W. Adams Street and, later, at 136 W. Adams (where Finley Peter Dunne was born); Edward, at 105 W. Adams; William Sr. at 107 W. Adams; Patrick at 134 W. Adams; James at 139 W. Adams; Matthew Riordan at 141 W. Adams; and William Dunne Jr. at 149 S. Desplaines Street.

17. *Chicago Weekly Times*, January 8, 1857; *Chicago Times*, November 29, 1857 and November 7, 1875.

18. For a critique of Protestant church-building, see Daniel Bluestone's classic work, *Constructing Chicago* (New Haven, Conn.: Yale University Press, 1991); *Chicago Tribune*, November 23, 1857.

19. *Chicago Daily Journal*, March 19, 1857.

20. *Chicago Daily Times*, July 1, 1859.

21. *Chicago Daily Times*, October 23, 1859.

22. *Chicago Tribune*, July 20, 1861.

23. *Chicago Times*, January 9, 1867.

24. The Christian Brothers succeeded the Brothers of the Holy Cross from South Bend, Indiana, who had staffed Saint Patrick's Boys School since 1856. Alfred T. Andreas, *History of Chicago, from the Earliest Period to the Present Time*. 3 vols.

(Chicago: A. T. Andreas Co., 1884–86), 2: 400.

25. In *Constructing Chicago*, Bluestone documents the withdrawal of Chicago's "first" Protestant churches and synagogues from the center of the city.

26. "Old and New Saint Patrick's," newspaper articles (1877?), Saint Ignatius College Prep Archives.

27. Ibid.

28. The debate over commercial education in Chicago has a long history. On May 24, 1865, the *Chicago Times* noted that, "Two years time is as long as the sons of most of our citizens can afford to spend in [Chicago's public] High School; and these two years should be spent in preparing themselves for the active, practical arduous duties of life." For information on Saint Patrick's schools see Andreas, 3: 767–68, and Sister Mary Innocenta Montay, C.S.S.F., *The History of Catholic Secondary Education in the Archdiocese of Chicago* (Washington, D.C.: Catholic University of America Press, 1953), 189–93; 202–204.

29. See especially "Catholic Chicago: The Church of Rome in the Great City of the West," *Chicago Times*, June 22, 1873.

30. By 1885 the mother parish of the Chicago Irish was struggling to maintain its position on the Near West Side. In nearby Saint Jarlath parish, Irish Catholics were building a new Gothic church on Jackson Boulevard at Hermitage Avenue. Two other impressive houses of worship were dedicated in the neighborhood in 1885: the Episcopal Church of the Epiphany at Adams and Ashland, and Zion Temple, designed by the noted architectural firm of Adler and Sullivan, at Ogden and Ashland. For information on improvements to Saint Patrick's Church see the *Chicago Daily News*, October 31, November 2, 1885; and

Chicago Record-Herald, November 1, 2, 1885.

31. William Lill received 3,557 votes and was awarded a gold-headed cane inscribed to "the most popular brewer in Chicago, as decided by ballot, at a Fair held for the benefit of Saint Patrick's Church, September 4, 1869." See news clippings on Saint Patrick's parish in the West Side Community Collection, box 9, folder 5, Chicago Public Library Special Collections.

32. I owe a special debt to Charles Fanning for introducing me to the genius of Finley Peter Dunne in his 1972 doctoral dissertation from the University of Pennsylvania, published as *Finley Peter Dunne and Mr. Dooley: The Chicago Years* (Lexington, Ky.: University Press of Kentucky, 1978).

33. "Some Ancient Business Mariners," *Chicago Record-Herald*, June 12, 1910.

34. Mary Onahan Gallery, "The New Saint Patrick's Church," *Chicago Citizen*, March 16, 1912.

35. Ibid.

36. Alexander Burke and his wife, Margaret Moore, were the parents of eleven children, including Judge Richard Burke, chief justice of the superior court, and Dr. Alexander Burke. When he died in 1914, *The New World* noted that Alexander Burke's "home was his club, and his family, his society." Special thanks to Reverend James P. Burke, O.P., for providing crucial details of his grandfather's life in Ireland and Chicago. Members of the Burke family generously restored the Saint Finbar window in Old Saint Patrick's as part of the recent Renaissance campaign.

37. The decline in the fashionable residential district along Jackson Boulevard presented a unique opportunity for the Daughters of Charity. With the assistance of prominent Chicagoans, in 1914 they established a social center at 308 S. Sangamon Street that included a day nursery for the children of working mothers. When the sisters relocated the center three miles west on Jackson Boulevard in 1947, they renamed it Marillac House.

Chapter 3. Walking Nuns: Chicago's Irish Sisters of Mercy

I extend special thanks to Sister Patricia Illing, R.S.M., archivist, for her generosity and hospitality; Ellen Skerrett, editor of this volume, for her insights and enthusiasm; and Walter Nugent, Andrew V. Tackes Professor of American History at the University of Notre Dame, for his unflagging support and avid interest.

1. William J. Onahan, *A Little History of Old Saint Mary's Church, Chicago* (Chicago: Privately published, 1908), 24. For the term *walking nuns*, see M. Angela Bolster, R.S.M., *Catherine McAuley: Venerable for Mercy* (Dublin: Dominican Publications, 1990), 55.

2. Sister Mary Carmel Bourke, R.S.M., *A Woman Sings of Mercy: Reflections on the Life and Spirit of Mother Catherine McAuley, Foundress of the Sisters of Mercy* (Sydney, Australia: E. J. Dwyer, 1987), 8; and E. A. Ryan, S.J., "The Sisters of Mercy: An Important Chapter in Church History," *Theological Studies* 18 (June 1957), 259–60.

3. The Daughters of Charity came to Saint Patrick's School on September 11, 1871. Sister Cornelia Markey served as first principal; her companions were Sisters Leopoldine Judge and Euphemia Tuttle, who remained only a month. Following the Chicago fire in October 1871, the Daughters of Charity from Holy Name (whose school was destroyed) moved to Saint

Patrick's. Since many of their former pupils followed them, the Daughters of Charity from Holy Name replaced the first group of sisters (they received new assignments). The second principal was Sister Mary McCarthy; her companions were Sisters Cephas Byrne, Ellen Connaughton, Anastasia Ryan, Elizabeth Newman, Mary Owings, and Ann Tobin (three of them were born in Ireland). From 1871 to 1967, the Daughters of Charity conducted the grade school; their high school remained open until 1970. See Sister Bernice Brennan, D.C., "History and Activities of Three Schools, Elementary and Secondary, of the Daughters of Charity in Chicago" (master's thesis, De Paul University, 1953). I am also grateful to Lois Martin for biographical data from the Daughters of Charity Archives, Mater Dei Provincialate, Evansville, Indiana.

4. It is important to name these pioneers: Mother Agatha (Margaret) O'Brien, Sister Gertrude (Catherine) McGuire, Sister Vincent (Mary Ann) McGirr, Sister Josephine (Elizabeth) Corbett, and Sister Veronica (Eva) Schmidt. All were either born in Ireland or were the children of Irish immigrants. Biographical data can be found in the Sisters of Mercy Archives, Province Center, Chicago.

5. Mother Mary Austin Carroll, R.S.M., *Leaves from the Annals of the Sisters of Mercy in Four Volumes, vol. 3: Containing Sketches of the Order in Newfoundland and the United States* (New York: Catholic Publication Society, 1889), 245. On lay sisters, see Caitriona Clear, *Nuns in Nineteenth-Century Ireland* (Dublin: Gill and Macmillan, 1987), 91–99.

6. This description of the new building appeared in the 1848 *Catholic Directory*. It is quoted in Sister Mary Eulalia Herron,

R.S.M., *The Sisters of Mercy in the United States*, 1843–1928 (New York: Macmillan Company, 1929), 56.

7. William K. Beatty, "When Cholera Scourged Chicago," *Chicago History* XL (spring 1982): 5–8 (quote); Sister Mary Fidelis Convey, R.S.M., "Mother Agatha O'Brien and the Pioneers" (master's thesis, Loyola University, 1929), 126; Roland Burke Savage, *Catherine McAuley: The First Sister of Mercy* (Dublin: M. H. Gill and Son, 1950), 147–53; and Joy Clough, R.S.M., *In Service to Chicago: The History of Mercy Hospital* (Chicago: Mercy Hospital 1979), 18. Mother Agatha realized the risks in taking control of the hospital. They did not, however, prevent her from doing so. She remarked in a letter: "I am fearful & uneasy because an Hospital is such an arduous undertaking, but if Heaven aids us all will be right." Mother Agatha O'Brien to Sister Scholastica Drum, February 7, 1851, Sisters of Mercy Archives.

8. These quotations are taken from four letters written by Mother Agatha O'Brien on November 12, 1850; February 7, 1851; September 4, 1851; and November 12, 1851, Sisters of Mercy Archives.

9. On the Galena foundation, see Carroll, *Leaves*, 247. Sister Gertrude McGuire died of tuberculosis and Sister Veronica Schmidt of typhoid fever in Galena. See Clough, *In Service to Chicago*, 13. Mother Agatha O'Brien to Charles O'Brien, September 4, 1851, Sisters of Mercy Archives (quote). According to the 1860 manuscript federal census, for example, fifty-seven Sisters of Mercy lived on Wabash Avenue, of whom thirty-nine were born in Ireland.

10. Clough, *In Service to Chicago*, 18–19 (quotes). On the average number of patients in 1852, see "General Hospital of

the Lake," *Western Tablet*, February 28, 1852. The total number admitted between February 20, 1851 to February 20, 1852 was 220.

11. Convey, "Mother Agatha O'Brien and the Pioneers," 203, 228. Convey believes that Saint Patrick's free school for girls opened in 1854; however, according to two pieces in the *Western Tablet*, it began in 1852 (quite possibly late 1851). See "Catholic Education in Chicago," February 21, 1852, and "Catholic Directory," March 27, 1852.

12. Mother Agatha O'Brien to Sister Elizabeth Strange, June 28, 1851, Sisters of Mercy Archives.

13. "Reception of Nuns," *Western Tablet*, August 21, 1852.

14. John Gilmary Shea, *A History of the Catholic Church within the Limits of the United States from the First Attempted Colonization to the Present Time* (New York: John G. Shea, 1892), 617–18. For a thorough discussion of the incident, see Thomas M. Keefe, "Chicago's Flirtation with Political Nativism, 1854–1856," *Records of the American Catholic Historical Society of Philadelphia* 82 (September 1971): 149, 156 (quote).

15. Convey, "Mother Agatha O'Brien and the Pioneers," 212–13; and A Sister of the Community, "The Sisters of Mercy: Chicago's Pioneer Nurses and Teachers, 1846–1921," *Illinois Catholic Historical Review* 3 (April 1921): 353.

16. Beatty, "When Cholera Scourged Chicago," 10; Suellen Hoy, *Chasing Dirt: The American Pursuit of Cleanliness* (New York: Oxford University Press, 1995), 62; Onahan, *A Little History of Old Saint Mary's Church*, 24 (quote); and Convey, "Mother Agatha O'Brien and the Pioneers," 338.

17. Carroll, *Leaves*, 271–72; Convey, "Mother Agatha O'Brien and the Pioneers," 343; Reverend Monsignor Harry C. Koenig, ed., *A History of the Parishes of the Archdiocese of Chicago*, 2 vols. (Chicago: Archdiocese of Chicago, 1980), 1, 753; "Cleaning of the Streets—Health of the City," *Chicago Daily Tribune*, June 7, 1854 (quote); "The Streets —Health of the City, ibid., June 16, 1854; "Quarantine," ibid., May 1, 1855; and Beatty, "When Cholera Scourged Chicago," 10.

18. "Mother Mary Agatha (Margaret O'Brien)," *The Metropolitan Catholic Almanac and Laity's Directory, for the Year of Our Lord 1855* (Baltimore: Lucas Brothers, 1856), 285.

19. Ellen Skerrett, "Chicago's Irish and 'Brick and Mortar Catholicism': A Reappraisal," *U.S. Catholic Historian* 14, no. 2 (spring 1996): 53–71 (quote on p. 53).

20. Quoted in Charles Shanabruch, *Chicago's Catholics: The Evolution of an American Identity* (Notre Dame, Ind.: University of Notre Dame Press, 1981), 130.

21. "Saint Angela's Female Academy" Prospectus, 1857, Sisters of Mercy Archives; and Julia Marie Doyle, "Saint Angela's First," *The New World*, 1936 (clipping), also in Sisters of Mercy Archives. Saint Angela Merici is one of the saints "to whom the Sisters [of Mercy] are recommended to have particular devotion." See *Rule and Constitutions of the Religious Sisters of Mercy* (Philadelphia: H. L. Kilner and Company, n.d.), 33–34. On Saint Angela's works of charity and teaching, see Michael Walsh, "The Teacher Saint," *Book of the Saints* (Mystic, Conn.: Twenty-Third Publications, 1994), 13–15.

22. The first quotation is from "Saint Angela's Female Academy" Prospectus, 1857. On the place of religion in the curriculum, see Eileen Mary Brewer, *Nuns and the Education of American Catholic Women, 1860–1920* (Chicago: Loyola Press, 1987), 48 (quote)–51; and "Saint Agatha's

Academy for Young Ladies" Prospectus, n.d., Sisters of Mercy Archives (for quote on Christian principles and morality).

23. A Member of the Order, *Life of Mary Monholland: One of the Pioneer Sisters of the Order of Mercy in the West* (Chicago: J. S. Hyland and Company, 1894), 130–31. On use of a carriage, see Doyle, "Saint Angela's First." Although Julia Marie Doyle's mother remembers the Mercy sisters leaving Saint Patrick's in 1862, it appears that they left in 1863. See Carroll, *Leaves*, 273. The Sisters of Loretto, under the direction of Sister Ferdinand Sweeney, did not come to Saint Patrick's until 1864. They had been a part of the Sisters of Loretto of Nerinx, Kentucky; however, Sister Ferdinand and three other sisters left this community in 1864 to form a "new reformed Society of Loretto." Bishop James Duggan, who knew the family of one of the sisters, invited them to Saint Patrick's, where the need for sisters was great. They remained until 1871, when they were replaced by the Daughters of Charity of Saint Vincent de Paul. See Anna C. Minogue, *Loretto Annals of the Century* (New York: American Press, 1912), 181–84. I am grateful to Sister Florence Wolff, Loretto Archives, Nerinx, Kentucky, for this information.

24. Carroll, *Leaves*, 273 (quote), 277. On bad timing, see Member of the Order, *Life of Mary Monholland*, 132; the author remarked: "During the rebellion it was not easy for Mother Francis to meet emergencies. She had but lately returned from the seat of war, herself, and filled as she could the vacancies formerly held by her absent children [sisters]." See also Suellen Hoy, "Caring for Chicago's Women and Girls: The Sisters of the Good Shepherd, 1859–1911," *Journal of Urban History* 23 (March 1997); and Ellen Ryan Jolly, "Sis-

ters of Mercy, Chicago, Illinois," in *Nuns of the Battlefield* (Providence, R.I.: Providence Visitor Press, 1927), 223–39. According to Jolly, ten Irish-born Mercys nursed during the war (p. 239). Colonel James Mulligan's wife, Marian Nugent, had been a student at Saint Xavier's Academy.

25. "The Sisters of Charity," *Chicago Tribune*, June 21, 1862 (quote); "Obituary—Sister Anne Regina," *Chicago Times*, March 19, 1867; and Jolly, *Nuns of the Battlefield*, 67–68, 232–36.

26. Member of the Order, *Life of Mary Monholland*, 107–13; Carroll, *Leaves*, 276; George Levy, *To Die in Chicago: Confederate Prisoners at Camp Douglas, 1862–1865* (Evanston, Ill.: Evanston Publishing, 1994), 22–23, 28, 183; "Honor Their Dead: . . . Reminiscences of Miss Sweet," *Chicago Tribune*, May 26, 1895 (quote).

27. On Chicago's Sisters of Mercy as "ministering angels," see "Nurses for the Western Army," *Chicago Tribune*, October 18, 1861. On the respect earned, see David Gollaher, *Voice for the Mad: The Life of Dorothea Dix* (New York: Free Press, 1995), 414.

28. Protestant Female Nurse Association, "To the Ladies' Hospital Aid Societies of the Northwest," *Chicago Tribune*, May 23, 1862 (for both quotes). On Dorothea Dix, see Gollaher, *Voice for the Mad*, 413–14.

29. Robert E. Riegel, "Mary Ashton Rice Livermore," in Edward T. James et. al., eds., *Notable American Women, 1607-1950: A Biographical Dictionary*, II (3 vols., Cambridge, Mass.: Belknap Press of Harvard University, 1971), 410–13. The 1883 Livermore quotation can be found in Sister Mary Denis Maher, *To Bind Up the Wounds: Catholic Sister Nurses in the U.S. Civil War* (New York: Greenwood Press, 1989), 39. See also pages 155–60 for a fine discussion of the significance of these sis-

ter-nurses.

30. In 1851, for example, Catharine Beecher pointed with envy to the Catholic Church, which had "posts of competence, usefulness and honor . . . for women of every rank and of every description of talents." Catharine Beecher, *The True Remedy for the Wrongs of Women* (Boston: Phillips, Sampson, and Company, 1851), 51. In James Hurt's introduction to a recent edition of *Twenty Years at Hull-House*, Jane Addams and Ellen Gates Starr are described as "fashionable young ladies" who moved to "a dilapidated mansion in the heart of Chicago's slums determined to be 'good neighbors.' " Jane Addams, *Twenty Years at Hull-House: With Biographical Notes* (Urbana, Ill.: University of Illinois Press, 1990), *ix*. See also Donald L. Miller, *City of the Century: The Epic of Chicago and the Making of America* (New York: Simon and Schuster, 1996), 417–20. In an interview on National Public Radio (May 1996), Miller called Jane Addams a "gutsy" woman for living and working among Chicago's poor.

It should be known that Ellen Gates Starr (who spent her last years in a Benedictine convent) was the niece of Eliza Allen Starr, one of Chicago's foremost Catholic converts. She had "the greatest childhood influence on Ellen" and always considered the Sisters of Mercy her "old and true friends." See Allen F. Davis, "Ellen Gates Starr," in James et. al., eds., *Notable American Women*, 3, 351 (quote)–53; and Reverend James J. McGovern, *The Life and Letters of Eliza Allen Starr* (Chicago: Lakeside Press, 1905), 169 (quote).

31. Leonard I. Sweet, *The Minister's Wife: Her Role in Nineteenth-Century American Evangelicalism* (Philadelphia: Temple University Press, 1983), 88–90 (quote).

32. Ibid., 91 (quotes). On Emily Judson, see Barbara Welter, "She Hath Done What She Could: Protestant Women's Missionary Careers in Nineteenth-Century America," in Janet Wilson James, ed., *Women in American Religion* (Philadelphia: University of Pennsylvania Press, 1980), 114–15.

33. Suellen Hoy, "The Journey Out: The Recruitment and Emigration of Irish Religious Women to the United States, 1812–1914," *Journal of Women's History* 6 (winter-spring 1995): 65–72. On the severe inadequacies of the Famine refugees, see Lawrence J. McCaffrey, "Forging Forward and Looking Back," in Ronald H. Bayor and Timothy J. Meagher, eds., *The New York Irish* (Baltimore: Johns Hopkins University Press, 1996), 214.

34. Marta Danylewycz, *Taking the Veil: An Alternative to Motherhood and Spinsterhood in Quebec, 1840–1920* (Toronto: McClelland and Stewart, 1987), 105 (quote)–09. See also Hoy, "The Journey Out," 84.

35. Danylewycz, *Taking the Veil*, 85 (quote)-87; Hoy, "The Journey Out," 68. In the baptismal registry at Saint Patrick's Church, Sister Callista's name appears as "Mary Ellen Mangin." She was born on November 19 and baptized on November 21, 1855. She died of consumption on October 9, 1883, Sisters of Mercy Register, Sisters of Mercy Archives.

36. Joseph G. Mannard, "Converts in Convents: Protestant Women and the Social Appeal of Catholic Religious Life in Antebellum America," *Records* (of the American Catholic Historical Society of Philadelphia), 104 (winter-spring 1993): 90 (quote); and James K. Kenneally, *The History of American Catholic Women* (New York: Crossroad, 1990), 43.

37. Convey, "Mother Agatha O'Brien and the Pioneers," 190–91; 212–14; and Mary Liv-

ermore, *My Story of the War: A Woman's Narrative of Her Personal Experience as Nurse in the Union Army* (Hartford, Conn.: A. D. Worthington and Company, 1887), 436 (quote). Historian Lori D. Ginzberg notes that, although middle-class Protestant women rarely discussed incorporating, their very interest in doing so (and some did) "challenges their insistence on a protected female sphere." Catholic sisters, who made incorporation an essential business tool, escape her notice. Lori D. Ginzberg, *Women and the Work of Benevolence: Morality, Politics, and Class in the Nineteenth-Century United States* (New Haven, Conn.: Yale University Press, 1990), 48.

38. See the fine discussion of the nineteenth-century "worldview" of Irish men and women in Hasia R. Diner, *Erin's Daughters in America* (Baltimore: Johns Hopkins University Press, 1983), 139–53, especially pages 139–40 (quotes) and 145–46.

Chapter 4. Preserving the Union, Shaping a New Image: Chicago's Irish Catholics and the Civil War

1. *Chicago Tribune*, February 26, 1855.
2. Information on Mulligan's wake and funeral is taken from the *Chicago Tribune*, July 30, 31, August 2, 1864; *Chicago Times*, August 2, 3, 1864; and *Chicago Evening Journal*, July 29, August 2, 1864. In September 1861 Lincoln offered Mulligan the rank of brigadier general. He turned it down to stay with his men, expecting that his regiment would expand into a large Western Irish Brigade. Later, Mulligan unsuccessfully lobbied for a star on his shoulder, blaming his failure to achieve it on anti-Irish bigotry in Washington. Immediately after his death, the government breveted him brigadier general. Twenty years later a grant from the Illinois state legislature and local donations financed an impressive monument crowned with a Celtic cross close to the western entrance of Calvary Cemetery in Evanston, next to Mulligan's final resting place. It was formally dedicated on May 30, 1885. In 1899 Chicago began construction of the James A. Mulligan School at 1800 N. Sheffield Avenue in what is now the Lincoln Park neighborhood. It is no longer in use.

3. For a discussion of Chicago's economy, population, and atmosphere on the eve of the Civil War see *Theodore J. Karamanski, Rally 'Round the Flag: Chicago and the Civil War* (Chicago: Nelson-Hall Publishers, 1993), *xi–xiv*. Studies of the Chicago Irish include Lawrence J. McCaffrey, Ellen Skerrett, Michael F. Funchion, and Charles Fanning, *The Irish in Chicago* (Urbana, Ill.: University of Illinois Press, 1987); Ellen Skerrett, "The Development of Catholic Identity among Irish Americans in Chicago, 1880 to 1920," *From Paddy to Studs: Irish-American Communities in the Turn of the Century Era, 1880 to 1920*, Timothy J. Meagher, ed. (New York and Westport, Conn.: Greenwood Press, 1986), 117–38; Charles Fanning, Ellen Skerrett, and John Corrigan, *Nineteenth Century Chicago Irish: A Social and Political Portrait* (Chicago: Center for Urban Policy, Loyola University of Chicago, 1980); Paul Michael Green, "Irish Chicago: The Multiethnic Road to Machine Success," *Ethnic Chicago*, Peter d'A. Jones and Melvin G. Holli, eds. (Grand Rapids, Mich.: William B. Eerdmans Publishing, 1981), 212–59; and Michael F. Funchion, "Irish Chicago: Church, Homeland, Politics, and Class—The Shaping of an Ethnic Group, 1870–1900," *Ethnic Chicago: A Multicul-*

tural Portrait, Jones and Holli, 57–92.

4. *Chicago Tribune*, July 30, 1864. Seventeen years to the day Colonel Mulligan lectured on the battle of Lexington at New York's Cooper Union, Reverend John McMullen delivered a paper about Chicago's Civil War hero to the Chicago Historical Society. James A. Mulligan Papers, December 17, 1878, Chicago Historical Society.

5. For examinations of early nineteenth-century anti-Irish Catholic nativism see Ray Allen Billington, *The Protestant Crusade, 1800–1860* (Chicago: Quadrangle Books, 1964) and Dale T. Knobel, *Paddy and the Republic: Ethnicity and Nationality in Antebellum America* (Middleton, Conn.: Wesleyan University Press, 1986). Knobel argues that anti-Irish prejudices were more ethnic than religious. Considering that they did not include Irish Protestants or Scots-Irish Presbyterians, his thesis is questionable.

6. Carl Wittke, *The Irish in America* (reprint New York: Russell and Russell, 1970), 123–34 contains valuable information on black-Irish conflict in the period under discussion. Other studies that emphasize Irish and African-American rivalry are Robert Ernst, *Immigrant Life in New York City, 1825–1863* (New York: Kings Crown Press, 1949); Florence E. Gibson, *The Attitude of the New York Irish toward State and National Affairs, 1848–1892* (New York: Columbia University Press, 1951); and Phyllis F. Field, *The Politics of Race in New York: The Struggle for Black Suffrage in the Civil War Era* (Ithaca, N. Y.: Cornell University Press, 1982). In *The Irish in New Orleans, 1800–1860* (New York: Arno Press, 1976), 51–54, Earl F. Niehaus discusses Irish versus African-American rivalry in that important southern city preceding the Civil War. But Graham Hodges,

" 'Desirable Companions and Lovers': Irish and African Americans in the Sixth Ward, 1830–1870," *The New York Irish*, Ronald H. Bayor and Timothy J. Meagher, eds. (Baltimore: Johns Hopkins University Press, 1996), 107–24, presents a different story in one part of New York City where tolerance existed in the community and workplace and African-American men and Irish women mated and often married.

7. Statement in the House of Representatives by New York City congressman Mike Walsh, quoted in William V. Shannon, *The American Irish* (New York: Macmillan, 1963), 55.

8. See Billington and Knobel cited in note 5. Anti-Catholic nativism in 1850s Chicago is discussed in Thomas M. Keefe, "Chicago's Flirtation with Political Nativism," *Records of the American Catholic Historical Society of Philadelphia* 82 (September 1971): 131–58; "The Catholic Issue in the *Chicago Tribune* Before the Civil War," *Mid-America* 57 (October 1975): 227–45; and Michael Funchion, "Political and Nationalist Dimensions," *The Irish in Chicago*, 62.

9. For a discussion of the "devotional revolution," see Emmet Larkin, *The Historical Dimensions of Irish Catholicism* (Washington, D.C.: Catholic University of America Press, 1984). Lawrence J. McCaffrey, *Textures of Irish America* (Syracuse: Syracuse University Press, 1992), 47–88, discusses the significant role of Catholicism and the Catholic parish in Irish America. In a number of publications, Ellen Skerrett has described the parish and the importance of "brick and mortar" Catholicism in shaping Irish Chicago. Her works include "The Catholic Dimension," *The Irish in Chicago*, 22–60; "The Irish in Chicago: The Catholic Dimension," Ellen Skerrett, Edward R. Kantowicz, and Steven M. Avella, *Catholicism,*

Chicago Style (Chicago: Loyola Press, 1993), and "Chicago's Irish and 'Brick and Mortar Catholicism': A Reappraisal," *U.S. Catholic Historian* 14, no. 2 (spring 1996): 53–71.

10. According to Joseph M. Hernon, *Celts, Catholics, and Copperheads: Ireland Views the American Civil War* (Columbus, Ohio: Ohio State University Press, 1968), 11: "In the Union armies there were at least 150,000 soldiers of Irish birth. Young Irelander John Mitchel claimed there were 40,000 Irish born Confederate soldiers." In *The Irish in America*, 134–35, Carl Wittke writes "The number of Irish in the Union army has been estimated from 150,000 to 170,000, but report of the United States Sanitary Commission in 1869 placed the figure at 144,221 natives of Ireland, about five thousand more than might have been expected in proportion to the total Irish-American population. Of this number 51,206 came from New York, 17,418 from Pennsylvania, 12,041 from Illinois, 10,007 from Massachusetts, 8,129 from Ohio, 3,621 from Wisconsin, and 4,362 from Missouri."

11. Hernon, *Celts, Catholics, and Copperheads* and Toby Joyce, "The American Civil War and Irish Nationalism," *History Ireland* 4 (summer 1996): 36–41 discuss the various reasons why Irish nationalists and Irish Catholic bishops in Ireland opposed support for the Union in the American Civil War. They point out that Fenians in America were far more interested in preserving the United States than were their Irish Republican Brotherhood counterparts in Ireland. In *The Fenian Movement in the United States, 1858–1886* (New York: Russell and Russell, 1971), William D'Arcy offers a detailed history of the American wing of the IRB, including the opposition of many American Catholic bishops such as Duggan (p. 49) to Fenianism.

12. After the 1860 election Douglas, though quite sick, with his last ounces of energy first tried to save the Union through compromise. When that failed he traveled through the North preaching solidarity behind Lincoln and the war. He died on June 3, 1861. Bishop Duggan led the funeral procession to the grave, near Lake Michigan on the south side of the city. Karamanski's valuable *Rally 'Round the Flag*, 60–65, describes Douglas's patriotic effort. Karamanski's work was an important source in the writing of this essay.

13. Information on Mulligan and the Irish Brigade comes from the following sources: A. T. Andreas, *History of Chicago*, vol. 2 (reprint New York: Arno Press, 1975), 190–95; Harold F. Smith, "Mulligan and the Irish Brigade," *Journal of the Illinois State Historical Society* 56 (summer 1973): 164–76; T. M. Eddy, *The Patriotism of Illinois*, vol. 2 (Chicago: Clark and Company, 1866), 567–79; William L. Burton, *Melting Pot Soldiers: The Union's Ethnic Regiments* (Ames, Iowa: Iowa State University Press, 1988), 11–13, 43, 136–38; "Ethnic Regiments in the Civil War: The Illinois Experience," *Annual Illinois History Symposium, Illinois State Historical Society, Selected Papers*, 31–39; and *Chicago Tribune*, July 30, 1864.

14. "In the Hour of Need," *Chicago Tribune*, April 24, 1861.

15. "Reception of Colonel Mulligan: Chicago Welcomes the Hero of Lexington," *Chicago Evening Journal*, November 9, 1861; and "Reception of Colonel Mulligan: Honors to the Defender of Lexington," *Chicago Tribune*, November 9, 1861.

16. Letter of James A. Mulligan, November 12, 1861, and "Proclamation from the City of New York," December 17, 1861, Mulligan Papers, Chicago Historical Society. For

accounts of Mulligan's activities in New York see *New York Times,* December 19, 1861, and *Chicago Tribune,* December 21, 1861.

17. Smith, 173. For a contrasting view of Mulligan at Camp Douglas, see Karamanski, 83–85. According to Ed Gleason's *Rebel Sons of Erin: A Civil War History of the Tenth Tennessee Infantry Regiment (Irish) Confederate States Volunteers* (Indianapolis, Ind.: Guild Press of Indiana, 1993), 40–41, Colonel Mulligan and Tennessee Irish prisoners at Camp Douglas shared a mutual respect.

18. Frederick H. Dyer, *A Compendium of the War of Rebellion*, vol. 1 (New York: Yoseloff, 1959), 40, lists the Irish Brigade's fatalities as four officers and fifty enlisted men killed or mortally wounded and two officers and ninety-three enlisted men dead of diseases.

19. *Chicago Tribune*, August 2, 1864.

20. *Chicago Tribune*, August 3, 1864.

21. Burton, 33. March 26, 1864 letter from William West to Secretary of State William Seward quoted in D'Arcy, 62. See also Michael Scanlan's letter, "The Fenian Brotherhood—An Explanation," *Chicago Tribune*, August 4, 1864.

22. *Chicago Tribune*, August 3, 1864.

23. Biographical information on Denis Dunne and his family is based on Len Hilts, "The Dunnes of New Brunswick and Chicago," unpublished manuscript. Articles on Dunne's life and funeral were published in the *Chicago Times*, December 24, 27, 28, 1868.

24. For additional information on Father Dunne see James P. Gaffey, *Citizen of No Mean City: Archbishop Patrick Riordan of San Francisco, 1841–1914* (Wilmington, N. C.: Consortium Books, 1976), 6–8; and Skerrett, *Catholicism, Chicago Style*, 35–38.

25. Information on the Irish Legion was gathered from *Chicago Tribune* and *Chicago Times* news reports; Andreas, *History of Chicago*, vol. 2, 249–52; and Burton, *Melting Pot Soldiers,* 139–40. According to D'Arcy, *The Fenian Movement in the United States*, 43, in 1864, the Irish Legion donated $507 to the Fenian Brotherhood.

26. *Chicago Tribune*, August 10, 1862.

27. For conflicts in the Irish Legion between Dunne and Snowhook supporters and between O'Meara and his officers see Burton, "Ethnic Regiments," 33–34, 38.

28. Bruce Catton, *Reflections on the Civil War,* John Leekly, ed. (New York: Berkeley Publishing Company, 1994), 41–42, 68–69, 161, 177–78, 232 discusses food problems and the toll of disease on troops. Peter Casey to his wife from Irish Legion Ninetieth Regiment Illinois Headquarters, May 13, 1863, Mulligan Papers, Chicago Historical Society.

29. Iver Bernstein, *The New York City Draft Riots: Their Significance for American Society and Politics in the Age of the Civil War* (New York: Oxford University Press, 1990).

30. *Chicago Tribune*, August 1, 1863.

31. O'Connell's position on slavery and Irish Americans who opposed it is discussed in Lawrence J. McCaffrey, *Daniel O'Connell and the Repeal Year* (Lexington, Ky.: University of Kentucky Press, 1966), 72–75. O'Connell's 1843 denunciation of slavery and its Irish-American friends was reprinted in the *Chicago Tribune*, August 11, 1863, to encourage Irish-American Catholics to support the black emancipation aspect of the Civil War.

32. May 11, 1863, Mulligan Papers, Chicago Historical Society.

33. Karamanski, 213–14. Earlier, 179–80, Karamanski describes Irish hostility to blacks in Chicago in the wake of the Emancipation Proclamation.

34. *Chicago Tribune*, July 2, 1863. See also

Karamanski, 210–20, 233.

35. Karamanski, 223.

36. Karamanski, 238–39; *Chicago Tribune*, June 13, 1865.

37. *Chicago Tribune*, June 14, 1865; *Chicago Times*, June 14, 1865.

38. James P. Gaffey, "Patterns of Ecclesiastical Authority: The Problem of Chicago Succession, 1865–1881," *Church History* 42 (June 1973): 257–70; and *Citizen of No Mean City*, 22–23.

39. After Duggan was institutionalized for a mental breakdown and Bishop Thomas Foley took charge in Chicago, Dunne's allies were restored to good standing. McMullen became diocesan vicar-general and rector of Holy Name Cathedral and then the first bishop of Davenport, Iowa. McGovern became pastor of Holy Trinity, Bloomington, and Roles pastor of Saint Mary's, Rock Island.

40. Quoted in Gaffey, *Citizen of No Mean City,* 32.

41. The Dunne funeral is described in the *Chicago Times*, December 25, 27, 28, 29, 1868, and *Chicago Tribune*, December 27, 1868.

Chapter 5. Mr. Dooley Reconsidered: Community Memory, Journalism, and the Oral Tradition

1. Len Hilts, *The Dunnes of New Brunswick and Chicago* (unpublished ms, 1996), 20; James P. Gaffey, *Citizen of No Mean City: Archbishop Patrick Riordan of San Francisco, 1841–1914* (Wilmington, Del.: Consortium Books, 1976), 8; and Elmer Ellis, *Mr. Dooley's America: A Life of Finley Peter Dunne* (New York: Alfred Knopf, 1941), 5.

2. Parnell spoke in Chicago on February 23, 1880. New York *Irish World*, February 21, March 6, 1880; Philip H. Bagenal, *The American Irish and Their Influence on Irish Politics* (Boston: Roberts Brothers, 1882), 191–204. For the Dillon/O'Brien meeting see *Chicago Tribune*, November 29 and November 30, 1890. On the Cronin case see Charles Fanning, *Finley Peter Dunne and Mr. Dooley: The Chicago Years* (Lexington, Ky.: University Press of Kentucky, 1978), 152–55 and Michael F. Funchion, *Chicago's Irish Nationalists, 1881–1890* (New York: Arno Press, 1976).

3. Ellis, 3–15. *Proceedings of the Board of Education of the City of Chicago, September 1879 to September 1880* (Chicago: n. p., 1880), 186.

4. Ellis, 16–57; Fanning, *Chicago Years*, 5–23.

5. This piece and all of the other Dooley pieces quoted in the essay are collected in Charles Fanning, ed. *Mr. Dooley and the Chicago Irish: The Autobiography of a Nineteenth-Century Ethnic Group* (Washington, D.C.: Catholic University of America Press, 1987).

6. Ellis, 58–76. Fanning, *Chicago Years*, 23–36.

7. For Dunne's central position in Irish-American literature in general see Fanning, *The Irish Voice in America: Irish-American Fiction from the 1760s to the 1980s* (Lexington, Ky.: University Press of Kentucky, 1990), 214–37.

8. The Chicago Dooley pieces are arranged thematically in Fanning, ed., *Mr. Dooley and the Chicago Irish*. The chapters are as follows: The Past: Ireland, Emigration, Early Bridgeport; Daily Life in Bridgeport in the Nineties; Assimilation and Dissolving Community; Bridgeport as a Culture of Poverty; Chicago Politics: The View from Archey Road; Cathleen ni Houlihan in Chicago: Irish-American Nationalism; Mr. Dooley's Philosophy.

9. On Count Taafe see *Chicago Sunday Post*, December 4, 1892. On the Home Rule Bill see *Chicago Evening Post*, February 13, April 22, May 4, and September 2, 1893.

10. *Chicago Evening Post*, December 9 (editorial), December 12 (editorial), and December 13, 1893. On March 21, 1896, the Chicago archdiocesan paper *The New World* ran an editorial deploring the habit of "rushing the can" by children.

11. The piece began with the names of the four dead firemen: "O'Donnell, Sherrick, Downs, Prendergast," Mr. Dooley repeated slowly. "Poor la-ads. Poor la-ads. Plaze Gawd, they wint to th' long home like thrue min. 'Tis good to read th' names, Jawn. Thanks be, we're not all in th' council." (*Chicago Evening Post*, November 23, 1895)

12. "Finley Peter Dunne at Bedside of Sister," *Chicago Tribune*, November 13, 1914.

13. Father McLaughlin died on July 31, 1854. Reverend Monsignor Harry C. Koenig, ed. *A History of the Parishes of the Archdiocese of Chicago*. 2 vols. (Chicago: Archdiocese of Chicago, 1980), 1: 753. See Charles E. Rosenberg, *The Cholera Years: The United States in 1832, 1849, and 1866* (Chicago: University of Chicago Press, 1962), 192–97, 211.

14. Walter J. Ong, *Orality and Literacy: The Technologizing of the Word* (London and New York: Methuen, 1982), 145–46, 117–55.

15. Frank O'Connor, *The Lonely Voice: A Study of the Short Story* (London: Macmillan, 1963), 13, 14.

16. O'Connor defines "primary" literature as that which is "in the main original, not derivative, and expresses the joys and fears of man confronted with an unfamiliar universe." *A Short History of Irish Literature* (New York: Capricorn Books, 1968), 40.

17. Lincoln Steffens remembered Dunne as an endlessly entertaining office-mate who "could not master himself. He could not make himself write. I never knew a writer who made such a labor of writing; he seemed to hate it; he certainly ran away from it whenever he could." *The Autobiography of Lincoln Steffens* (New York: Grosset and Dunlap, 1931), 537–38.

18. "In the Interpreter's House," *The American Magazine*, May 1907, quoted in Ellis, 231.

19. Dunne to Herbert Small, September 25, 1899, and an undated letter of 1899, Dunne Letters, Chicago Historical Society.

20. "Finley Peter Dunne at Bedside of Sister," *Chicago Tribune*, November 13, 1914. While principal of the Howland School on the ethnically-changing West Side, Amelia Dunne Hookway wrote several plays, including one on the voyages of Columbus and, in 1912, one that drew on Bohemian folklore and dance. Ella Flagg Young, *Sixty-First Annual Report of the Board of Education for the Year Ending June 30, 1915* (Chicago, n.d.), 35; Playbill, "The Fount of Gold, A Play in One Act, Adapted from a Bohemian Folk Tale" (Hilts Collection, June 3, 5, 7, 1912).

21. The first two collections were *Mr. Dooley in Peace and in War* (Boston: Small, Maynard, and Company, 1898), and *Mr. Dooley in the Hearts of His Countrymen* (Boston: Small, Maynard, and Company, 1899).

22. "Irish-American Literature and Why There Isn't Any," *Irish Writing* (Cork) 3 (November 1947): 76.

23. Quoted in Seamus Heaney, "The Sense of Place," *Preoccupations: Selected Prose, 1968–1978* (New York: Farrar, Straus, Giroux, 1980), 139.

Chapter 6. Celtic Revived: The Artistry of Thomas O'Shaughnessy

I thank Ellen Skerrett and Joseph O'Shaughnessy for their assistance with this essay. Ellen's research over the years has illuminated the history of Saint Patrick's Church and the life of its illustrious artist, Thomas A. O'Shaughnessy. Joseph O'Shaughnessy's recollections of his father have deepened my admiration for the genius of Thomas O'Shaughnessy's artistic vision. I am also grateful to Julie Sloan for her comments on the history and technology of stained glass. Finally, I thank my wife Julia Versau for providing encouragement and clarity.

1. Cheryl Washer, "The Work of Edmond Johnson: Archaelogy and Commerce," *Imagining an Irish Past: The Celtic Revival, 1840–1940*, T. J. Edelstein, ed. (Chicago: David and Alfred Smart Museum of Art, 1992), 115.

2. "An Exhibition of One Hundred and Fifty Drawings in Color and Black and White by H. R. Boehm, H. Von Hofsten, T. A. O'Shaughnessy, Wm. Schmedtgen, J. T. McCutcheon. November 3, to November 10, 1902. Anderson Galleries, Wabash Av. & Madison St." Roger Flaherty Papers, box 1, March 1910–October 1917, Chicago Historical Society. Ellen Skerrett located this reference and a good many others for the essay. I thank her for sharing the fruits of her diligence with me.

3. "Columbus Day Is Fruition of a Celt's Labor," *Chicago Tribune*, October 12, 1955; "An O'Shaughnessy Behind Columbus," *Chicago Sun-Times*, October 6, 1961.

4. The attention the ships received even inspired the Selig Polyscope Company, one of Chicago's early feature film studios, to include them in the first multireeled motion picture ever made. I am grateful to Joseph O'Shaughnessy and Attracta Parr, Thomas O'Shaughnessy's children, for this information.

5. He designed the float, "Ireland Educating the World," for the Fourth of July Parade, *Chicago Record-Herald*, June 23, 1910. See also the "Feis of King Guaire" at Orchestra Hall, *Chicago Record-Herald*, May 22, 1910.

6. The early history of the church is compiled from various accounts in "Saint Patrick's Church (Roman Catholic), HABS No. ILL-1033," Historic American Buildings Survey (U.S. National Park Service, 1963), 1–9; Reverend Monsignor Harry C. Koenig, ed. *A History of the Parishes of the Archdiocese of Chicago*, 2 vols. (Chicago: Archdiocese of Chicago, 1980), 1: 751–3; Henry F. Whithey and Elsie Rathburn Whithey, *Biographical Dictionary of American Architects (Deceased)*, (Los Angeles: Hennessey and Ingalls, 1970), 112. Figures based on *Fifth Annual Review of the Commerce, Manufactures, and the Public and Private Improvements of Chicago, With a Full Statement of Her System of Railroads, and a General Synopsis of the Business of the City for the Year 1856* (Chicago: Daily Democrat Press, 1857), 7–14.

7. Quoted in Marcus Whiffen and Frederick Koeper, *American Architecture, 1607–1970* (Cambridge, Mass.: MIT Press, 1980), 167.

8. Ibid.

9. Copy of undated newspaper article from a scrapbook in the archives of Saint Ignatius College Prep.

10. Eliza Allen Starr, "History of Ecclesiastical Art," *The New World*, December 12, 1901, 4; Commission on Chicago Landmarks, "Holy Family Church and Saint Ignatius High School" (preliminary summary of information), 1982, 6, 8. The pulpit and its canopy and two side altars were removed in 1996, as part of the extensive rehabilitation of the

church. The railing was removed in the 1980s.

11. *Chicago Evening American*, March 18, 1912.

12. There are no specific references to the completion dates of the sanctuary windows. However, some of the glass and wall decorations were in place by 1917 when an article was published discussing Dr. James J. Walsh's address to the American Institute of Graphic Arts in New York:

Years ago he visited St. Patrick's church in Chicago, with its most dingy interior, as all our churches were that were built fifty years ago. He recently visited St. Patrick's again and there was a complete transformation. He saw the influence of the "Book of Kells" all over the walls. On inquiry, he found that Thomas A. O'Shaughnessy, a Chicago artist, had taken the graphic art of the Celts of one thousand years ago, design, coloring and all, and placed it in the stained-glass windows and walls so that it glows with beauty. ("What the Graphic Arts Owe to Ireland," *Inland Printer*, June 1917, 381).

13. *Chicago Citizen*, March 16, 1912. I thank John Corrigan for this reference and all his help with the research in the *Citizen*.

14. Sharon Darling, *Chicago, Ceramics, and Glass* (Chicago: Chicago Historical Society, 1979), 103.

15. Beginning in 1890 windows by Tiffany, and one by LaFarge, were also installed in the Second Presbyterian Church at 1936 South Wabash Avenue.

16. Unidentified article, "McSwiney [sic] Memorial Window Masterpiece by O'Shaughnessy," in research materials on the artist at the Chicago Historical Society, Department of Decorative Arts; letter from Bernard E. Gruenke, Jr., Conrad Schmitt Studios to George Maher, Saint Patrick's Church, December 18, 1992.

17. Marilyn Stokstad, "The Art of Prehistoric and Early Christian Ireland," *Irish History and Culture: Aspects of a People's Heritage*, Harold Orel, ed. (Lawrence, Kans.: University of Kansas Press, 1976), 46.

18. "A memorial canopy of Celtic Mosaic is being made in the Art Glass Studios of Thomas A. O'Shaughnessy, 108 North State Street, Chicago, Illinois. This canopy will be made of the same glass used in the windows of St. Patrick's Church. No painted glass will be used and yet this Canopy will be the most elaborately decorative and most beautifully colored decorative panel ever made of glass." *Fifty First Annual Commencement Exercises*, Saint Patrick's School, 1913: 30. The windows were announced in the *Chicago Citizen* of May 17, 1913.

19. I am grateful to Sister Alice Whitehead, I.B.V.M. archivist, and Suellen Hoy for providing biographical information and a portrait of Rose McGuire taken when she entered the convent in 1919. At the time of her death in 1955, Mother Ambrose, I.B.V.M., was a member of the Loretto order's general council in Toronto.

20. *The New World*, November 19, 1920.

21. *Catalogue of Ecclesiastical Art and Architecture*, XXVIII. International Eucharistic Congress exhibition, Municipal Pier, Chicago, June 19–26, 1926, Joseph J. O'Shaughnessy Collection.

22. The stencils appear to have been completed in 1922: "The ancient building itself has, during the past eight months, been redecorated in the classic style of seventh and eighth century Gaelic art." (*The New*

World, March 10, 1922). The ceiling was redecorated some time after 1943, without O'Shaughnessy's participation and a new scheme for the walls, including paintings of large medallions over the chancel arch, was carried out by Mr. and Mrs. Bertrand Murray. (*Chicago Tribune*, March 17, 1960). Large portions of O'Shaughnessy's original design were recreated in 1996.

23. *Chicago Evening Post*, March 17, 1922.

24. See, for example, *Imagining an Irish Past*, Edelstein, ed., 145–48.

Chapter 7. Saint Patrick's Daughter: Amelia Dunne Hookway and Chicago's Public Schools

I wish to give special thanks to Ellen Skerrett and Suellen Hoy, whose tireless detective work in Chicago's archives and lively lunch-time conversations over the past year helped shape this essay. I also wish to thank Kay and Len Hilts, whose cherished collection of family photographs helped make Katherine Dunne Flood and Amelia Dunne Hookway's story come alive.

1. "SLC to Mrs. Hookway, October 1908," Mark Twain Papers, The Bancroft Library, University of California, Berkeley. Mark Twain's previously unpublished words are © 1997 by Chase Manhattan Bank as Trustee of the Mark Twain Foundation, which reserves all reproduction or dramatization rights in every medium. Quotation is made with the premission of the University of California Press and Robert H. Hirst, General Editor, Mark Twain Project. For Amelia Dunne Hookway's views on children's theater see, "The Drama at the Schools and Universities," *Chicago Record-Herald*, June 14, 1908.

2. "Amelia Dunne Hookway to Samuel L. Clemens, Chicago, May 31, 1909," Mark Twain Papers, The Bancroft Library, University of California, Berkeley. Used with permission of the copyright owner.

3. Quoted in Albert Bigelow Paine, *Mark Twain: A Biography: The Personal and Literary Life of Samuel Langhorne Clemens*, Vol. 4 (New York: Harper and Brothers Publishers, 1912), 1412n.

4. James O'Donnell Bennett, "Dramatics at Howland School," *Chicago Record-Herald*, May 23, 1909, 4.

5. The chronicle of the origins of the Saint Patrick's schools has been pieced together from the following unsigned and undated sources located in the Daughters of Charity of Saint Vincent de Paul Archives in Evansville, Indiana: "Saint Patrick Grammar and Girls' High School, Chicago, Illinois" [slide script]; "History of Saint Patrick Girls' High School;" "Saint Patrick Grammar and Girls High School, Chicago, Illinois;" and "Saint Patrick's Girl [sic] School . . . by An Alumna" [memoir], 1930–31. In addition, "The Sisters of Mercy by a Sister of the Community," *Illinois Catholic Historical Review* 3: 4 (April 1921): 356, and "Registration for Saint Patrick's Girls' High, Grade School Will Be Open All Summer," *The New World*, June 20, 1952, were consulted.

6. Quoted in Sister Bernice Brennan, D.C., "History and Activities of Three Schools, Elementary and Secondary, of the Daughters of Charity in Chicago" (master's thesis, De Paul University, 1953), 58, Daughters of Charity Archives.

7. Elmer Ellis, *Mr. Dooley's America: A Life of Finley Peter Dunne* (New York: Alfred A. Knopf, 1941), 11.

8. George Howland, "Report of the Superintendent," *Twenty-Ninth Annual Report of the Board of Education for the Year End-*

ing June 30, 1883 (Chicago: Jameson and Morse, 1884), 61.

9. Ellis, 15; Charles Fanning, ed., "Introduction," in Finley Peter Dunne, *Mr. Dooley and the Chicago Irish: The Autobiography of a Nineteenth Century Ethnic Group* (Washington, D.C.: Catholic University of America Press, 1987), *xvi*.

10. Table 3, "The Training and Salary of Chicago Public School Teachers," in Mary J. Herrick, *The Chicago Schools: A Social and Political History* (Beverly Hills, Calif.: Sage Publications, 1971), 404.

11. "Amelia Dunne Hookway," *The New World*, November 20, 1914.

12. "Finley Peter Dunne at Bedside of Sister," *Chicago Tribune*, November 13, 1914.

13. *The New World*, November 20, 1914.

14. *Chicago Tribune*, November 13, 1914.

15. Table 14, "Female Employment Percentages in Selected Occupations, by Nativity, United States, 1900," in Janet A. Nolan, *Ourselves Alone: Women's Emigration from Ireland, 1885–1920* (Lexington, Ky.: University Press of Kentucky, 1989), 82.

16. For a discussion of the unusual patterns of Irish women's immigration to the United States in the late nineteenth and early twentieth centuries see Nolan, *Ourselves*.

17. By 1910, almost 85 percent of the unmarried women who identified themselves as Irish had jobs, a percentage far higher than that of any other ethnic group. See Table B.1, "Females Ages 10–64 in the Labor Force, by Marital Status, 1910," in Susan Cotts Watkins, ed., *After Ellis Island: Newcomers and Natives in the 1910 Census* (New York: Russell Sage Foundation, 1994), Appendix B, 374.

18. In 1910 only slightly over 7 percent of all Irish-born married women in the United States were working for pay outside the home. This low percentage mirrors those found among married women in other ethnic groups in that year. See Watkins, *After Ellis Island*.

19. Almost half of all Irish-American girls between the ages of fourteen and eighteen, the high school years, were in school in 1910. See Table B.1, "School Enrollments," Watkins, *After Ellis Island*, 380.

20. Table 13, "School Attendance Percentages among Children Aged Six to Sixteen, by Nativity of Father, United States, 1900," in Nolan, 81, and Table 7.4, "Enrollments, by Race and Ethnicity, by Sex and Age Group, 1910," in Jerry A. Jacobs and Margaret E. Greene, "Race and Ethnicity, Social Class and Schooling," in Watkins, 232–33.

21. See Nolan, "The National Schools and Irish Women's Mobility in the Late Nineteenth and Early Twentieth Centuries," *Irish Studies Review* (spring 1997, forthcoming) for a fuller discussion of girls' education in the national schools.

22. Table 14, Nolan, *Ourselves*, 82.

23. "130 Get Certificates to Teach in Chicago," *Chicago Record-Herald*, June 13, 1908. While no exact count of Irish-American public school teachers in Chicago at the turn of the century yet exists, reliable estimates of the numbers of Catholics (and by inference the number of Irish Americans) teaching in Chicago's public schools can be found in James W. Sanders, *The Education of an Urban Minority: Catholics in Chicago, 1833–1965* (New York: Oxford University Press, 1977), 131. According to Cardinal Mundelein, by 1920 fully 70 percent of Chicago's teachers were Catholics. See Ellen Skerrett, "The Catholic Dimension," *The Irish in Chicago* (Urbana, Ill.: University of Illinois Press, 1987), 46. Other cities with large Irish-American populations also had high numbers of Irish-American teachers. For instance, in 1908

one quarter of the teachers in Providence and Boston were Irish Americans, and one third of New York City's teachers with foreign-born parents were Irish Americans. See Joel Perlmann, *Ethnic Differences: Schooling and Social Structure Among Irish, Italians, Jews, and Blacks in an American City, 1880–1935* (New York: Cambridge University Press, 1988), 55, 56.

24. *Proceedings of the Board of Education, City of Chicago*, June 23, 1915, 1282.

25. George S. Counts, *School and Society in Chicago* (New York: Harcourt, Brace, Jovanovich, Inc., 1928; reprint New York: Arno Press, 1971), 239–40.

26. Sanders, *Education of Urban Minority*, 27, 130, 131; "130 Get Certificates to Teach in Chicago."

27. Timothy Walch, *Parish School: American Catholic Parochial Education from Colonial Times to the Present* (New York: Crossroad Publishing Company, 1996), 25–29; and David Galenson, "Determinants of School Attendance of Boys in Early Chicago, " *History of Education Quarterly* 35:4 (winter 1995): 397.

28. Walch, "Catholic Education in Chicago: The Formative Years 1840-1890," *Chicago History* 7: 2 (summer 1978): 87.

29. Lotus D. Coffman, *The Social Composition of the Teaching Population* (New York: Teachers College, Columbia University, 1911), 1, 14, 37, 69, 70.

30. See Walch, "Catholic Education," and "Catholic School Books and American Values: The Nineteenth Century Experience," *Religious Education* 73: 3 (September–October 1978): passim.

31. Nolan, "A Patrick Henry in the Classroom: Margaret Haley and the Chicago Teachers' Federation," *Eire-Ireland* 30: 2 (summer 1995): 106.

32. Table 3, Herrick, *Chicago Schools*, 404–405.

33. Margaret A. Haley, "Why Teachers Should Organize," *Addresses and Proceedings of the National Education Association*, 43rd Annual Meeting, St. Louis, 1904, in Margaret A. Haley, *Battleground: The Autobiography of Margaret A. Haley*, edited with an introduction by Robert L. Reid (Urbana, Ill.: University of Illinois Press, 1982), Appendix B, 286.

34. *Proceedings of the Board of Education, City of Chicago*, June 30, 1915, 1420, 173.

35. Nolan, "Irish-American Teachers and the Struggle Over American Urban Public Education, 1890–1920," *Records of the American Catholic Historical Society of Philadelphia* 103: 3–4 (winter 1992): 15.

36. Marjorie Murphy, *Blackboard Unions: The AFT and the NEA, 1900–1980* (Ithaca, N.Y.: Cornell University Press, 1990), 177–79.

37. Ella Flagg Young, "In Memoriam" in "Report of the Superintendent of Schools," *Public Schools of the City of Chicago: Sixty-First Annual Report of the Board of Education for the Year Ending June 30, 1915* (Chicago, n.p., n.d.), 35.

Suggestions for Further Reading

Avella, Steven M. *This Confident Church: Catholic Leadership and Life in Chicago, 1940–1965.* Notre Dame, Ind.: University of Notre Dame Press, 1992.

Brewer, Eileen Mary. *Beyond Utility.* Chicago: Loyola Press, 1987.

Burton, William. *Melting Pot Soldiers: The Union's Ethnic Regiments.* Ames, Iowa: Iowa State University Press, 1988.

Clough, Joy, R.S.M. *In Service to Chicago: The History of Mercy Hospital.* Chicago: Mercy Hospital, 1979.

Cronon, William. *Nature's Metropolis: Chicago and the Great West.* New York: W. W. Norton, 1991.

Diner, Hasis. *Erin's Daughters in America.* Baltimore: Johns Hopkins University Press, 1983.

Fanning, Charles. *Finley Peter Dunne and Mr. Dooley: The Chicago Years.* Lexington, Ky.: University Press of Kentucky, 1978.

———. *The Exiles of Erin: Nineteenth Century Irish-American Fiction.* Notre Dame, Ind.: University of Notre Dame Press, 1987.

———. *The Irish Voice in America: Irish American Fiction from the 1760s to the 1980s.* Lexington, Ky.: University Press of Kentucky, 1990.

———. *Mr. Dooley and the Chicago Irish: The Autobiography of a Nineteenth-Century Ethnic Group.* Washington, D.C.: Catholic University of America Press, 1987.

Funchion, Michael F. *Chicago's Irish Nationalists, 1881–1890.* New York: Arno Press, 1976.

Holli, Melvin G., and Peter d'A. Jones, eds. *Ethnic Chicago: A Multicultural Portrait.* 4th ed. Grand Rapids, Mich.: William B. Eerdmans Publishing Company, 1995.

Hoy, Suellen. *Chasing Dirt: The American Pursuit of Cleanliness.* New York: Oxford University Press, 1995.

Hoy, Suellen, and Margaret MacCurtain. *From Dublin to New Orleans: The Journey of Nora and Alice.* Dublin: Attic Press, 1994.

Kantowicz, Edward R. *Corporation Sole: Cardinal Mundelein and Chicago Catholicism.* Notre Dame, Ind.: University of Notre Dame Press, 1983.

Karamanski, Theodore J. *Rally 'Round the Flag: Chicago and the Civil War.* Chicago: Nelson-Hall Publishers, 1993.

Koenig, Rev. Msg. Harry C., ed. *A History of the Parishes of the Archdiocese of Chicago and A History of the Institutions of the Archdiocese of Chicago.* 4 vols. Chicago: Archdiocese of Chicago, 1980.

Lane, George A., and Algimantas Kezys. *Chicago Churches and Synagogues: An Architectural Pilgrimage*. Chicago: Loyola Press, 1981.

McCaffrey, Lawrence J. *Ireland from Colony to Nation State*. New York: Prentice Hall, 1979.

———. *The Irish Diaspora in America*. Reprint. Catholic University of America Press, 1983.

———. *Textures of Irish America*. Syracuse, N.Y.: Syracuse University Press, 1992.

———. *The Irish Question: Two Centuries of Conflict*. Lexington, Ky.: University Press of Kentucky, 1995.

McCaffrey, Lawrence J., Ellen Skerrett, Michael F. Funchion, Charles Fanning. *The Irish in Chicago*. Chicago: University of Illinois Press, 1987.

McGreevy, John T. *Parish Boundaries: The Catholic Encounter with Race in the Twentieth-Century Urban North*. Chicago: University of Chicago Press, 1996.

Maher, Sister Mary Denis. *To Bind Up the Wounds: Catholic Sister Nuns in the U.S. Civil War*. New York: Greenwood Press, 1989.

Miller, Donald L. *City of the Century: The Epic of Chicago and the Making of America*. New York: Simon and Schuster, 1996.

Nolan, Janet. *Ourselves Alone: Women's Emigration from Ireland, 1885–1920*. Lexington, Ky.: University Press of Kentucky, 1989.

Pacyga, Dominic A., and Ellen Skerrett. *Chicago: City of Neighborhoods*. Chicago: Loyola Press, 1986.

Sanders, James W. *The Education of an Urban Minority: Catholics in Chicago, 1833–1965*. New York: Oxford University Press, 1977.

Shanabruch, Charles. *Chicago's Catholics: The Evolution of an American Identity*. Notre Dame, Ind.: University of Notre Dame Press, 1981.

Skerrett, Ellen, Edward R. Kantowicz, Steven M. Avella. *Catholicism, Chicago Style*. Chicago: Loyola Press, 1993.

Walch, Timothy. *Parish School: American Catholic Parochial Education from Colonial Times to the Present*. New York: Crossroad Publishing Company, 1996.

Contributors

Eileen Durkin is a writer and storyteller who follows in what Robert and Kelly Wilhelm have identified as "the ancient Irish tradition of the *fer comgne,* the synchronizer." She takes contemporary experiences, folklore, and history and weaves them together into "storytelling for a new generation." Since 1987 her work has been featured on Saint Patrick's Day at Saint Patrick's Church as well as during conferences, retreats, reunions, and other communal celebrations.

Ellen Skerrett is the co-author of *Catholicism, Chicago Style* (Loyola Press, 1993), *The Irish in Chicago* (University of Illinois Press, 1987), and *Chicago: City of Neighborhoods* (Loyola Press, 1986).

Suellen Hoy teaches American history at the University of Notre Dame. She is the author of *Chasing Dirt: The American Pursuit of Cleanliness* (Oxford University Press, 1995) and co-author of *From Dublin to New Orleans: The Journey of Nora and Alice* (Attic Press, 1994).

Lawrence J. McCaffrey is professor emeritus of Irish and Irish-American history at Loyola University Chicago and co-founder of the American Conference for Irish Studies. He has published numerous books and articles on Ireland and Irish America, including *The Irish Question: Two Centuries of Conflict* (University Press of Kentucky, 1995), *Textures of Irish America* (Syracuse University Press, 1992), *The Irish Diaspora in America* (reprint, Catholic University of America Press, 1983), *Ireland from Colony to Nation State* (Prentice Hall,

1979), *Daniel O'Connell and the Repeal Year* (University of Kentucky Press, 1966), and *Irish Federalism in the 1870s: A Study in Conservative Nationalism* (American Philosophical Society, 1962).

Charles Fanning, director of Irish Studies at Southern Illinois University, is the author of many books and essays on Irish-American writers, including *The Irish Voice in America: Irish-American Fiction from the 1760s to the 1980s* (University Press of Kentucky, 1990), *The Exiles of Erin: Nineteenth Century Irish-American Fiction* (University of Notre Dame Press, 1987), and *Finley Peter Dunne and Mr. Dooley: The Chicago Years* (University Press of Kentucky, 1978).

Timothy Barton, an attorney, is research director for the Landmarks Division of the Chicago Department of Planning and Development. He has written many articles on Chicago history and architecture.

Janet Nolan, associate professor of history at Loyola University Chicago, is the author of *Ourselves Alone: Women's Emigration from Ireland, 1885–1920* (University Press of Kentucky, 1989) and several articles on Irish and Irish-American women's education. She is now working on a new book, *Saint Patrick's Daughters: Education and Women's Mobility in Ireland and Irish America, 1880–1920.*

Reverend John J. Wall is the pastor of Old Saint Patrick's Church. Recognizing the poten-

tial of this long-neglected urban church, Father
Wall turned four registered parishioners in
1983 into an associate membership of over thirteen thousand through a series of spiritually
and socially enhancing programs and special
events.

Index